Sleaze: The Corruption of Parliament

David Leigh is a contributing editor at the *Observer* and well known as an investigative author and TV producer. His programmes include controversial inquiries at *World in Action* into Cabinet minister Jonathan Aitken; and into the arms trade. He previously worked as a reporter on Thames Television's 'This Week', and as head of investigations at the *Observer*, where he was Granada Television's Investigative Reporter of the Year and won three other major press awards. His wrote a history of the Matrix Churchill scandal, which led to the Scott inquiry; other books include a study of MI5 and the former Labour leader Harold Wilson; biographies of Michael Foot and the drug smuggler Howard Marks; and books on the Chernobyl disaster; the Westland affair; the Jeremy Thorpe case; and official secrecy in Britain. He lives in Shepherds Bush, London.

Ed Vulliamy was born in Notting Hill, London, and educated at Oxford. He is a senior foreign correspondent for the *Guardian*, which he joined from Granada Television's *World in Action*, having won a Royal Television Society award for a film about Northern Ireland. He has been a bureau chief in Italy and the United States, specialising in corruption scandals and the Mafia, and also writes about painting and music. His coverage of the carnage in former Yugoslavia, where he found the Serbian concentration camps, won him Foreign Correspondent of the Year, International Correspondent of the Year and a prize from Amnesty International. In 1994, he won the James Cameron Memorial Award for journalistic excellence and published *Seasons In Hell: Understanding Bosnia's War*. He broadcasts regularly for CNN and the BBC, and is currently based in Britain.

Sleaze

The Corruption of Parliament

David Leigh and Ed Vulliamy

FOURTH ESTATE ● *London*

First published in Great Britain in 1997 by
Fourth Estate Limited
6 Salem Road
London W2 4BU

3 5 7 9 10 8 6 4 2

A catalogue record for this book is available from the British
Library.

ISBN 1–85702–694–2

Typeset by York House Typographic Ltd, London
Printed in Great Britain by Clays Ltd, St. Ives plc
Bungay, Suffolk

'The spirit of corruption is so inseparably inter-woven with British politics, that their ministry suppose all mankind to be governed by the same motive. They have no idea of a people submitting to even temporary inconvenience from an attach-ment to rights and privileges. Their plans and business are calculated *by* the hour and *for* the hour, and are uniform in nothing but the corrup-tion which gives them birth.'

Thomas Paine: 'The Crisis', *December 1776.*

'I do hope that in speaking about the various policies that we have to debate, we do so untram-melled by personal interests.'

Neil Hamilton MP, House of Commons, 13 April 1989

Contents

Acknowledgements

Although, naturally, the errors and infelicities are ours, a great deal of the material for this book was supplied by the participants in the events themselves, who gave us written or oral accounts of what they knew. To that extent, the named authors are merely editors of other people's stories. They were players: we are merely recorders. In particular, the contributions should be acknowledged at the *Guardian* of Peter Preston, editor when the original sleaze disclosures were published; Alan Rusbridger, who is editor now; David Hencke, the investigator who reported many of the original stories; David Pallister, his fellow investigator; Brian Whitaker, managing editor, who handled the Hamilton litigation; Richard Norton-Taylor, the *Guardian*'s Whitehall expert, who analysed the history of parliamentary corruption for us, and Jamie Wilson, the paper's skilful researcher. At the *Observer*, investigator Jonathan Calvert gave us the story of his personal involvement in the *Sunday Times*' 'Cash for Questions' story. Will Hutton, editor of the *Observer*, loaned David Leigh from his staff, and Simon Tisdall, foreign editor of the *Guardian*, released Ed Vulliamy from his duties to write this book.

The authors thank Karen Morgan and Paula Froelich for their long transcriptions of legal material. They would also like to thank: Jane Mulholland, Tom Beezer, the casualty department at Hammersmith Hospital (an Ian Greer client), Mark Hollingsworth, Keith Lockwood, Jeannie Mackie, Louisa Saunders, Geraldine Proudler and Nicki Schroeder.

Foreword

This is a vastly entertaining book. It is also an alarming book. Those with faith in the integrity of British democracy will look for the legend that all the characters are fictitious and any resemblance to real events merely coincidental. Can these rascals and humbugs really be prancing about the great Palace of Westminster, concealing the petty corruptions of their party in the elaborate mummeries of British parliamentary procedure? You bet they can. Our institutions are peculiarly vulnerable to the bold and litigious liar, and one who is already an MP has a head start on the scrutineers of power. The press may do its part, as the *Guardian* so ingeniously and courageously did in its exposure of sleaze, but look at the labryinth of law it had to run, at considerable expense and risk, and see how cumbrously Parliament now moves, even on a matter affecting its own reputation. A dinosaur trying to step on a lizard.

The precedents are not encouraging. I recall being summoned to the Privileges Committee, a sort of Star Chamber, to apologise, if I would, for the outrageous allegation by the *Sunday Times* that an honourable member had cooked the books of the Commons catering committee over which he presided. Mr Robert Maxwell MP graduated to grander thefts. When we and publisher Jonathan Cape fought Executive secrecy in the courts, in the matter of the Richard Crossman diaries, members of Parliament remained silent on the most significant constitutional protest of our generation.

It is quite true, as the writers suggest, that the American Congress would have unravelled the Hamilton–Greer–al-Fayed imbroglio long ago. Congressmen, one might say, have had more experience of the corruptions of lobbying and on a scale to match the size of the country, but Congress has at least equipped itself to try and cope, and of course the American press endures none of the restraints of the British. I think zealous scrutiny has gone too far in America, discouraging entry into public life. The system of independent counsel investigating office-holders has been distorted by partisanship, and too many newspaper reporters have become trivia cops. But these are hardly intolerable hazards in Britain where you can buy an MP for a few nights at the Ritz and live *not* to tell the tale.

Harold Evans
former editor of the *Sunday Times* and *The Times*

**Peter Preston, former Editor,
and Alan Rusbridger, Editor of the *Guardian***

Preface

On 20 October 1994, the *Guardian* published a lead story which told how two serving Government ministers had (in earlier backbench life) been paid covert bundles of cash for asking questions. One of the pair – Tim Smith – resigned and said he was sorry. Neil Hamilton struggled to stay in office for a while, waving a ginger biscuit of defiance. But after only a few days of agonising, John Major was finally forced to change the Commons scenery. The line couldn't be held. The hoary mantras of Westminster probity, the chummy conveniences of chaps regulating chaps, could not be defended any longer. Public anger and public derision had become irresistible: the Prime Minister called for Lord Nolan.

Within three months, the Nolan committee was up and running hard. Its hearings would be open to the public and broadcasters. No secrecy; no evasion. On 17 January 1995, the first witness played to a packed house in the Central Hall just across Parliament Square.

Professor Ivor Crewe – now Vice-Chancellor of Essex University – is one of Britain's pre-eminent political analysts. He told the Nolan team the latest Gallup Poll findings. Some 77 per cent of people polled reckoned that MPs 'cared more about special interests' than about ordinary people; 87 per cent believed that MPs 'will tell lies if the truth would hurt them politically'; only 28 per cent thought Members of Parliament lived up to 'a high personal moral code'. A full 64 per cent asserted that 'most MPs make a lot of money by using public office improperly'.

Crewe's bleak assessment rippled through the 18 open hearings of the committee, and informed its final report. There Lord Nolan told John Major directly about the need for urgent action. 'Unless corrective measures are promptly taken, there is a danger that anxiety and suspicion will turn to disillusion and growing cynicism.' He delivered a 96-page prescription for drastic change – including, uniquely in British history, the appointment of an outside Commissioner for Standards: a non-chum for the club.

This book is the fullest account of how the new owner of Harrods met Ian Greer and his two ad hoc associates, Mr Smith and Mr Hamilton: the businessman from Alexandria and the British gentlemen. It tells what happened and seeks to explain why it happened.

It begins far away in the wheeling and dealing frenzy of the eighties, when two tycoons wanted to buy the same department store. But it is not quite over yet. Neil Hamilton's long trek to the libel courts may have ended in ignominy, but the first great test of the Nolan revolution has yet to be passed. We don't yet know whether – when the last report is issued, the last haggle settled – ordinary people will look at the evidence and begin to have faith again.

Here are the facts to measure the outcome by. In the digging, they have the messiness of real life. Newspaper investigations are neither cheap nor easy: no pat scripts unravel to order. Mr Smith and Mr Hamilton asked the questions, wrote their letters to ministers and took their undeclared booty from Mohamed al-Fayed for years in newspaper silence. Nobody rumbled them at the time. Ian Greer built the most powerful lobbying firm in the land without press scrutiny – and fobbed off a Commons select committee inquiry along the way. Greer's repertory company of MPs saw the curtain rise on their activities time after time without a sniff of press concern. They all almost got away with it. They must have expected they could always get away with it. They'd have been the first to hymn the sanctity of British public life: See how few nasty cases there are; see our wondrous purity. When there is no exposure, there can only be such complacencies.

One random remark – by Fayed to the editor of the *Guardian*, long ago in the summer of 1993 – opened a tiny hole in that sanctified hypocrisy. It began 14 months of inquiries as a reporting team led by David Hencke began knocking on doors and pounding telephones. Yet even then, as the story hit the front page, forgetfulness might soon have returned. The chums tried to vote down Nolan's recommendations. The chums soothed Tim Smith's feathers and soon had the disgraced ex-minister back, sitting in state on the supreme financial watchdog of parliament, the Public Accounts Committee. The chums, finding that Neil Hamilton couldn't pursue his libel action without demolishing 300-year-old rules of parliamentary privilege, promptly changed the law to let him have a go – whilst chummily denying responsibility for the deed.

The Hamilton affair is the Westminster scandal of the decade because his mates had clubby faith in him, or would not whisper their doubts. It imploded because the court case he had told them would be his salvation collapsed in flames – and they were flames lit by sheaves of documents dragged from the heart of the Government machine by the *Guardian*'s demands. The former minister was a lawyer himself. He thought he knew what he was doing. He was ready to take the millions in damages he'd been told to expect. But, in a crunching four days of disillusion, he ended having to pay the paper instead.

So the libel case became not a footnote to drama, but the denouement of the drama itself. Without it, Neil Hamilton might gradually have edged along the Tim Smith road, working his passage, pretending nothing serious had happened, blaming an awful press. He was already back in the old Conservative trade and industry committee role he'd milked in the eighties. The pals were rallying round. Ian Greer had him back on the canapé circuit. If – as Hamilton blithely expected – the *Guardian* had folded, if one of those statements of apology on page two and accompanying cheques had got everyone off the hook of the grotesquely costly libel game, then he might have hoped to get his chauffeur-driven Rover back eventually. But the paper did not fold. There was faith in the story and, more than that, in the importance of the story. Money (though Neil Hamilton may find it difficult to credit) wasn't a factor. The editors believed that cheats and liars in powerful places could not be skirted or appeased.

Mr Hamilton returned to Nolan and the machinery of improved regulation which, perversely, his initial fall had sparked into life. He chose to be judged by his chums. He went back round the track.

We do not, as this book goes to press, know how the final lap will end. Thus far it has taken longer for Sir Gordon Downey and the revamped Privileges Committee to investigate than it took to set up Nolan, his committee, his office staff and his hearings, from scratch. The newly-formed Standards and Privileges Committee took the best part of twenty hours of meetings to analyse the first document which came their way. It remained to be seen how they would cope with the thousands of pages of evidence about to come their way. What you have in these pages are the tools for your judgement, not neatly knotted history. But the *Guardian* team – the reporters, the researchers, the editors, the long-suffering managers and the beavering lawyers – think this the only relevant way. We're not concerned with pretty packages. We have all lived and breathed and fretted over this story because it reaches to the heart of our system of government.

Many democracies around the world have bulwarked their credibility by inviting outsiders in, by building judicial tribunals into the system. They are not clubs. They try to relate directly to the people they serve. Westminster has always chosen another way. Westminster may still be trying to choose another way. The case of Neil Hamilton, we believe, is the test of that self-regulatory way, perhaps to destruction. After this, can it be business as usual? After this, will anyone heed the clipped warnings of Ivor Crewe? The *Guardian* cites the public interest. And we believe we do it on behalf of you, the ultimate jury.

Peter Preston
Alan Rusbridger
London, December 1996

Putting on the Ritz

'This refinement, this perfection, is not a super-
fluous luxury, nor abusive privilege, but truly an
art of knowing how to live.'

Jacques Chirac on the Paris Hotel Ritz, 24 July 1986

Shattering the silence of an autumn dawn, green fleets from
Mayor Jacques Chirac's *Propreté de Paris* cleaning department
fanned out across the cobblestones of the Place Vendôme.
The dogs on the streets of distant London, where municipal
subsidy was not a political priority, may have been tugging as
usual at bits of decomposed Kentucky Fried Chicken for
breakfast, out of bags of uncleared rubbish. But by the time
the Paris of the mid-1980s went to work, battalions of men
and women in green tunics driving green vehicles and carrying
green hosepipes or fluorescent green plastic brooms had
swept and hosed down the French capital until it glistened.
There were even special green scooters kitted out with
vacuum-cleaner units to pick up the dog turds. But the sounds
of this fastidious cleansing in the elegant eighteenth-century
square reached only faintly up to the bedrooms on the third
floor, where a British Conservative MP was snoring.

When he awoke in the gleaming brass bed, the first thing
Neil Hamilton could see was a terracotta bust, in the *belle
époque* style, of a sweetly enticing French courtesan. It had
been studiously placed there by the management. The bust
had an elaborate *pompadour* hairstyle and two little roses
peeping out beneath her exposed breasts. Perched on the
windowsill of Room 356 at the £400-a-night Paris Hotel Ritz,
the sculptured lady turned a honeyed glance slightly sideways,
her eyelids lowered. It was a gesture of respectful unseeing, as
though to offer both pleasure and discretion. Of course,

Hamilton's profession deployed different skills – the parliamentary question rather than the tease of a fingertip – but he would have understood the young lady's codes of practice.

From 8 to 14 September 1987, Hamilton was having all his bills paid at the Paris Ritz. This trip, with his wife Christine who was sleeping beside him, was what the Conservative MP was to term one of his 'little indiscretions', and he was determined to get the most out of it. Room 356 is not the best at the Ritz, not by a long chalk. And indeed, Hamilton complained that it was a room without a view of Paris. His pique was greeted with a Gallic shrug. The Ritz was a former aristocratic town house in the heart of the city, close by the Tuileries Gardens, and 'a view' was not the point. It was the interior fantasy-scape that mattered. The dilapidated hotel had been restored, from tapestry-panelled wall to gilt lavatory chain, by its owner, Mohammed al-Fayed, who also owned Britain's élite department store, Harrods. For some time, since 1985, Fayed had hired Hamilton to pursue his interests at Westminster. As a result, the Hamiltons were now in an orchard of opulence, with permission to pick the fruit.

They were waved each night through the antique-look mirror doors of the hotel's Espadon restaurant, by the debonair, chisel-jawed young man who checked reservations from behind a lectern. The demand from gourmets for Espadon bookings was such that non-residents had to book a week in advance. The Hamiltons' table, in cream linen, had a porcelain vase of miniature roses and two huge waiting menus, printed on board in gold-leaf and blue. There was space for only 50 diners in the intimate but well-proportioned room, plus a discreet string quartet.

The music of Mozart accompanied the 'scrambled eggs *Périgourdine* in cassoulette with shredded truffles', and '*pastilla* of warm foie gras with sliced black truffles and a chicken aspic'. To the sound of Haydn's Esterhazy quartets, whole lobsters were dished up warm in 'an aromatic broth with an orange sauce'. '*Les Viandes*' ensued in handsome portions, served by waiters gliding like swans across the floorspace, in tails and cream-coloured bow ties, carrying plateloads of the '*premières de côtes d'agneau tranchés*', '*jeunes pousses à cru et jus de homard*'. Like circus jugglers' props, in arrangements that defied gravity, the 'double chop of milk-fed veal studded with cracked grey peppercorns and *Guérande* sea salt' competed with 'breast of *Bresse* chicken larded with foie gras cooked in *vin jaune* served with a *quenelle* of polenta with San Daniele ham'.

More Mozart. Then, the 'tray of cheeses selected by our traymaster' and finally the coda, '*Les Desserts*', perhaps the 'Savarin cake with seasonal fruit, a sorbet of *fromage blanc* and a passion fruit sauce'. Gourmandising for two, washed down every single night with a bottle of the Ritz's own house-brand champagne. The Hamiltons never left the Espadon after a meal without an unpaid bill of more than £200 being totted-up in their wake. Only once during this gluttony did they decide against the string quartet, ordering up a £232 dinner to eat in their room instead. But never did they consider a night off, with a more cardiac-friendly menu in a local *brasserie*, at their own expense.

After dinner, the couple ran a gauntlet of luxury the management called 'Temptation Alley' to return to their room. Temptation Alley is a shopping arcade of glass cases with up-market trinketry on display and a musk perfume pumped through the air vents. And more Mozart. At each end of the mall is a mirror wall, to make it look three times the real length. It was almost liturgical – the Ritz religion; a nave in the cathedral of Mammon with gleaming side chapels. *Marc de Morandes Parfums* came first. Then, at the next showcase, Christine Hamilton might have paused by a designer cling-fit peacock-blue sequined mini-dress. Was it quite her style? She could order her initials to be fashioned in *diamanté* for an earring, choker or brooch. The next glass altar was consecrated to *Lorid* – and that was full of silver sea shells and snails.

The Hamiltons asked to stay six nights here at the Ritz, walking up and down, through the scent-soaked air. Their own room was like a stage-set for a periwigged farce – Beaumarchais without the wit or satire: one of those dreadful domestic dramas in which dandies and music teachers are forever hiding behind sofas then jumping into bed with the chambermaid or out of the *boudoir* window. The pastel blue walls had neo-classical *bas-reliefs* with lutes and laurel leaves.

The fireplace was an extraordinary gilt-and-marble structure, and on the mantelpiece was a vast gold clock with cherubs supporting a brass lyre. It looked like something stolen from a rococo cathedral altar. Next to these monuments was a mock-marble minibar full of champagne and Swiss chocolate, to which the Hamiltons laid siege. Their daily bill from the fridge averaged some £35 (1987 prices), rising to a valedictory £72.16 on the last day.

In the bathroom, the mixer taps on the 'His and Hers' basin suite were silver swans, water bursting forth from their open mouths. There was a vase of purple orchids by the vanity mirror. The Hamiltons may have snickered over the two china-handled bell-pulls that hung down into the bath itself. One said 'valet', the other 'maid'. Beside the bed too, were buttons with illuminated coloured lights: '*Sommelier*/Waiter' (red); '*Femme de Chambre*' (green) and '*Valet de Chambre*' (yellow). The Hamiltons breakfasted there most mornings, at £30 or £40 a throw. By the door was a picture called '*Le Baiser*', of two pubescent *putti* kissing one another with titillating, naughty-naughty innocence. Above their bed, a reproduction Corot. 'It would have to be repro,' said one of the Ritz managers drily. 'Anything original in here would be stolen.'

Neil and Christine Hamilton managed to run up an impressive total bill of £4,221. On a crisp autumn evening, with the leaves of the Parisian plane trees just turning to gold, the MP could have stepped on to the balcony of Room 356 after supper and told himself this was only the beginning. A future of 'little indiscretions' may have seemed to beckon from across the slate rooftops of the Ritz, and the Parisian night beyond, across the gardens of the Ministry of Justice. Courtrooms and justice would certainly have been the last things on his mind.

**Mohammed al-Fayed, Egyptian multi-millionaire,
alights from his company vehicle, a Harrods carriage**

2

Zero Hour

'The English ships passing, with the officers on deck in their white uniforms. They were a dream to me.'

Mohammed al-Fayed

An unforgiving anger moved across the owner of Harrods' mind as he scanned the business page of that Sunday's *Observer* newspaper. Despite his protests to the paper's 'independent directors'; despite the long letters of complaint to the Secretary of State for Trade and Industry; despite the writs for libel which his expensive lawyers had served the previous month . . . despite all this, his opponent kept coming at him. That Sunday morning, Mohammed al-Fayed decided to counter-attack.

The date was October 1985, two years before Neil Hamilton's free trip to the Paris Ritz, and it was as a result of this article in the *Observer* that the MP was recruited by the Egyptian. The article was written by the paper's City editor. It repeated a claim by the *Observer*'s proprietor, Tiny Rowland – chief executive of the giant Lonrho trading company – that the present proprietor of Harrods had unfairly snatched the purchase of the 'top people's store' in Knightsbridge. Rowland had been trying to acquire the store for himself, and the two tycoons had been locked in a bitter duel ever since. Fayed was accused of having bought this emblem of establishment London by using someone else's money – that of the Sultan of Brunei, who was so ridiculously rich that if one of his financial advisers had ever borrowed a few hundred million pounds for a while, the billionaire autocrat would probably not even have noticed.

The *Observer* article also carried a threat of battle to come:

'Rowland,' it said, 'has raised the matter, in a letter sent by hand last Monday, with the Prime Minister, Margaret Thatcher.' Moreover, the piece went on, the Government's Office of Fair Trading (OFT) had not closed the file on Mohammed al-Fayed's claims of immense family wealth, which had persuaded the Government to wave through his purchase of Harrods in the first place. 'Few City observers expect Rowland to let the matter rest,' trumpeted the paper, on behalf of its owner. 'The fact that the OFT file is officially open will inevitably lead to further pressure from Lonrho. And presumably further disclosures.'

If Fayed's reaction was in character with his normal temperament, he would have sworn until the air was blue. But he then also decided, on that day in his palatial penthouse on Park Lane, that it was time to act. Time to stop this relentless campaign over his origins – that exotic story which Rowland was so determined to unearth, which had begun more than 40 years before in the Egyptian city of Alexandria. Fayed's sensitivity about his early career in Egypt was now to raise the curtain on a drama of bribery and corruption which would last a decade and turn British political life upside down.

'No subject of conversation except money,' Lawrence Durrell, the British Embassy's press attaché in Alexandria, complained to his American friend in 1944. Durrell, one of many European writers entranced by the fabulous history of Egypt's second city, was writing to the author Henry Miller. At that time there were few remains of the city's classical antiquity, as Durrell discovered, seeking out the whispers of Alexandria's past with the help of a famous guidebook by E. M. Forster. 'No, I don't think you would like it,' he wrote to Miller, 'this smashed up, broken down shabby Neapolitan town, with its Levantine mounds of houses peeling in the sun'. There was, he complained, 'no music, no art, no real gaiety. A saturated middle-European boredom laced with drink and Packards and beach cabins.' That, of course, was the view of the privileged and bored who eyed with disdain what they saw as the Alexandrian 'morass of venality and money'.

But the city was also a place of exotic romance. In Durrell's imagination, entering it from the harbour 'is like walking the plank for instantly you feel, not only the plangently Greek city rising before you, but its back cloth of deserts stretching far away into the heart of Africa. You hear nothing but the noise of the sea and the echoes of an extraordinary history.' And what an extraordinary history: the royal city of the Ptolemies and Cleopatra, the intellectual birthplace of Christianity and the world's seat of learning for 700 years. When the Arab general Amr rode through the Gate of the Sun with his 4,000 cavalry in AD 642, past the tomb of Alexander and the Pharoah's Lighthouse – one of the seven wonders of the world – he sent an understated message back to the Caliph in Arabia: 'I have taken a city of which I can only say that it contains 4,000 palaces, 4,000 baths, 400 theatres, 1,200 greengrocers and 40,000 Jews.'

The three Fayed brothers – not Jews, but Arabs – were born into this city between 1929 and 1933. The future was pregnant with promise and adventure for these brothers: they were going to own famous things, be flattered by rulers, outsmart tycoons and, in the end, reveal the humbug at the heart of British political life. Led by Mohammed al-Fayed, they were traders and commission-takers. Like so many other Arab fixers, once the world oil price went up in the 1970s, they would surf on a tidal wave of new money flowing into Paris and London, as individuals of astonishing wealth.

In the Alexandria of their birth, while sensitive expatriates lounged in the luxury of the Cecil Hotel, drank cocktails in the Union Bar or took cakes at the *art deco* Pastroudis café, the real Alexandria hummed on commerce as it had done more than 2,000 years before. It was essentially a city of the Levant, facing the Mediterranean rather than the desert. The cool breezes from the north and the expansive beaches that swept along a 15-mile Corniche to the east made Alexandria the summer escape from the heat and dust of Cairo. There were perhaps half a million Egyptians, but the dynamism of the city's commerce came from its cosmopolitan atmosphere: Alexandria counted 80,000 foreigners, including wealthy Jewish families, and Greeks who dominated the war-time black market.

Mohammed al-Fayed and his four brothers and sisters grew up in the old quarter, not far from the docks and great cotton warehouses. Their father, a teacher of Arabic and later an inspector at the Ministry of Education, arrived in the early 1920s with his wife from a village in the Western Delta of the Nile. The Fayeds were blitzed and bombed throughout the second world war. Although Egypt had formally been an independent country since 1922 – after 50 years of domination from London – Britain remained a guarantor of Egypt's defence, with troops stationed along the Suez Canal. Alexandria was an important British naval base and her docks were the target of Luftwaffe bombing. In the summer of 1942, Field Marshal Rommel's Afrika corps was within a day's march of the city, and forced the British fleet to evacuate the port. Montgomery's victory at the battle of El Alamein was Alexandria's deliverance.

Years later, Rommel's businessman son, Manfred, would approach Fayed about the possibility of opening a branch of Harrods in Stuttgart. Fayed wrote back asking:

'Why did your father bomb my home town?'

'It was not my father,' replied Rommel Jnr., 'it was the air force.'

In later life, Fayed liked to recall the military activity which added a sense of excitement and glamour to the city: 'When I was a small boy in Alexandria I used to stand on the quayside and watch the English ships passing, with the officers on deck in their white uniforms. They were a dream to me. They were men of efficiency and men of honour. I dreamed of being like them.' He would add, with a twist of irony: 'They seemed incorruptible.' Despite the air raid sirens, black-outs and the dull thud of the explosions, the city lived on through war. Entire families would head down to the *brasseries* on the Corniche to drink beer and eat *mezze*. Young people roamed in noisy gangs to the beach, the café and cinema. In dilapidated Sister Street, the red light quarter boomed, as did Mary's House, the most famous brothel in Alexandria, where the girls were said to accommodate 35 men a night each.

Egypt emerged from the turmoils of war only to be plunged into the 1948 conflict with Israel, the 1952 revolution that brought Nasser to power, and the Suez invasion of 1956. Fayed, meanwhile, embarked on the traditionally Alexandrian pursuit of making money. His entrée into business came through the omnipresent Saudi Arabian fixer, Adnan Khashoggi. Khashoggi's father, a devout Muslim from Mecca, was a physician and confidant of King Ibn Saud, conqueror of modern Saudi Arabia. Adnan and two of his brothers were sent to Alexandria for their education at Victoria College, modelled on a British public school. After they left in 1952, Adnan set up in business in Riyadh, then took off for university in California. Fayed also went to Saudi Arabia, at that time a brutal, backward, feudal expanse. He became Khashoggi's manager, soon trusted with major contracts. In 1954, he married Adnan Khashoggi's sister, Samira. His brother Ali al-Fayed, then aged 20, followed Khashoggi to the United States to college near San Francisco. The families thus entwined, Khashoggi helped the Fayeds towards commercial success, even though they fell out within four years and Mohammed divorced Samira in 1958.

During the 1960s, the Arabian peninsula saw the real beginning of the oil revenues that would turn its deserts into a great black lake of money. Its rulers were persuaded that much of it would be wisely spent on Western guns, missiles, tanks and planes, which is how Khashoggi became one of the most ubiquitous arms dealers of the century, taking millions on commission. Meanwhile, the Fayed brothers acquired a string of companies and interests: hotels, transport and shipping, with agencies in Genoa and half a dozen eastern Mediterranean ports. Some of their Egyptian interests were lost between 1961 and 1964, as Nasser launched a widespread programme of 'nationalisation', but by then the brothers were moving away from their city of origin.

Local newspapers published in the poorest country in the Western hemisphere recorded the arrival in 1964 of 'Sheikh' Mohammed al-Fayed, said to be of Kuwait. Fayed had come to Port-au-Prince, capital of Haiti, for an audience with the island's dictator, Papa Doc Duvalier. Haiti is one of the world's most remarkable corners – Voodoo isle, where the fabulous villas that rise above the Caribbean look out over the banana trees that line the silver beaches – and over the sprawling, stinking shanty towns of Cité Soleil and Carrefour, where dwellings are built on landfills of packed rubbish and children play in open sewers.

This was an inauspicious start for Fayed's brokerage in politics. One of the features of life in the teeming slums of Port-au-Prince was that as the hot sun sank, the rich young men from Papa Doc's *tonton macoute* militias would start their patrols of the emptying streets. By the time the city rose early for work, the remains of that night's *macoute* victims, mutilated with machetes, were already drawing the flies, steaming in the early sunshine.

Fayed's introduction to Papa Doc, ruler of this nightmare-in-paradise, had been made by Clemard Joseph Charles, Duvalier's banker and bagman who siphoned off Haitian money to Swiss banks. 'Sheikh' Mohammed, he said, wanted to invest $6 million in the impoverished country by building an oil refinery and modernising the harbour.

One of the journalists who wrote about the intriguing Arab visitor rather than the usual violence one morning was Aubelin Joliceur, a character who had attracted the attention of Graham Greene while the novelist was writing his masterpiece *The Comedians*. 'It was the most critical year of Papa Doc's rule,' wrote Greene, 'and perhaps the cruellest . . . Though the curfew had been raised no one ventured out after dark.' In the novel, Joliceur became Petit Pierre who showed 'an odd satirical courage – perhaps he depended on the police not to read between the lines'. Understandably, Fayed did not stay long in Haiti. Eight months later, he disappeared; the Haitian dictator later claiming he had spirited away $100,000 from the harbour authority. Fayed says he lost money on the initial works and withdrew when Duvalier had demanded a $5 million bribe. It was a plausible story, but a sorry start.

So Fayed turned his trader's eye back to the Arabian Gulf, to Dubai. This was an obscure desert sheikhdom surviving on pearl fishing, trade with Iran and smuggling. Sheikh Rashid bin Said al-Maktoum, a canny merchant ruler, decided to improve the port, even before oil was discovered in 1966. By the end of the 1970s, Dubai was an oil state and a shipping and industrial hub. Some called it the Hong Kong of the Middle East. Much of the early construction work was done by British firms – Costain, Taylor Woodrow, Bernard Sunley – and financed by banks, principally Morgan Grenfell, from the City of London. The Fayed brothers were pivotal to this development, and began to acquire a fortune. From 1967 Fayed was retained as Costain's agent; within ten years he was also in a joint venture agreement with Morgan Grenfell for a share of commission fees on new business. The backward sheikhdom was dragged into the twentieth century in little more than two decades. Fayed built a skyscraper there, which was fully let even before it was completed. The boom involved billions of pounds, and for British executives involved in the construction works, Fayed was a crucial facilitator, on good terms with the sheikh and the power-brokers of Dubai. It was Fayed's connections with Costain that took him to another big player on the international business scene. The brothers started to invest in Costain in 1970, and by 1974 controlled 25 per cent of the shares. Then they linked up with one of the most colourful and controversial trading firms in Britain: Lonrho.

Lonrho grew out of an African mining business in Rhodesia, and was controlled by R. W. 'Tiny' Rowland, a tall tycoon of German origin who had pale blue eyes and flew into dangerous rages when crossed. In Britain, Mohammed al-Fayed was not only to cross Tiny Rowland, but to outsmart him at his own game. Although Rowland's boardroom table was decorated with senior British Tory politicians such as Duncan Sandys and Edward du Cann, disclosures about secret payments to directors in the Cayman Islands and bribes to foreign rulers led to Rowland being branded by Conservative Prime Minister Edward Heath in 1973 as 'the unpleasant and unacceptable face of capitalism'.

The Fayeds sold most of their Costain stake to Lonrho. Mohammed took a seat on the Lonrho board. He and Ali eventually bought a total of 10 million Lonrho shares. But the relationship failed to thrive and the Fayeds sold out in 1976, to Sheikh Nasser al Sabah of the Kuwaiti royal family, for £12.5 million. Mohammed and Tiny (who used to refer to the Egyptian trader as 'Tootsie') went their separate ways for seven years. With his growing pile of money, Fayed acquired a symbol of Manhattan, part of the celebrated Rockefeller Centre. In 1979 he bought the *fin-de-siècle* Paris Hotel Ritz, a gloriously fading badge of French cultural history. Sparing no expense, Fayed set about restoring this venerable monument to the Parisian *belle époque* as a gilt extravaganza, to such an extent that President Jacques Chirac treated him to the freedom of the French capital, the prized medal, the *Légion d'Honneur*, and some very flowery speeches: 'The feelings of esteem and friendship that I have for you . . . your innate sense of business, your art of human relations, and the unity and solidarity of your family surroundings . . . your success is exemplary and envied . . . you are no ordinary businessman. In a world in which everyone thinks in a more and more ferocious way in terms of basic profit, you bring an unusual note of unselfishness and charity . . . how could I not feel an infinite gratitude?'

This passion for re-building the decaying curios of imperial Europe was an interesting side to Fayed's character. The newly-rich deal maker made his long-term residence not in France, however, but in Britain. In 1970 Fayed set himself up as the Scottish MacFayed. He was visiting a tanker ship he owned, run aground in the North Sea off the coast of Scotland. Returning, he caught sight of the fairy-tale, 600-year-old Balnagown Castle near Invergordon, dilapidated seat of the eccentric Clan Ross. He sought out the owner and made an offer, there and then. Having bought the castle, he set about restoring that too, while extending its estate to take in an expanse of forestry and mountains. His bulging bank-accounts were good for any quantity of stags' heads, fire-irons, repro Gothic Revival furniture and stuffed golden eagles. Fayed says that his 'greatest wish' is 'to see the golden eagle sweep once again around the towers of Balnagown'. Here, Fayed also bought his first shop, a small store and post office in the neighbouring village. He walked in one day, spent £30 (the highest single bill in the shop's history), met the two ladies who owned it and bought them out. It took 30 minutes.

In London, the Fayeds bought a more ambitious property: a spectacular penthouse in the most famous street in Mayfair, overlooking Hyde Park and rapidly being colonised by the new Middle Eastern millionaires. On the eighth floor of No 60 Park Lane, they created an atmosphere of neo-Alexandrian opulence, while fitting the walls with oak panels stripped from English castles. As Tiny Rowland put it: 'Between the potted palms and the perfume-injected air was the delicious smell of lots of money.' At nightfall from Fayed's windows, it is said, he could see the lights of the famous Harrods store, glittering like a gaudy jewel, to the west across the park in Knightsbridge. In a special way, for Mohammed al-Fayed, Harrods stood for England. It was the high altar of that England he had imagined as a boy in Egypt. It was also the temple of money; and Fayed longed to buy it. The English establishment came to get its silk pyjamas from whoever owned Harrods, and Fayed craved such a role.

What was the attraction of weary Britain for Fayed and so many of his newly-rich Middle Eastern colleagues who thronged the Dorchester Hotel, the casinos of the West End, and the mansions of 'Millionaires' Row' in Hampstead? Partly, of course, it was simply that England was more interesting. Who would not prefer the champagne and opera of temperate London to a grim vista of baking Arabian sand? Partly, there was an attraction in the City of London's financial skills: for many years, the Fayeds used the blue-blooded money-managers of Morgan Grenfell to handle their deals. But there was something else. London represented the heart of an empire to which Fayed and his compatriates had once been expected to kow-tow. 'The English ships passing, with the officers on the deck in their white uniforms. They were a dream to me.' Britain and its institutions – the Navy, the Queen, Big Ben – still stood, in the imagination of people like Fayed, for efficient sobriety. With the arrogance of the British, they thought, went a reputation for probity. Fayed says this is what he had been brought up to admire in them. There is no reason to disbelieve him: it is what the Empire taught and what British politicians after all, claim to admire about themselves: 'Mother of Parliaments'; 'fount of democracy', etc., etc. The clichés, though mouldering and decades past their sell-by date, are well known.

From his London base, Fayed operated on a big map. He obtained an introduction to the fantastically wealthy young dictator of Brunei, a jungle state near Borneo with an economy built round Shell Oil. The revenues were so big and the country so small that the Sultan could not spend the money fast enough, although he tried. He bought 11 Rolls-Royces and Bentleys, seven Mercedes, four Ferraris and a jumbo jet. He built a 1,788-room palace bigger than the Vatican, and still had plenty left – enough to tilt the economy and currency of a country like the Britain of Prime Minister Margaret Thatcher. The Sultan had a cash surplus of $15 billion, some of which was managed for him by Morgan Grenfell. He took away $5 billion from the British-run Crown Agents after Brunei won its independence and handed it over to rival American banks Morgan Guaranty and Citibank. These were big enough sums to affect the health of sterling, and were desperately important to the bankers' wallets. Fayed travelled to Brunei in the summer of 1984 and came successfully away with powers of attorney to handle the Sultan's business deals. He was adorned with the useful sobriquet 'the Sultan's personal adviser'. With the Sultan's money, Fayed bought the run-down Dorchester Hotel close by his Park Lane penthouse, on the Sultan's behalf.

Fayed, now an influential figure in the Middle East, was still unknown to the British public. But in the autumn of 1984, he broke on to the British scene like an unexpected starburst from a firework display. He did so as a beaming, avuncular and fabulously rich Egyptian entrepreneur from nowhere – or as Tiny Rowland would furiously dub him, the Hero from Zero. The cause of the astonishment was that Fayed and his brothers suddenly offered to pay £615 million cash for Britain's deluxe retail group, House of Fraser. The jewel in this company's crown was the famous Knightsbridge storefront of Harrods itself, gleaming across the park. Rowland himself had been scheming to control House of Fraser for seven years, frustrated by boardroom opposition and a hostile Conservative Government which blocked his bids at every turn. His rage at the Fayeds' bid was increased by the fact that he himself sold the Fayeds the initial 30 per cent of the House of Fraser shares, thinking to buy them back later and unaware that the Fayeds had acquired huge funds with which to make their own bid. Indeed, how could the claim by a trio of unknown Egyptians that they were financially stronger than most British corporations be taken seriously by anyone?

Fayed was soon surrounded by a cloud of PR men, City lawyers and bankers who assured the public and the authorities, particularly Trade Secretary Norman Tebbit, that the Fayeds were the Egyptian equivalent of Old Money, sound as the Bank of England. Inspectors from the Department of Trade and Industry were later to report: 'The image they created of their wealthy Egyptian ancestry was completely bogus.' But even at the time, this hype was not enough to win the deal. Fayed did more. He had the ear of the Sultan of Brunei throughout the bid, and he spoke into it.

While his bid was being prepared in 1984, Fayed approached Prime Minister Margaret Thatcher (he was employing her PR adviser, Gordon Reece). Fayed settled down to meetings with Mrs Thatcher's newly-appointed foreign affairs adviser, civil servant Charles Powell, who had been seconded from the Foreign Office. As events progressed, Powell and his gregarious Italian wife Carla became friendly not only with Mohammed al-Fayed, but with his wife, Heini. Powell, a linguist once based in Helsinki, had the ability, unusual anywhere, to converse with Heini in her native Finnish. It developed a bond which would have repercussions. A feature of British foreign policy at the time was Mrs Thatcher's attempts to strike deals with oil-rich foreign countries, particularly in the Gulf, and to sell them advanced weapons, banking services, or practically anything else they could be persuaded to buy with the fortunes they held in sterling. This banana-republic economics led to a procession of colourful characters through the doors of Downing Street, like the Syrian Wafic Said, 'man of affairs' for the royal family of Saudi Arabia, who helped to negotiate a controversial £20 billion deal in 1985 to sell Tornado fighter aircraft to the Saudis.

Now Fayed's friend, the Sultan of Brunei, was due to visit Britain. While visiting Mrs Thatcher, the Sultan had money on his mind. The pound was in dire straits, level with the US dollar. The Sultan's billions might be better stashed in dollars. It would be better for Britain's economy if they were not. Moreover, the Sultan had £500 million to spend on arms, and should be prepared to buy British – but was just now pondering an option for a mix'n'match French and German hardware package. Fayed stepped into the breach, 'helpful' to Her Majesty's Government, as Charles Powell agrees. Fayed claims that he persuaded the Sultan to switch back his $5 billion of funds into British management, despite the poor state of sterling. Fayed was present at the Sultan's side as his 'personal adviser' when he arrived at Downing Street for his January state visit. Furthermore, according to Fayed, it was he who cemented the eventual £500 million arms sale for the British, via the Chief of the Defence Staff, Field Marshal Lord Bramall. So anxious was Defence Secretary Michael Heseltine for his help that 'he went to Park Lane, waiting for me two hours with a letter', says Fayed.

It is an unlikely-sounding story – except that Bramall is perfectly happy to confirm it was true: 'Mohammed al-Fayed was very useful to us at this time. It was known he had a lot of influence with the Sultan ... Michael Heseltine and I, at the insistence of Mrs Thatcher, went to see him at Park Lane. It was quite a brief chat, but the Sultan did return to his traditional links with us. We did hope that defence contracts would follow because we knew the Sultan wanted an air force.' Eventually, in 1989 a £500 million deal did emerge for Hawk jets and warships.

Fayed works on the trader's principle: 'To give is to receive.' In the end, his bid for Harrods was waved through on 2 November 1984 by a friendly Government, with only a flimsy inquiry into his wealth. As to whether the Fayed brothers manipulated the Sultan of Brunei's powers of attorney in a shrewd juggling of loans that got them control of the department store, no-one knows. The Sultan says he has no evidence they did – and adds, rather cryptically: 'If they did so, either in connection with the House of Fraser negotiation or in any other context, they did so totally without my authority.'

The source of the Fayed brothers' wealth and their origins became the kernel of one of the most bitter duels in British corporate history. Tiny Rowland's failure to anticipate the Fayeds' strategy led him, with the help of the *Observer*, which he then owned, to launch a relentless assault on the Egyptian brothers, trawling the world with an open cheque book for any damaging material. He said: 'This company can never forgive or forget.'

It was Rowland's vendetta which spawned the ominous

Observer article in October 1985 that now lay open at the offending business pages, in front of an angry Fayed in his London penthouse. It became plain to Mohammed al-Fayed that Rowland would not cease his attacks until the tycoon had successfully persuaded the politicians of Britain to take Harrods away from him again. Fayed had pulled off a spectacular coup in acquiring the store, with its shimmering lights, its cornucopian food hall, the famously well-groomed girls at the perfume counter. But for Fayed to protect his gains in Britain from interference, it was now going to be necessary for him to purchase some local political influence of his own. The next day, Fayed sent for the lobbyist, Ian Greer.

Ian Greer, lobbyist, at his offices near Westminster
where he keeps an MP's division bell.
Born a redhead in Glasgow,
he re-invented himself to achieve this gilded executive image

3

Maximum Pressure

'We don't pay MPs.'

Ian Greer, 1984

The 52-year-old who walked into Fayed's Park Lane pent-house suite on 28 October 1985 had a lot of straight grey hair, over-expensively styled so that it sat on his head rather like a wig. He liked to shop for shirts in Bond Street at Swaine Adeney Brigg, at Asprey for silver cufflinks and at Floris for scent. He had a Baume watch, to consult when it was time for lunch at Mark's Club, or in one of the discreet, over-priced booths at Wiltons in Jermyn Street so favoured by Conservative politicians. He was short and slight; insipid, a little dandy-ish with dark, slightly scary, eyes. He spoke with a well-bred accent, but his speech was marked by a slight simper. The lobbyist's business card said: 'Ian Greer Associates'. It told Fayed that his office was in St James's, at Catherine Place, within Division Bell distance of the House of Commons (he had had the Division Bell installed either to accommodate the needs of those who used his place as a hub of activity, or else to give that impression).

Fayed's friend Lord King, the hard-boiled chairman of British Airways, had recommended Greer as the best political 'fixer' he knew. King's British Airways was a notably predatory company, and they flourished as schoolyard bully of the airline business – in no small degree thanks to Greer's black art of lobbying. With Greer at his elbow, King had just sabotaged an attempt by the Civil Aviation Authority to force BA to hand over lucrative routes to a minnow of a rival, British Caledonian. British Airways did not like domestic competition, as companies such as Laker had found – and Richard Branson's Virgin would find – to their cost. King kept Greer on his books as a well-paid expert, who could recommend influential MPs for BA free trips and holidays, keep Conservative ministers sweet and throw champagne parties for politicians. Greer's weighty friends could chat about free enterprise one minute, and about crushing British Caledonian the next. To Greer, it was all good business.

At Park Lane, confronted with a new and wealthy potential client, Greer launched into his sales pitch. He proposed a renewable one-year contract with Ian Greer Associates. To improve the Egyptian's political profile, he envisaged 'a carefully prepared programme of meetings with Ministers and senior backbenchers . . .' Fayed cut him off. What the owner of Harrods wanted was the problem of Tiny Rowland solved and the attacks in the *Observer* stopped, right away. Greer should speak to his lawyer Michael Palmer to understand the facts. Greer got the message. He hit the phone. Within 48 hours, he despatched Fayed a letter saying he was now positioned on Fayed's behalf to put 'maximum pressure' on Leon Brittan, who had taken over as Trade Secretary. With that move, Ian Greer's most dangerous lobbying contract was in the bag. How could he have known it was a deal that would ultimately unveil the corruption of Westminster and in the end destroy both him and his firm?

Greer's organisation, only three years old, had a growing list of blue-chip clients. As well as British Airways, there was the Whitbread brewery, DHL the couriers, the food-and-drink giant Cadbury Schweppes and the store chain, Kingfisher. Immaculately dressed and mannered, Ian Greer liked to portray himself to these clients as the quintessential English Conservative gentleman. But it had not always been like that.

In fact the diminutive Ian Bramwell Greer was born in 1933, in Glasgow, and brought up among the tenement blocks of a city ravaged by the great depression at its harshest. Unemployment, poverty and drink were hallmarks of Glasgow in the slump. But Ian Greer was born into a family engaged in God's war against the misery, the son and grandson of Salvation Army preachers who came originally from Ireland. With that sort of faith, it would have been a more rigid and ambitious household than most of the Greers' neighbours. The family moved to a new 1930's council house estate a welcome stone's throw (about five minutes' walk) away from the infamous Gorbals. It was in the southern part of the city centre, a step up from the slums. Upon the outbreak of war, he went to Victoria Primary School, said to have been a place of decent education for the upright working-class families.

Contemporaries remember Ian Greer with a broad Glaswegian brogue and a ginger mop of hair. Eventually, Greer's parents moved south with the Salvation Army to the outskirts of London, and sent the young Ian to Cranbrook College in Ilford, Essex. It was an independent school, taking day boys, and young Ian Greer stayed for just 11 months. However, he manages to include it in the *Who's Who* entry he eventually acquired in the 1990s. Old boys describe Greer as an 'unmemorable pupil'. Whatever education Greer did receive remains a mystery, and is kept out of his public record. A now-hostile, once-close, colleague said he would be surprised if Greer left with any noteworthy examination record: 'he was a poor performer and not that intelligent'.

Greer had another cross to bear: he was gay, in a world where homosexuality was a crime. It was not until 1967 that homosexual acts between men were de-criminalised in Britain and for a homosexual, London in the fifties was a place of shared secrets, shame and potential blackmail. In the Conservative party, homosexuality was a meeting point between people like Greer, who came as new arrivals into the establishment and the capital city, and the stalwart traditions of beating and buggery at the 'better' schools of England. Throughout his later career Greer was to develop connections with a number of gay MPs, in a circle with a marked – often overt – homosexual flavour. This may well have been cogent to his eventual system of payments to politicians – not because the ethics of homosexuals vary from those of others, but because a sense of shared secrets can sometimes make a special bond. British politicians and homosexuals from that period sometimes found there was also a common professional survival value in lying. A politician learns automatically to obscure the awkward truth, just as gay men did.

Greer's first known employment, which he took in 1953,

was as a clerk at Conservative Central Office where he took an interest in organising the Young Conservatives. His first entry into the political fray as a voluntary 'trainee agent' took him to Dartford, Kent, in 1955 – the constituency where Margaret Thatcher once stood unsuccessfully for parliament. Here in 1959, Peter Walker ran for the Conservatives, and the 26-year-old Greer was his paid agent – 'the youngest agent at Central Office', he used to say.

The campaign brought him together with the youthful Michael Grylls, Walker's 25-year-old personal assistant. It was the beginning of a long and lucrative friendship between the lowly Glaswegian preacher's son and the groomed, almost *bouffant* offspring of a brigadier – chalk and cheese. Grylls had been an officer in the Marines, educated at the Royal Naval College in Dartmouth and universities in Paris and Madrid.

The key to Greer's rise was his intimate experience of the organised Conservative party – a formidable election-winning and influence-peddling machine, which Greer learnt to operate. His next job was as agent to Trevor Skeet, incumbent MP for Willesden East, who had won the marginal seat in Harold Macmillan's landslide victory of 1959. Greer was unsuccessful. When Harold Wilson overturned 13 years of Tory rule in 1964 and Labour moved into Downing Street, Skeet lost his seat. Now Sir Trevor Skeet, he is not a close friend of Greer, though he was on a list of MPs who agreed to be lobbied by Philip Morris, tobacco giant and Greer client, as late as 1994.

His tail between his legs, Ian Greer moved on to become agent for the Essex seat of Basildon and Billericay. Here he made a significant connection, working for Sir Edward Gardner, then a recently appointed QC. He met and became acquainted with Sir Edward's secretary, Barbara Wallace, who would one day be extremely useful: in 1979 she was made secretary to the newly-elected MP for Huntingdonshire, a clumsy figure called John Major.

Greer did not prosper as an agent, however. In 1966, Sir Edward, just like Sir Trevor before him, lost his seat and Greer's brief career fighting constituencies for losing Tories came to an abrupt end. He quit politics for a job in the charity world, as director of the Mental Health Trust. This was a small charity to which few people gave money, but which nevertheless had an illustrious list of trustees, including the banker Sir Evelyn de Rothschild, and Jocelyn Stevens, at the time editor of *Queen* magazine and a personal assistant to the managing director of Beaverbrook Newspapers. Greer might have enjoyed networking among the trustees, but this venture was not a success either. The organisation had large administrative expenses, and in 1968 was taken over by a rival mental health charity. Ian Greer lost out again.

This was the moment of metamorphosis for Ian Greer. His personality and appearance changed; little, ginger, Glaswegian Greer re-invented himself. The heavy accent disappeared. Now, plummy English tones flowed from the Greer mouth, a voice that would not sound out of place at an old-school-tie dinner. A darkened and more sombre hairstyle took over from the ginger mop. Then, at the end of 1968, Greer formed a public relations company with the new influence in his life: PR man John Russell, who was to become his long-standing homosexual partner. This re-invention plainly helped to launch Greer into the sphere where he was to be ultimately influential: Government and public relations. Ian and John enjoyed a successful personal and professional partnership for 14 years, before a venomous split.

At first, even if life was sweet back at the flat in Kensington, business was bad at the Mayfair office of Russell Greer Associates. Their aim was to create not just another public relations company but a new brand of lobbying business. Commercial firms and other organisations might have wanted to change the law, but rarely had any idea how to do it. They were not even regularly informed about what was going on in parliament or Whitehall. Russell and Greer believed they had spotted a gap in the market. Industry and interest groups needed access to legislative clout and influence. Politicians had influence. And despite the many acolytes who hung around the Westminster beehive, the agent who could put the right businessman on to the right politician seemed to be missing. The language of influence was money, of course.

Britain's infant lobbyists faced the problem that most businesses did not see the slightest reason why they needed to be informed, let alone pay fees to be so. So there was no interest.

For six months, Greer and Russell failed to find a single client. 'The directors of a company,' Greer concluded, 'felt they would be able to follow what was going on in ... the *Financial Times*. Or ... one of the directors had been close personal friends of an MP ... Many of the people I met at this time seemed to have great confidence in the old boy network.'

Greer set out to build his own 'new boy' network and to appoint a hand-picked staff dependent on him. The seeds of that network, which would one day bring in an annual turn-over of £3.5 million, were sown in the 1970s, before Greer fell out with John Russell. After seven lean years, he began to get the first of the blue-chip lobbying clients he was desperate to attract. During this period the Unitary Tax Campaign, Whit-bread (the brewers), DHL (the private mail couriers), the Midshires Building Society, Associated Octel (manufacturers of lead in petrol) and the white-collar trade union, ASTMS, were all recruited. These clients produced further contacts and provided the framework for the ensuing operation.

Greer's limited links with the Labour party were forged when ASTMS wanted to lobby MPs over flexible working hours. This gave Greer access to Clive Jenkins, then general secretary, to Muriel Turner, then assistant general secretary and to Doug Hoyle, then MP for Nelson and Colne and president of ASTMS. Muriel Turner, created a life peer in 1985, was later a director of Ian Greer Associates. Doug Hoyle was given a Greer employee, John Roberts, as research assistant after winning Warrington North in a 1981 by-election. But two crucial clients were the Unitary Tax Campaign and DHL.

The Unitary Tax Campaign began with the Foseco Minsep mining company. The company was suffering from legisla-tion being passed in various American states which meant British companies active there were taxed on the basis of worldwide earnings. It was a policy which some states, notably California and Florida, originally developed to avoid being cheated of tax revenue by big railroad companies that passed through their territory, claiming exemption from tax because their financial headquarters were elsewhere. In British eyes, it was an unacceptable imposition on foreign companies. Fose-co's finance director, Peter Welch, launched his campaign to counter this practice, and in 1979, in search of clout at Westminster, approached Ian Greer. The campaign involved 50 major companies and brought Greer in touch with international firms, including the cigarette barons British American Tobacco (BAT). It also gave him his first taste of having sufficient resources to pay for British MPs to fly to America – not on freebie junkets, but to lobby senators on Capitol Hill. The transformed Glaswegian redhead had gone multinational.

Among the politicians who quickly scrambled aboard was the dapper Michael Grylls, Greer's friend from the Dartford campaign in 1959 and now MP for Surrey North West. Almost immediately upon being elected in 1974, Grylls became an officer of the Conservative backbench trade and industry committee, and from 1981 he was its chairman. Grylls, described by one observer as having 'the looks of a 1930s matinee idol', was recruited as chief parliamentary front man for the Russell-Greer tax campaign, which was to run, nicely profitable, for years.

Grylls procured a pass to the Commons for Andrew Smith, Greer's young lieutenant and a former clerk in the Agriculture Ministry, as his 'research assistant' on the tax campaign. Smith, according to colleagues, became like a son to Greer and eventually his deputy in the company. A second young staffer, Anthony Mayes, got a Commons 'research assistant' pass from another of Greer's long-standing friends, Conservative MP Andrew Bowden. This enabled both men, inside the edifice of humbug, to get parliamentary papers and rub shoulders with the MPs.

The propriety of this was questionable, but the practice of commercial organisations suborning MPs to get access to the Commons was increasing. Many outsiders felt it ought to be diminished. But equally, some MPs thought they were so poorly paid and given such meagre resources by the taxpayer that they were driven to be less than fastidious about the rules, which require an MP to declare financial interests.

The lobbyists paid Michael Grylls steady sums of money. This was not against the undemanding parliamentary rules, in so far as Grylls declared on the MPs' Register of Interests that he was paid unspecified amounts as a 'consultant' to the tax

campaign. But the exact financial link between Grylls and
Greer himself was always opaque.

The second big break for the lobbyists came in 1981, when
DHL, a small private air courier company, approached
Russell-Greer. They did so in the form of Dave Allen, head of
DHL – a debonair playboy, who loved and lived with the jet
set. He was not the smooth Greer type at all. But for Allen,
Greer pulled off his biggest coup to date. He successfully
collared Kenneth Baker, then a junior minister, to break with
decades of history and push through a bill which scrapped the
postal monopoly on deliveries costing more than £1. That law
transformed a small courier company into a multimillion
earner and household name by the end of 1981. Part of Allen's
gratitude would be shown through £11,000 in donations,
given six years later to Ian Greer's company – allowing him to
spread his munificence among both Tory and Labour contacts, ranging from the Conservative Kenneth Warren (later
chairman of the all-party trade and industry committee) to
trade unionist Doug Hoyle.

With business beginning to boom, Greer recruited his first
team of youthful whizzkids, without paying overmuch attention to John Russell's views: John Rhys Sale, who later left for
America, John Roberts, a clerk from the Foreign Office, and
Charles Millar, who moved on to form his own company.
Relations with Russell began to deteriorate. Greer was always
the fawning 'meeter and greeter' while Russell, more reserved,
was backroom boy and researcher. By 1981 they were sitting
at opposite ends of the office. Russell said he was increasingly
unhappy at the way Ian Greer was developing the business –
and discontented with the accounts. Matters came to a head
just before Christmas 1981, when at an extraordinary board
meeting Russell accused Greer of spending the firm's money
to help his MP friends. Greer amazed the assembled company
by exploding into a rage. He accused his business partner and
lover of making 'outrageous allegations'. Most of the board,
except for business partner Derek Hart, the late BBC presenter, walked out. Millar, Roberts and Sale left with Greer
and founded their own company, Ian Greer Associates. Russell later found that two days before the meeting, files for all
the big accounts – DHL, the Unitary Tax Campaign, Whit-

bread and Associated Octel – had already been removed from the office. Greer had planned the coup weeks before. A legal agreement was signed later banning any mention of details of the 'divorce' for ten years. It was a vindictive parting with daggers drawn: those who stayed on with 'The Russell Partnership' claim that Greer tried to prise the last remaining clients away. Greer is said to have made bitchy telephone calls to former friends and colleagues to damage his former partner. Of course, the bad blood became worse as Ian Greer's success reached new heights.

Greer's estranged friends (of whom there are plenty) offer some insight into this curiously blank but clever mind. 'He is a dull and uninteresting person,' said one, 'who gets a turn-on from politics and being in the thick of it. He has no interest in anything else. He doesn't like opera, music, theatre, films or football matches, but he would arrange anything for his clients. He would go to the opera but he'd hate every minute of it.' Greer's unenlightening *Who's Who* entry specifies 'gardening' as a hobby. Former colleagues say, however, that he would spend very little time working on the grounds of Medley, his £750,000 residence on Kingston Hill on the River Thames, just outside London. 'Call in the expert' was his reaction to a horticultural problem. Greer liked to present himself as genteel. His taste was displayed at his Catherine Place business premises. Staff sat at bogus-antique tables, under oil-paintings depicting the Palace of Westminster. His own office was oppressively decorated in an ersatz country-house manner, with the affectation of a couple of poodles snoring on a sofa. Greer's favourite little dogs were called Sacha and Humphrey.

The large and genial Keith Lockwood is a professional PR man who likes to play it straight – may the best man win, and all that. Lockwood now works for Vauxhall, but in the early 1980s he was one of Greer's competitors in the public relations business. He encountered Greer's method of operation firsthand, as the Thatcher Government and its new crop of MPs were just getting into their stride. Lockwood was advising the big office supplies company, Rank Xerox. The corporation needed political support on a European 'antidumping' case against Japan, and wanted to contact the chairman of the Conservative backbench trade and industry committee. Lockwood helped them make contact: the chairman was the MP for North West Surrey, Michael Grylls.

Lockwood set up a meeting between Grylls and the Rank Xerox executive at the House of Commons. Grylls knew that it was Lockwood and his company, Shandwick, who had arranged the meeting and who were working with Rank Xerox. The Rank Xerox executive felt that he could handle the meeting alone, particularly since the UK parliament was somewhat peripheral to what was essentially a European Commission issue. But it was important to keep key UK MPs informed nevertheless.

The day after the meeting, Lockwood visited Rank Xerox to discuss progress. While he was there, Grylls rang the executive. Over the phone speaker, Lockwood heard Grylls say that on reflection he could be of help, but only if Rank Xerox employed a good lobbying company, 'and I know the very one – Ian Greer Associates . . . their telephone number is . . .' The Rank Xerox man explained that he already had such a company working for him: Shandwick. Grylls said that in that case, there was little he could do to help.

'The most blatant piece of commission-hunting I have ever come across,' says Lockwood. 'To have the audacity to suggest that the only way a large British company could effectively pursue European trade justice through the Conservative backbench trade and industry committee was by employing Ian Greer Associates is beyond belief. Knowing some of the other Conservative MPs on the committee very well, I do not believe that they were aware of this "sideline".'

Lockwood continued, 'Even ignoring the affront to democracy, the business advice was hopelessly off-line too. At that time, Greer did not have an operation in Brussels, concentrating solely on Westminster, and this was above all a European issue! I was so amazed I called Grylls myself next day. I told him: "Guess what: someone in your office has been commission-hunting and putting my clients on to Greer. What's going on?" Grylls pretended to be mystified. "How awful," he said, and promised me there'd be an internal inquiry to find out who it was. Well, I felt that I had made my point if nothing else.'

But the Grylls/Greer factor struck again some time later while Lockwood was still at Shandwick. As part of Shandwick's work for British Airways prior to privatisation, it was essential to involve Grylls in his Conservative backbench trade and industry committee position. Lockwood continued ruefully, 'The gods were not smiling on Shandwick that day – the BA executive absolutely insisted on meeting Grylls alone. A pure coincidence, I'm sure, but shortly after that meeting Shandwick lost the BA business to Greer.'

Lockwood goes on to say, 'I would be the first to admit, against the trend, that as a group politicians are overworked and underpaid. It will continue to be necessary for them to have outside business interests both to pay the mortgage and, more importantly, to keep them in touch with the "real world". However, I strongly draw the line at any suggestion that MPs earning commission by exploiting businessmen whose knowledge of parliament is slight is somehow acceptable.' The role of Michael Grylls was to be at the heart of Greer's lobbying system as it developed over the coming decade in Westminster. It was a discreet one.

Greer's old friend from the Dartford election in 1959 had now become his main connection. Grylls and he were, he said, 'Good and close friends.' It was a relationship that would thrive on undeclared 'introduction fees'.

With other MPs, the financial relationship was more bluntly expressed: Greer promised a free holiday to Labour backbencher Walter Johnson, in return for help with the interests of Greer's valued client, Associated Octel. The firm's future income making lead additives for petrol was in doubt. Awkward environmentalists were arguing that the lead should be reduced because lead fumes were poisoning the nation's infants by causing them brain damage, and that this was undesirable. Associated Octel and the socialist Johnson begged to differ. Johnson wrote candidly to Greer in 1983:

'Dear Ian, As you will recall, you kindly agreed to pay me a fee of £1,000 for services to your company, and that this would be paid in the form of paying a bill for a holiday. Will you confirm that this arrangement still stands?'

Johnson said, 'It was a chance to earn some extra cash – nothing wrong with that.' And in this way, the nucleus of a taxi rank of willing politicians was formed around Ian Greer. As Greer said in 1984: 'It's useless writing to 650 MPs. That's not good lobbying. A good lobbyist should know 12 to 20 MPs who are key, and who are important.'

If one of Greer's tactics was to offer 'sweeteners' to politicians, then another was to be unblushingly untruthful in public about the nature of the connection. A Thames Television journalist interviewed him in 1984 about his connections with Michael Grylls. He replied: 'As far as our company's relationship with him is concerned, it is one of friendship. Hopefully, he finds the briefings we give him, and the discussions we have, of use.' Grylls' interest in the Unitary Tax Campaign, said Greer winningly, sprang from his chairmanship of the backbench trade and industry committee:

'It is pertinent to his interests . . .'

'Do you pay him?'

'No, we don't pay MPs. I've been a parliamentary adviser now for 15 years and we have not in fact paid MPs, we have not had MPs as advisers of the company. One has a substantial number of friends in the House of Commons and it is unnecessary to do so.'

The biggest catch of 1984 was Lord King and British Airways. As rival PR man Keith Lockwood had gloomily predicted, the fishing was done by Grylls. Grylls would eventually admit that he went privately to Lord King and said, 'Why don't you approach Ian Greer Associates?' Grylls took money from Greer for doing so, and could subsequently be spotted with Mrs Sarah Grylls, in May 1985, occupying first-class seats aboard a sumptuous BA freebie to Rio de Janeiro.

Some may have seen British Airways' conduct as that of a predator and bully. Not apparently Michael Grylls. His Surrey constituents no doubt concluded he was speaking strictly on their behalf when he told the Mother of Parliaments in 1987 that BA should be allowed to swallow up its rival, British Caledonian: 'Perhaps BCal is not big enough to compete on the international routes, and that may be a very good reason for allowing the merger to go ahead.' Lord King was so taken with Greer's lobbying skills – and the way they produced

Grylls' impeccable logic in parliament – that he reportedly recommended Greer to every company with which he was subsequently connected.

By 1985, when Mohammed al-Fayed of Harrods approached him on King's recommendation, Greer could thus claim to be the father and master of the novel art of political lobbying in Britain. He had even produced a book, *The Right To Be Heard*, on the subject. It is a tedious publication, in effect a sales brochure promoting a sanitised version of his campaigning skills. Unsurprisingly, Greer wrote little of it. He relied on one of his Whitehall contacts, Stanley Godfrey, recently retired head of the Treasury press office. Greer acknowledged this: 'The skills and expertise [Godfrey] acquired over many years in Fleet Street and Whitehall enabled him to conduct the extensive and detailed research required.' The book bountifully acknowledges the help of his MP friends Michael Grylls and Andrew Bowden, and a new-found acquaintance, Transport Minister Lynda Chalker. It even has a glowing foreword from Bernard Weatherill, who was Speaker of the House of Commons.

Hidden in the flat tedium of Greer's book, however, is a short section that is highly revealing, and gives a genuine clue as to how he would proceed. While the conventional view was that the House of Commons had become irrelevant to the business of government, that civil servants took decisions which ministers rubber-stamped, Greer's insight, gleaned from years in the engine-room of the Conservative party, was different. Certain backbench MPs, he believed, had real influence on the political process, particularly those organised into specialist committees and those who, as Parliamentary Private Secretaries (PPSs), had the ear of ministers. Greer wrote: 'Opinion within the backbench committees is always taken seriously by ministers and party Whips, and the early signs of backbench unrest can often be identified and appeased at this level.'

The Right To Be Heard does also have one moment of entertaining effrontery. Greer affects to complain that it is the media who peddle a 'dishonest and damaging image' of his trade. What they do, he wrote, is to 'portray the lobbyist as a somewhat shady or sinister individual, working furtively behind the scenes on behalf of equally shady clients whose objectives are not always seen to be in the best public interest'. This was exactly what Greer was doing. He was in the process of constructing a machine in the Commons to 'work furtively behind the scenes'. And as events were about to demonstrate, Ian Greer's Westminster sleaze machine was still merely a prototype design. The lobbyist continued to develop it to influence and pervert the House of Commons, a parliament whose venerable age and pomp masked an increasingly rotten reality.

The revolutionary Oliver Cromwell,
the only British parliamentarian to govern as head of state

4

The Mother of All Parliaments

'What shall we do with this bauble? There, take it away.'

Oliver Cromwell, on the Mace, dismissing parliament, 1653.

The House of Commons that Ian Greer set out to infiltrate with his sleaze machine was once a symbol of freedom against tyranny, but by the middle of the 1980s, it had become a weak and cynical institution. One senior Tory backbencher recalls that the motto of those years on his side of the House was: 'Enrich yourselves!' Throughout the 1980s, he said, the party Whips positively encouraged MPs to make money. 'All they asked is that we returned to the Commons to vote at 10 pm.'

For decades, MPs revelled in the evocative schoolbook description of the House of Commons as the Mother of Parliaments. Its members jealously guarded their privileges in the comforting knowledge that they were established as a bulwark against absolute monarchy and unelected barons. Indeed, one of the key parliamentary committees was called the Privileges Committee, and its role was to protect Westminster against the assaults of outsiders. Repeated scandals that suggested the House of Commons was becoming corrupt were glossed over. The stance of too many complacent MPs was that satirised more than a century earlier, in Thomas Love Peacock's *The Misfortunes of Elphin*, published just before the first great parliamentary Reform Bill of 1832 swept 'Old Corruption' away. In Peacock's political satire, a defender of the failure to maintain the kingdom's flood-defences speaks up. To those warning of impending disaster, he says:

Decay is one thing, and danger another. Everything that is old must decay. That the embankment is old, I am free to confess; that it is somewhat rotten in parts I will not altogether deny; that it is any the worse for that, I do most sturdily gainsay. Our ancestors were wiser than we: they built it in their wisdom; and if we should be so rash as to try and mend it, we should only mar it.

Hiding behind the increasingly anachronistic notion of 'parliamentary sovereignty', MPs had resisted attempts to make them accountable to independent scrutiny. But as they had demanded reverence, perversely they had abandoned their role of scrutinising the executive. They deferred to ministers and to unelected civil servants.

Thus they were to back away in embarrassment from proposals by Sir Richard Scott, author of the arms-to-Iraq report, to give the Commons more authority in dealing with an over-secretive, overweening administration. Open admissions that in the 1980s and 1990s parliament was not up to the job were only to come late in the day, in John Major's eventual decision to ask Sir Richard Scott, a judge, to investigate the arms-to-Iraq scandal and to appoint Lord Nolan, a Law Lord, to conduct an inquiry into standards in public life.

Unelected judges had to be called in to stand up as independent tribunes of the people. This was because, throughout the 1980s, during the long years of uninterrupted one-party rule, many of the elected MPs at Westminster who should have been doing the job were resorting to lining their own pockets, peddling influence, or seeking preferment from the Government, as one of the 116 lucky members of the 'payroll vote'. The Nolan committee was to identify a 'culture of moral vagueness' among the holders of public office.

By 1989, it was estimated that the mushrooming lobbyists' firms – of which Greer's was merely the biggest – were taking £10 million a year from outside commercial bodies for the sale of political influence. In increasing numbers, MPs were cutting out the middlemen and openly selling themselves. An analysis of the 1995 Register of Members' Interests was eventually to suggest that 26 MPs had acquired 'consultancy' agreements with public relations or lobbying firms and a further 142 in total, almost 30 per cent, had 'consultancies' with other types of company or with trade associations. An estimated 389 MPs – nearly 70 per cent of all backbenchers – had financial relationships with outside bodies which directly related to their membership of the Commons.

As the oral sessions of Question Time became predictable theatre, shedding more heat than light, the flock-wallpaper corridors of parliament were becoming infested by the new commercial lobbyists, pressing elbows, paying inducements. The parliament in which they did so became a place of unwritten rules and arcane ceremonies, of style rather than substance. Bemused critics from outside were silenced with the put down, 'You don't understand, old boy, how West-minster works.' As Lord Blake, the Tory historian, was to say in subsequent evidence to the Nolan committee: 'The public is inclined to think that the House of Commons is a rather cosy body, it regulates itself . . . it is all a little bit too much like a private club.'

One of the characteristics of British private clubs is a frantic rush to sweep scandal under the carpet whenever it appears. Or, as Dr Michael Pinto-Duschinsky of Brunel University, an academic student of party corruption, puts it: 'Over the past century British politics has been far from sleaze-free, but compared to other countries the British are adept at dealing with corruption quietly.'

Corruption has really been the political norm – it was honesty at Westminster, or at least the attempt at achieving it, that was a late Victorian novelty. Whenever the efforts to exterminate it relaxed, misconduct spread like a weed. Gen-erations of students have been steeped in tales of 'rotten boroughs' in the eighteenth century, of landowners telling their tenants how to vote, of the distribution of gifts and titles. Cornelius O'Leary, in his book, *The Elimination of Corrupt Practices in British Elections 1868–1911*, describes how bribery flourished all over the place. At Beverley, for example, a Royal Commission inquiring into the 1868 campaign found that one-third of the voters were known as 'rolling stock' – they would roll to the side offering the largest bribes.

By the end of the nineteenth century, largely thanks to parliament handing over the enforcement of election law to the courts, politics became relatively clean. Then, in 1911, came the Marconi scandal. Two ministers, one of them David Lloyd George, the Chancellor of the Exchequer, the other Rufus Isaacs, bought shares in the American Marconi Company before they went on sale to the public but after the British Government – as the ministers knew – had signed a large and lucrative contract with the separate British Marconi Company. The Chief Whip also bought shares on behalf of the Liberal party. After going on sale, the American Marconi shares doubled in value.

The ministers initially tried to conceal their share-dealing. When they were found out, they denied they were guilty of any wrongdoing. A Commons committee set up to investigate the affair divided on party lines, in the ministers' favour, as did the House of Commons itself. There was little interest in the affair among the press or the public. Lloyd George went on to become Prime Minister, Isaacs the Lord Chief Justice.

After the first world war, many questions were raised about the way war-time contracts had been handed out. The Coalition Government's sale of honours to boost party funds also became a scandal. Ministers repeatedly misled parliament, denying that knighthoods and peerages were for sale, much as they do today. Lloyd George's sale of honours left him with a personal fortune estimated at £1.5 million – £40 million in today's money. And Lloyd George was not alone. Gladstone, despite being the symbol of probity, had cleaned up electoral practices in the 1870s and 1880s while all the time selling honours. The Tory prime ministers, Lord Salisbury and Arthur Balfour, sold knighthoods in return for contributions to party funds, a practice followed ever since by their successors. It was 1922 before the Government finally agreed to establish a Royal Commission on Honours, which recommended that political candidates for honours should be vetted by three privy councillors, none a member of the Government. The procedure remained in place in the 1980s: its efficiency was uncertain.

Immediately after the second world war, John Belcher, a junior minister at the Board of Trade where his responsibility included issuing Government licences at a time of tight controls, accepted gifts from a number of businessmen in return for favours. Attlee, the Prime Minister, set up a full-scale Tribunal of Inquiry under Mr Justice Lynskey to investigate the affair. It concluded that Belcher had behaved improperly. Belcher resigned his office and subsequently his Commons seat. The Belcher affair remained a lighthouse for the next 50 years, marking just how sternly an upright administration could deal with sleaze – if it wanted to.

In the 1970s, the Poulson scandal showed that corruption had returned to flourish in Westminster, parts of local government, the police and the health service. John Poulson, a Yorkshire architect, was the centre of a web of bribery which reached the Commons. Bankruptcy proceedings revealed documents which had been long and successfully hidden by all the parties. Those eventually prosecuted included T. Dan Smith, Labour leader of Newcastle upon Tyne Council, and William Pottinger, a senior civil servant at the Scottish Office. They, and others, were jailed. However, three MPs who had accepted financial favours from Poulson – the Tory MPs, Reginald Maudling and John Cordle, and the Labour MP, Albert Roberts – escaped prosecution. Maudling resigned his post as Home Secretary in 1972 as the scandal unfolded – he had been chairman of a Poulson company and lobbied for a Poulson company negotiating for a hospital contract in Malta without declaring his interest.

Maudling said he decided to resign only because as Home Secretary he was responsible for the Metropolitan Police, which was investigating the Poulson affair. In a ploy all too typical of beleaguered corrupt politicians at Westminster, he issued libel writs against the media. He successfully sued the *Observer* and the BBC. In 1978, the *Observer* paid him £12,500 and read a statement in open court saying it never intended to suggest that Maudling escaped prosecution because of parliamentary immunity. Other writs, against Granada Television and the *Daily Mirror*, were outstanding when he died in 1979.

A Commons committee set up to consider what to do about the three MPs met in secret – again a forerunner of how corruption would be treated in the 1980s. Only the Liberals and a handful of backbench MPs argued for public hearings, on the grounds that secret hearings would damage the name of the Commons. In 1977, the committee concluded that Cordle had 'abused his membership of parliament', and that Maudling's and Robert's failure to declare their connection with Poulson 'constituted conduct inconsistent with the standard which the House is entitled to expect from its members'. The report provoked a passionate debate, but in the end the Commons merely 'took note' of it. The Tories saved their MPs, Labour theirs.

The sanctimonious Cordle retired shortly after, telling the Commons that he had 'decided on reflection . . . that if a group of my colleagues decide unanimously that I was at fault in the matter, I must bow to their judgement'. But he said he did not believe he had done anything wrong and had a clear conscience.

The Poulson case was the biggest post-war scandal to afflict the body politic until the affair upon which Ian Greer and Neil Hamilton were about to embark. It was similar to the scandal to be provoked by Mohammed al-Fayed, in that the eventual explosive revelations emerged from a courtroom, not from parliament. The embarrassment caused by Poulson led to the launching of the Royal Commission on Standards of Conduct in Public Life under the Law Lord, Lord Salmon. This Royal Commission brought about the first Register of MPs' Interests, but otherwise many of the issues it raised were quietly forgotten at Westminster. In fact, when the subsequent Nolan committee on standards in public life was set up in the 1990s, much of its initial report consisted of a catalogue of how inadequate self-regulation of their conduct by MPs had proved to have been.

As far back as 1947, prompted by an attempt by a trade union to instruct an MP, the Commons had resolved that:

> it is inconsistent with the dignity of the House, with the duty of a member to his constituency, and with the maintenance of the privilege of freedom of speech, for any member of the House to enter into any contractual agreement with an outside body, controlling or limiting the member's complete independence and freedom of action in parliament or stipulating that he shall act in any

way as the representative of such outside body in regard to any matters to be transacted in parliament; the duty of a member being to his constituency and to the country as a whole, rather than to any particular section thereof.

Outsiders – the public – could be forgiven for believing that the resolution is quite clear and that MPs have repeatedly ignored it. Unravelled, it allows MPs to slip between loopholes. For it only prevented, it seemed, an MP from entering into a consultancy agreement which imposed, in return for payment, 'a binding obligation' to speak, lobby or vote in accordance with the client's instructions, or to act as the client's representative in parliament. It did not prohibit a binding obligation 'to advise' the client on parliamentary matters. Nor did the resolution appear to prevent MPs from 'voluntarily' speaking, lobbying, or voting in support of their clients' interests.

The distinction between voluntary advocacy and advocacy as a result of instructions and binding obligations could, in practice, be meaningless. The phrase, 'We'll see you're all right' comes to mind. How would the electorate know that an MP's decision to speak, lobby, or vote in a particular cause was truly voluntary? Money was surely the key, and any member of the public sitting in the gallery watching MPs make debating points on behalf of those who were paying them, might have reasonably concluded: — 'money talks'.

It was also hard for an outsider to distinguish between 'advocacy' (forbidden if done under orders) and 'advice' (lucrative, and apparently perfectly acceptable). The newly-established Register of Members' Interests, designed to reassure the public that MPs were not corrupt, made matters worse. In theory at least, it required declaration of 'any pecuniary interest or other material benefit which a member receives which might reasonably be thought by others to influence his or her actions, speeches or votes in parliament'. At the end of a decade of activity by Ian Greer and his fellow lobbyists, it was to be acknowledged (by Nolan) that the register 'has tended to create a false impression that any interest is acceptable once it has been registered, and so to add to the confusion . . .'

In 1969, the Select Committee on Members' Interests, known as the Strauss Committee, had reviewed the rules. It proposed a code of conduct, including a resolution stating that 'it is contrary to the usage and dignity of the House that a member should bring forward by any speech or question, or advocate in this House or among his fellow members any bill, motion, or cause for a fee, payment, retainer or reward, direct or indirect, which he has received, is receiving or expects to receive'. The Strauss Committee's report was shelved without debate. The proposal for a register of interests was blocked. It was only the exposure of the Poulson scandal that forced the new Labour Government to take action in 1974. William Whitelaw, then Leader of the House, may not have known it, but he spoke for continued tolerance of corruption when he argued in 1971: 'There is widespread support in the House for the view that it is right to rely on the general good sense of members rather than on formalised rules.'

Many years on, after the activities of Ian Greer had made a mockery of the register, Nolan concluded: 'It has taken members 20 years to accept the register fully, with senior members even in recent years feeling free to defy a resolution of the House in respect of entries in the register; and doubt has been expressed about whether justice has always been done to members whose conduct has been judged by the House in recent years.'

One of the opportunities for Greer to penetrate parliament so successfully as a lobbyist was that MPs got away with almost completely uninformative entries in the register. One MP, when he asked a parliamentary question in return for payment, suggested how he would misleadingly record the £1,000 fee: 'What I shall say is something like this,' he told his paymaster. 'I would put "Consultancy project carried out".'

'It is clearly unsatisfactory,' the Nolan committee recorded, 'that such opaque descriptions are routinely being entered so there is disclosure in appearance but not in practice.' The committee's eventual report decried what it called the 'culture of slackness' and warned of the 'tolerance of corruption'.

This state of affairs spread well beyond parliament. In local government, Westminster Council was found by the Audit Commission to have indulged in outrageous gerrymandering during the 1980s. Among quangos, the Welsh Development Agency was caught up in a fraud scandal. There were widespread allegations of ministers placing Tory supporters on the boards of these non-elected executive agencies for partisan reasons rather than merit, and instructing civil servants to undertake party-political tasks in breach of their political neutrality. Ministers were also criticised for taking on directorships immediately after they left office in the 'revolving door' syndrome. They accepted top jobs in companies which had directly benefited from the Government's privatisation policy and used their previous privileged position as advisers for private companies and banks.

It was the 'slack atmosphere' in the Commons itself in the mid-1980s, however, which provided the opportunity for lobbyists such as Greer to flourish. They had large sums of money at their disposal from their commercial customers. All that Greer needed to do in 1985 to promote the secret interests of his new client Mohammed al-Fayed, the owner of Harrods, was to identify those Members of Parliament whose services might be for sale – rather as one might, for example, find and flag down a passing taxi.

Neil Hamilton tearing up EEC directives

5

B'stard MP

'I have the essential streak of vanity.'

Neil Hamilton

The wild-eyed comedian Rick Mayall starred in a television series in the 1980s, built around the character of a Westminster politician called Alan B'stard MP. The joke – an audacious one in the days of a domineering Conservative administration – was that there was no deed so unscrupulous that B'stard would not gleefully do it. He revelled in his own lack of scruple, and generally came through triumphantly in the end. For some reason, those who recalled that fictional series, a satire on Thatcherite selfishness, often found a picture swimming into their mind of Neil Hamilton MP.

In the mid-1980s, the recently elected MP for Tatton in Cheshire wore floppy bow-ties and colourful shirts. He was a little podgy in the face, and a falling lock of hair over the forehead gave him scope for his droll Hitler impersonation, popular at some parties. This was the backbencher whom Ian Greer pushed forward to Mohammed al-Fayed in 1985, in order to demonstrate his control over politicians. Greer wrote: 'I have spoken to Neil Hamilton MP, vice-chairman of the Conservative party's trade and industry committee, who has agreed to table a question.'

Hamilton was a protégé of Greer and Grylls, two older men who had operated the Westminster system to their advantage for years. Indeed, Hamilton was almost their Frankenstein creature. They had helped provide the young aspirant with political support, assistance to write a book, a job while he hunted for a winnable seat, and even with a timely wife. It was Michael Grylls' secretary, Christine Holman, who married Hamilton the Conservative candidate five days before the

1983 election which took him to parliament. This enabled him to campaign successfully in Cheshire with a spouse, regarded as a valuable election accessory by most professional politicians.

While the young candidate had searched for a safe seat, he was given a full-time job at the Institute of Directors, in their parliamentary and European affairs department. This windfall was undoubtedly thanks to the support of Michael Grylls – the MP had recently acquired the title of 'Parliamentary Spokesman' for the IoD, and headed their 'Parliamentary Panel'. In the 1983 general election, when Hamilton entered parliament for Tatton in Cheshire, he was immediately installed as an officer of the backbench committee on trade and industry chaired by his mentor, Michael Grylls.

Earlier, as a newly-qualified barrister of 31, Hamilton had already been helped by Ian Greer to write a book on US/UK tax law. The lobbyist was assembling supporters for his industrial clients' Unitary Tax Campaign against the tax policies of American states, so a volume analysing the newly-passed US/UK Double Taxation Treaty was relevant and handy. Nor did it hurt the aspiring young politician to have an important-sounding treatise under his belt. It was the first step in a waltz between Hamilton and Greer which would make and break them both.

Hamilton was rancorous, un-moneyed, and Welsh. Although he could be wittily provocative, his mimicry and his jibes hardly qualified him for the world that John Major was later to eulogise – 'a nation at ease with itself'. He was at his best on the attack, savaging anti-apartheid campaigners, 'health fascists', bureaucrats, leftists, the wet, the windbags and the weak. Already he was locked in a truculent libel battle with BBC Television, who had called him a near-Nazi. It was Greer's strategy in 1985 to woo this barking dog of a politician, and set him on the enemies of Mohammed al-Fayed. Hamilton proved the type of person who was responsive to offers of cash.

Mostyn Neil Hamilton was born in 1949 in South Wales into one of those aspiring post-war families that were in the process of tentatively shedding their origins. They were Welsh miners by history. The valleys are a proud but sad country, and have become sadder since the closure of the coal mines that fed Hamilton's family. Back in 1966, when Hamilton was a sixth-former, the tragedy of a generation occurred down the road. A slagheap tumbled into a primary school playground at Aber-fan nearby, killing 116 infants; the slaughter cast a shadow over Wales for a decade. But his western edges of the valleys, where the mountains descend towards Llanello and the Loughor vale, have always been a step aloof from the harsher, militant mining heartland around Rhymney and Merthyr. The air of Ammanford and the Loughor valley is pleasant, breezier, more suburban, with easy access to breathtaking scenery. The Loughor valley's people – they say of themselves – are a cut above the *hoi polloi* of deepest pit country. Hamilton went to grammar school at Ammanford at the foot of the Black Mountains, and even in his teenage years yearned to be an MP – not for the Labour party, for whom this area was a fortress, but for his father's party. Both his grandfathers worked in the valley pits that were the cradle of the British Labour party, but his father rose to become the chief engineer of the National Coal Board in Wales and a convinced Conservative.

Hamilton went to study economics and politics at the windswept seaside town of Aberystwyth, not far from home, in west Wales. With only 2,000 students and a local pop-ulation of around 10,000, the new campus on the hills overlooking Cardigan Bay was an isolated community. These were the high days of sixties student revolt. In the United States, campuses were ablaze with draft-resistance to the Vietnam War. In Paris, rioting students took to the barricades. And in London, thousands besieged the American Embassy, berated Labour's Harold Wilson for betraying socialism or, at the very least, sang along with the Beatles and the rest of the generation: 'All You Need Is Love'. But student radicalism at Aberystwyth was a late starter, since the students themselves were generally uninterested, or else middle-of-the-road Labour. On the fringe, there was a raucous rugby crowd, a reportedly first-class tiddlywinks team, some hard-core Welsh language activists – and the Tories. While others caught the zeitgeist of insurrection, the undergraduate Hamilton locked on to a miscellaneous bunch of far-right would-be Conservative politicians. They were regarded patronisingly by some of their fellows as immature or weird.

Hamilton's university days were later to be the subject of controversy and attack from those who thought that his activities, many of them merely infantile, showed he was not a responsible politician. Hamilton threw himself into the Conservative Association, the Federation of Conservative Students (FCS) and the Monday Club. The Monday Club backed the pariah white regime of Ian Smith in Rhodesia and campaigned against black immigration. The Conservative politician Enoch Powell, building up to his notorious 'rivers of blood' speech against immigration in April 1968, was hero of the hour.

The Monday Club was going through a particularly unsavoury phase at the time. One of Hamilton's mentors there was George Kennedy Young, former deputy director of MI6, who had been involved in plotting a coup in Iran in 1953 and the attempted assassination of President Nasser of Egypt. Although his friends called him 'patriotic', there was an unavoidable racism in Young's rhetoric. In a Monday Club pamphlet, *Who Goes Home?*, published in March 1968, Young called for a minister for repatriation and a ban on immigration. He argued for the compulsory removal of blacks from Britain. 'We have got to get down to studying without fear or favour the whole question of repatriation,' he told a conference in Birmingham on 18 April 1968, two days before Powell's more famous speech in the same city. 'The immigrants came in on vouchers. They can go out on vouchers.' Years later, after Neil Hamilton took the BBC to court over a programme that examined the MP's political leanings, Hamilton explained his relationship with Young: 'Gerald [Howarth] and I both met Young through the Monday Club, which we joined in the late 1960s. With his distinguished war record and service to his country he was an impressive figure to a young student.'

Gerald Howarth, from Southampton University, was to become Hamilton's closest friend as well as a fellow Conservative MP. He was one of a political circle which was also to include three students from York – Christine Holman, a doctor's daughter reading sociology, and two homosexual ultra-right-wing activists, Michael Brown and Harvey Proctor. Brown and Proctor too were to become Conservative MPs. All four men in the group would become controversial figures: Howarth joined Hamilton in successfully suing for libel after being accused of far-right connections. Brown resigned as a whip after his homosexuality was revealed, and was subsequently discovered to have been taking undeclared commission payments as well. Harvey Proctor was forced to leave the Commons in 1987 after a conviction for gross indecency – a very public scandal involving spanking rent boys. Hamilton remained loyal to his friend of college days, despite Proctor's shame. The outcast Proctor went on to open a shirt shop in south west London, into which a pair of louts burst one afternoon in 1993, on a 'gay-bashing' spree. Proctor was entertaining two visitors, one of whom suffered a broken nose in the fray that ensued, while the other helped to shoo the intruders away. The broken nose was that of Neil Hamilton MP, and the counter-attacker was the only lady in the old student quintet, Christine Holman.

Christine was by then Neil Hamilton's wife. In the old days, she had been impressed by the student Hamilton's mutton chop sideburns and 'frightfully hilarious' mimicry. 'All he has to do,' she noted, 'is pull down his fringe a little, blacken a cork with a candle and paint on a moustache and he looks like Hitler.' When it came to an election for the chairmanship of the Federation of Conservative Students, however, Christine supported Hamilton's opponent, to whom he lost the vote: Andrew Neil, future editor of the *Sunday Times*.

Hamilton's comic impressions were a regular feature of the FCS annual revues between 1968 and 1972. His penchant for buffoonery was a talent he never abandoned. He became the local leader of the 'loopy right'. Mike Levin, a young politics lecturer at the time says: 'He was no fool. He was intellectually a good student.' He recalls Hamilton's vigorous proselytising about the free market: 'He was entertaining and lively company. There was an element of self-mockery about his right-wing antics.' To the young history lecturer, Deian Hopkins: 'He was an ebullient student, but as the agent for the Labour party I found his views offensive. He seemed to have a grandiose view of history.' Jonathan Smith, the editor of the student newspaper, the *Courier*, recalls: 'He described himself as Welsh but he spoke with a very English accent . . . The right were talking of privatising the water and the post office. We thought they were loopy.'

Hamilton's semi-facetious manifesto when he ran for the student union presidency read: 'The constitutional pedants, the ledgerbook minds will be resolutely crushed beneath the iron heel of a victorious people marching on the road to destiny.' There followed a 'message of support' from 'His Highness the Maharaja of Jaipur' (who is alive and well and living in Bradford): 'I am most happy to be commending Neil Hamilton for the post of Supreme Autocrat. Long Live King Victoria! Move right down de bus please. Hold tight.'

Each candidate was required to make a speech. Thunderous music heralded the arrival of Hamilton to deliver his: the apocalyptic opening bars to Richard Strauss's 'Thus Spake Zarathustra', inspired by Nietzsche's text on the Superman. Accompanied in this manner, the candidate strode towards the podium sporting a black cloak, black trousers with riding boots and a white jacket crossed with a red sash and large medallion. He was accompanied by several 'bodyguards', one wearing dark glasses and carrying a toy pistol. Hamilton, illuminated by a spotlight, delivered another semi-comical rant calling for the abolition of parliament and the suppression of the working class.

Hamilton did secure a position in the union as editor of the *Courier*. He changed its name to *Feudal Times and Reactionary Herald* with a motif resembling the imperial German eagle. His first issue carried the front page headline: 'Sensation!!! President Hamilton?' above a spoof article about the proprietor of the paper: 'Selfless, universally loved, public servant No 1, Lord Hamilton to invest himself with the mantle of office.' After an interview with Lord Hamilton at Reaction House, the reporter declares: 'I felt once again that inner glow which told me that the great days of Britain's history were not past, that there would be one more name: HAMILTON, inscribed alongside the heroes of old – Lord Eldon, Horatio Bottomley, King Richard II, Lord North, the Duke of Cambridge, etc.' The same issue devotes two inside pages to a speech by Enoch Powell attacking the National Union of Students as a 'beast of disorder'.

In the early seventies, Hamilton lived in a block of student rooms where his eccentric humour was regarded with both amusement and suspicion. While mixing with students of all political persuasions, he combined an eagerness to inform on his fellow students with some percipient political toadying. Some of his colleagues discovered that he had sent names of left-wing 'subversives' direct to the Secretary of State for Education – Mrs 'Milk Snatcher' Thatcher. She replied thanking him for his efforts, saying how cheered she was to find people like him ferreting away in the grassroots.

As vice-chairman of the FCS, Hamilton launched an offensive against 'leftist' student unions around the country (at a time when they were not hard to find): 'I would be very grateful if you could send ... *immediately* any cases of which you know and can corroborate of the misuse of funds by your Students' Union,' he wrote. 'Such things as payment of fines of students convicted, contributions to dubious organisations, e.g. Anti-Springbok, Anti-Apartheid, etc. .... also I would like evidence of occasions where right-wing associations have been victimised or discriminated against ... This information is vital if the law is to be changed.' His move followed the Government's announcement of an inquiry into the 'misuse of Student Union funds'. The minister behind it, whom he was to idolise, was Margaret Thatcher.

The choice of the First Earl of Eldon as one of Hamilton's heroes was a provocative touch. Eldon, a reactionary Chancellor for most of the period 1801–1827, opposed Catholic emancipation, the abolition of the slave trade and reform of the House of Commons. Hamilton joined 'the Eldon League', a group of young men who met to commemorate Tzar Nicholas II, the last of the Romanovs, with champagne cork-popping duels.

Hamilton passed off many of his escapades as comic pranks. But sometimes these high jinks were playing with fire. In 1972, with two of his Monday Club chums, Hamilton was guest of the Italian Social Movement – the neo-fascist party – at its convention on the Adriatic coast, at Pescara. This was a time when the MSI, led by a former intimate of Mussolini, Giorgio Almirante, encompassed a fringe youth wing called the 'Front of Youth' which was implicated by examining judges in a right-wing terrorist campaign of train bombs and street fighting. Hamilton's pass to the conference hall shows him to have been on the Front of Youth guest list. He barked a Mussolini-esque speech: 'Where there is chaos order must be restored. We are the guardians of the future, we cannot afford to fail. Long live you of the right. Long live anti-communist Italy. Long live imperial England!' For the duration of the conference, Hamilton stayed among the potted palms and cocktail bars of the four-star Grand Hotel Adriatica by the beach. He affected to be bewildered by the subsequent fuss. He explained that the speech was a spoof and the student Monday Clubbers had gone merely to take advantage of the hospitality of their hosts. He was free-loading: 'As far as I was concerned, it was an opportunity to have a free week's holiday on the Adriatic.'

When George Young was ousted from the Monday Club in 1973, the 24-year-old Hamilton says he too dropped out. In the February 1974 general election, they were both hopeless Conservative candidates. The racist Young was trounced in Brent East and Hamilton did not dent the reputation of Abertillery, in the Welsh mining valleys, as the safest Labour seat in the country. He got 2,730 votes to his opponent's 20,068. While Hamilton spent the next few years studying for the Bar and practising Conservative politics, he insists that he did not keep up with George Young, who went on to set up an 'anti-wog' group called Tory Action.

The Egyptian Mohammed al-Fayed, the owner of Harrods and Hamilton's later paymaster, used to complain that the British establishment were racist and regarded him as a 'wog'. It is perhaps proof of Hamilton's innocence of the charge of racism of the George Young variety that he never showed the least reluctance to spend time with Fayed in later life. He was always willing to take his money.

Christine Holman, with her long blonde hair and bright, remorseless grin, could have stepped out of the pages of *Country Life* or the *Tatler*. After she graduated from York, she moved straight to Westminster as an MP's secretary. The relationship with Hamilton was left behind. 'I was working in the House of Commons and having a ball,' she said years later. 'Lots of people were inviting me out. Poor Neil was a perpetual student. He didn't want to go out into the big wide world, so he spent about eight years at university.' Intensely political and a ferocious organiser, Christine at first wanted to be an MP. The secretary's job was just meant to be a 'foot in the door'. But she found herself working for Sir Gerald Nabarro, the noisy and moustachioed Conservative MP for South Worcestershire. After his death in 1973, she moved over to Michael Grylls, the sleek Thatcher loyalist who was to team up with Greer, the lobbyist. Christine, flamboyant but relatively unsophisticated, was to become a fixture around the House of Commons, a familiar part of the landscape to MPs and journalists.

After being called to the Bar in 1978, Neil Hamilton moved to London and met up with Christine again. Eventually (after he found the safe seat at Tatton) they married. Christine continued to work as a secretary to an MP – him. Christine has maintained a reputation for being the one who wears the trousers in the Hamiltons' marriage and she happily admits to her nickname of 'Bossy Boots'. Their motto as a couple, she tells journalists, is 'WDTT' – We Do Things Together. In public, even now, she appears to treat him like some naughty, lost boy. But her characterisation of Hamilton as a perpetual student and shrinking violet is belied by his driving ambition to get into parliament. He returned to the hustings at Bradford in 1979, attacking a Labour majority of over 8,000. He came a respectable second, increasing the Tory vote by five per cent. A few years later, buoyed up by his double taxation book and the full-time salary from the Institute of Directors, Hamilton won Tatton in June 1983 with a majority of 13,960.

Neil Hamilton came into parliament as part of a landslide. He was one of the 'School of '83', to which the fictional TV figure of Alan B'stard MP also belonged. It had been an unpleasant election campaign, fought in the slipstream of victory in the Falklands War the previous year. Patriotic images transformed Mrs Thatcher's lacklustre standing in the polls to a commanding lead. Her opponent had been the elderly and intellectual but un-telegenic Michael Foot. The result had been the triumph, it seemed, of one kind of Britain over another. The campaign had culminated in a Conservative rally at Wembley, graced by Mrs Thatcher herself. The comedian Kenny Everett had entertained the crowd: 'Let's bomb Russia!' (cheers), 'Let's kick Michael Foot's stick away!' (loud cheers and laughter).

The 'School of '83' was a group of MPs who not only afforded Mrs Thatcher an unassailable majority, but, the old guard claimed, changed the tone of the Commons. They despised the old patrician, one-nation conservatism. They were what snobs on both sides of the House called the 'Terylene Tories' or the 'estate agents', who reflected the power of the new hard right within the lower middle class, and whose natural leader, Norman Tebbit, MP for Chingford, Essex, was the prototype for the new label 'Essex Man' – the people who put more emphasis on economic than on cerebral activity. As one Conservative minister put it: 'It's become a very classless party nowadays – more's the pity. Kind of chap who has only got two buttons on his suit' (a good suit, for those as fastidious as the minister, has four buttons on the cuff).

One of Hamilton's first acts as an MP was to support motions calling for a debate on the restoration of the death penalty. But his reputation as a right-winger had preceded him. In September 1982, well before the general election, the Young Conservatives had begun an investigation into allegations that their organisation and the party had been infiltrated by the far right. Their report, completed nearly 18 months later, co-incided with a BBC Television 'Panorama' programme on the subject on 30 January 1984 – 'Maggie's Militant Tendency'. In the final few minutes, Hamilton's burlesques came back to haunt him. His right-wing history – the Monday Club, his reactionary student capers, the visit to the MSI conference and his links with George Young of Tory Action – were all rehearsed. The programme also recounted a parliamentary visit to Berlin in August 1983, when Hamilton was alleged to have goose-stepped outside the Sylterhof Hotel and given a Nazi salute at the Reichstag. The programme caused intense embarrassment at Conservative Central Office, and four MPs including Gerald Howarth and Neil Hamilton issued writs for libel. Harvey Proctor and Roger Moat eventually dropped out, leaving Hamilton and Howarth to fight on.

At the High Court hearing in October 1986, with Christine at his side and occasionally breaking down in tears, Hamilton denied he was a racist. 'I am not a racist in the sense that I believe that a man is any better or worse for the colour of his skin. I am aware, as we all are, of human difference, and the differences which come about from having grown up in states with radically different customs and systems.' Addressing the jury, he went on: 'If it is racist to be aware of those differences, then we are all racist. I do not believe that a man is the better or worse for his nationality or race, although I am proud to be British.'

Hamilton also denied making any public Hitler impersonations and claimed the goose-stepping was done by two other delegates, who had been amazed at some Russian and East German soldiers goose-stepping at the Soviet war memorial. Hamilton showed the court his famous impression of Hitler. Even the judge, Mr Justice Simon Brown, smiled.

Next day, the case was adjourned for out-of-court talks. Then, sensationally, the Sunday papers reported that the BBC governors, who had met under the vice-chairman, Lord Barnett, had instructed the director general, Alasdair Milne, to settle. On Tuesday Charles Gray QC, the BBC's counsel, conceded that the allegations of links with racist groups 'were false and should never have been included' in the documentary.

Cocks of the walk, the two MPs called the result 'a magnificent triumph of David over Goliath'. Hamilton got £20,000 damages from the BBC, and cost them another £200,000 in legal fees. Phil Pedley, author of the Young Conservative report on which the programme was based, refused to climb down, however, and Hamilton quietly dropped his case against him. Pedley now says: 'I still think Hamilton is very right wing, but I don't think he's a Nazi. He just engaged in a pattern of behaviour that showed very poor judgement.'

This libel battle was important to Hamilton. It gave him an unquenchable belief that he could manipulate the erratic law of libel against the media to his advantage. It must also have given him confidence in the support available to him from the political forces of the right. Although 'Panorama' had been misguided in pressing too far their belief that Hamilton had neo-Nazi links, their programme was made in good faith. And they were reflecting anxieties inside Hamilton's own party about an important matter of public interest.

Hamilton's connections were unsavoury. As an MP, his behaviour was indeed worthy of criticism. Furthermore, it later became plain that the MP had not found it politic to tell the whole truth. It was several years before Peter Carter-Ruck, Hamilton's veteran solicitor, admitted in his autobiography that part of the MP's costs had actually been indemnified by the millionaire grocer Sir James Goldsmith. That revelation puts a different complexion on a letter to *The Times* from Hamilton on 29 October 1985: 'We were risking everything we owned to restore our good names . . . We never sought, nor were we offered, nor would we have accepted a penny of financial support from the party.'

Some discrepancies also emerged about the 'Hitler salutes' that Hamilton claimed he never gave in Germany. A copy of a letter Hamilton wrote to Party Chairman John Gummer emerged, in which he had repeated his denial: 'I make it absolutely clear that, while in Berlin, I did not do any goose-stepping nor did I at any time give Nazi salutes. Indeed, I have always thought the latter was a criminal offence in the Federal Republic.' But Tony Kerpel, then the leader of the Conservative group on Camden Council, had also been on the German trip. His evidence was never heard in court, but after transmission of the programme he had written to the reporter Michael Cockerell: 'I do recall Neil Hamilton gave Hitler impersonations, including one occasion during a visit to the Reichstag building. This impersonation was not a full-blown salute, but consisted of Mr Hamilton walking with his right forearm held upright, palm bent back, and left arm held across the body.' And Hamilton no longer seemed disposed to deny this fact about his antics. In a post-trial article for the *Sunday Times*, he wrote admitting: 'When we visited the Reichstag I made a short speech of welcome in German. Before I went out on to the balcony and out of sight of our hosts I gave a little salute with two fingers to my nose to give an impression of a toothbrush moustache. Somebody on the trip clearly did not share our sense of humour.'

The same cockiness which characterised Hamilton's behaviour towards the BBC was to emerge again in his dealings with Ian Greer. No sooner had he arrived in the Commons than he began to promote the interests of one of the lobbyist's existing clients – Associated Octel. Although they had a factory in his constituency, and therefore a right to be represented by him, Octel chose to work through Greer.

Under these circumstances, the MP gave a hostage to fortune in February 1984, a few days after the notorious 'Panorama' programme, when he told *Private Eye*: 'I have never received a penny piece from the company.' The letter was provoked by an article in the magazine mentioning Hamilton's name and revealing that Labour MP Walter Jonson had got £1,000 for pushing the cause of Associated Octel for Greer. Hamilton wrote:

> IGA is an excellent firm offering an excellent service to the client companies lucky enough to retain it. I have never received a penny piece from the company. Since I was elected last June, I have worked with IGA on behalf of Associated Octel, which has a plant in my constituency where 250 jobs will be lost because of the Government decision to phase out lead in petrol. My interest is solely to try and save jobs for my constituents.

It was not a reason that Hamilton could use the next time he was called in by Ian Greer Associates, however. For very few of his north-of-England constituents shopped at Harrods. And in Wilmslow, Knutsford, and the huge ICI works at Northwich that Hamilton supposedly represented, it would probably have been hard to find a single soul who gave a damn about who owned the London store. Yet Neil Hamilton, Member of Parliament, soon came to give the impression he cared a great deal.

The world's most famous shop

6

On the Game

'Since a politician never believes what he says, he is surprised when others believe him.'

Charles de Gaulle

The view from the illuminated rooftop of Harrods on the winter evening of 1985, when Hamilton took Fayed's brief, looked out across a cold-hearted city. The capital had new inhabitants, the sight of whom shocked foreign visitors leaving the theatres at the end of an evening – on the pavements where the car headlights glistened, were people sleeping, huddled under sodden cardboard. Over the river from the Palace of Westminster itself was a new, abysmal metropolis of the homeless and wretched, which came to be called 'Cardboard City'.

Although the gap between rich and poor was widening, the Government which Hamilton supported had ridden the crest of a patriotic wave. They used the flag for every slogan they could find. But the same Union Jack was coming to signify a new brutality. That year, charges by flag-waving English soccer fans through a beer-haze and across the terraces of the Heysel Stadium in Brussels had left 39 innocent Italian supporters dead. Europe was dumbstruck.

The pound was nearly level with the dollar. Britain was slipping down the economic premier league. The view from Harrods that winter was over a sombre townscape. But the shining bulbs strung down the sides of the store were lambent in the night. Harrods at least was a palace of abundance, where money talked, and where Christmas would soon be coming. The previous year, an IRA bomb had ripped through the store to mark the festive season. This year, the Egyptian proprietor had other worries.

The Westminster sleaze machine designed by Ian Greer was first set in motion to help Mohammed al-Fayed on the evening of Monday 28 October, when Greer presented himself to the frustrated proprietor of Harrods. He was instructed to demonstrate that he could exert political influence on the Egyptian's behalf. The danger that Fayed feared most was that his enemy, Tiny Rowland of Lonrho, would persuade the Government to start an investigation into the way he had acquired control of Harrods. Fayed and his lawyer, Michael Palmer, wanted 'maximum pressure' put on Trade Secretary Leon Brittan to prevent this.

Within 48 hours, Greer produced the proof of his lobbying powers, telling Fayed he had arranged a plan for the Conservative MP Neil Hamilton to table a parliamentary question.

Parliamentary questions, or PQs, are a means used by politicians to get information about their areas of special interest. They can prise information out of the administration of the day, since they oblige the minister to whom they are addressed to reply. This in turn means research work by civil servants, at the taxpayer's expense. For this reason, PQs are supposed, the public would assume, to relate to the pursuance of good government, or to constituents' interests. PQs have, in practice, also become a means whereby politicians make a point: no matter how reckless or defamatory. The publicly-tabled questions prepared by the Greer team were designed to be the first salvo in a campaign to discredit Tiny Rowland's Lonrho for abusing his *Observer* newspaper, which employed so-called 'independent directors' to protect its editorial freedom. Hamilton's first PQ would ask Brittan to say: 'Whether he is satisfied that the independent directors can effectively exercise the role ascribed to them.' In his letter to Fayed boasting of this initial success, Greer added pointedly: 'I look forward to our meeting next week, when hopefully we will be able to agree the financial basis on which we work.'

With the recruitment of Neil Hamilton, a saga of parliamentary corruption began that would test the condition of Westminster ethics to destruction. In later years, when they saw the havoc in Fayed's wake, many Conservative supporters were to blame the Egyptian for it all, accusing him of un-

English behaviour. That was to miss the point. Fayed's un-Englishness meant merely that he had unpractised fingers on the levers of corruption – sometimes even clumsy ones. Under his control, the machine was to veer off the road and ultimately spill its secrets. But when Fayed came along, the Westminster corruption engine was already constructed, polished and working, normally steered silently and discreetly by chaps who had been to the right schools. It just happened to fall for a while into the hands of Mr Toad.

Fayed's lawyer composed the draft PQs immediately after the first Harrods meeting in the autumn of 1985, and telexed them to Greer's offices near Westminster. The allegations of Rowland's interference in the *Observer* stories were duly handed over to the MP, Neil Hamilton, who took them to the Table Office upstairs in the Palace of Westminster. There, the Commons clerks accepted the form and had the questions printed under parliamentary privilege in the next day's Order Paper, for written answer by the Trade Secretary, the response to be published in *Hansard*, the official record of proceedings in the Mother of Parliaments.

Hamilton himself neither knew nor cared whether the *Observer*'s independent directors had been failing in their duties, as his questions alleged. The point of these questions was not to elicit an answer. There was not much that ministers could constructively say. But the fact that the issue was being raised in public served to put pressure on the minister – and pressure on the directors of the *Observer*. It was useful to Fayed. The virtue of PQs was their public nature: not only could Fayed observe how he was getting political value for money, but the newspapers could also write them up under privilege, without fear of libel suits.

Indeed, the City journalist Kenneth Fleet at *The Times* wrote about them straight away. The fairly obscure PQs had no doubt been drawn to his attention, perhaps by Greer himself. *The Times*' headline said: 'MP TO QUERY ROLE OF OBSERVER DIRECTORS' and the story included a further announcement that Leon Brittan had sent an official letter to Rowland, refusing to move against Fayed. 'The press this morning is good,' Greer crowed to Fayed. 'I am delighted.'

Neil Hamilton's willingness to act as a political catspaw on Greer's behalf paid immediate dividends for the lobbyist. Fayed signed up with Greer for a year's worth of further lobbying, at £25,000 – an unusually low figure. Greer's best contracts brought in £10,000 a month – £120,000 a year. His most moderate rate for lobbying was normally £4,000–£5,000 a month and anything cheaper bought only a news service of 'political intelligence'. But the Harrods deal was for little more than £2,000 a month. Fayed has an explanation for this: he says the true arrangement included another £20,000 a year, which he handed over quarterly to Greer in cash – wads of banknotes, £5,000 at a time, to make under-the-counter payments. It was Fayed's belief that this 'slush fund' was to pay bribes. As Fayed tells it, Greer had sought to educate him as to how British politics could be made to work: 'He said you need to rent an MP just like you rent a London taxi.'

Once comfortably on the payroll, Greer's next move was to demonstrate his special access to the Trade Secretary himself. This he did by producing Leon Brittan's Parliamentary Private Secretary, the Scotsman Gerry Malone. A PPS is only a backbench MP but his unpaid role as Westminster intelligencer and bag-carrier for his master, who personally selects him, makes a PPS a good conduit to a minister. Malone was 'a sharp and able young man', Greer wrote to his client. Greer collected Malone from the Commons in a taxi and delivered him to Fayed for a personal meeting at Park Lane on Monday 11 November. The very next day, Malone dutifully approached Leon Brittan about Fayed's problems. Or so Greer briefed his client: 'Leon would like Gerry to keep in touch with all of us . . . He believes that his letter to Rowland is as much as he can do at the present time and should be seen, as indeed it is, as a very good victory for you. Gerry's suggestion of a letter to the independent directors [of the *Observer*] . . . was considered to be a good and worthwhile idea.'

Greer's and Fayed's lawyers duly put their heads together, and composed a second appeal to the *Observer* directors. It did not get far. Moreover, the Malone connection proved a wasted effort. In January 1986, Leon Brittan was suddenly forced to resign for his part in leaking a letter designed to discredit Defence Secretary Michael Heseltine during the Westland affair – a political row over the takeover of a helicopter firm. Malone disappeared from Government office alongside his boss, although Greer would not forget his co-operative attitude: the MP got an undeclared donation of £1,000 from Ian Greer Associates for election expenses the following year.

Greer had a second string to his bow: to try to build up a group of backbenchers who would work for Fayed in parliament. The unscrupulous Hamilton was a prime candidate. Greer arranged a briefing for him with Fayed's lawyers on the morning of 13 November. The second MP whom Greer briefed was equally predictable: Michael Grylls, chairman of the Tory backbench trade and industry committee. Grylls was certainly likely to be responsive, and not merely because he and Greer were old partners. On 1 November 1985, just as Fayed and his problem materialised, Greer paid money to Grylls as one more undeclared commission for supposedly new 'introductions'. The MP would have been ungrateful to spurn Greer's new client under such circumstances.

Parliamentary friends were soon needed. For Rowland returned to the attack in the *Observer* in the New Year of 1986 with a sizzling set of new – and largely fabricated – allegations which he presented to the *Observer*'s then editor, Donald Trelford. Trelford personally wrote and published an unlikely story, to near-mutiny from his horrified journalists, that Mark Thatcher, the Prime Minister's son, had himself gone to Brunei in Fayed's company to do conspiratorial deals with the Sultan.

Greer the lobbyist was there to counter-attack. He drew up a list of a dozen MPs to whom he circulated a pained letter from Fayed, protesting anew that he was being made the innocent victim of a megalomaniac bad loser who was prostituting the British press. 'We want to build up in parliament a group of Fayed supporters,' Greer said, uninhibited. His group expanded to four MPs with the addition of Peter Hordern, who had long been openly paid as 'consultant' to the House of Fraser, the stores' holding company, and Tim Smith, the Beaconsfield MP who was vice-chairman of the Tory trade and industry committee and had already demonstrated his greed by openly taking money from accountants Price Waterhouse to lodge PQs on their behalf.

Smith was co-operative, but Hamilton and Grylls naturally provided the most immediately obliging responses. Grylls wrote to Fayed: 'I do think you have been treated deplorably and very much regret the suffering the *Observer*'s campaign has brought you.' After talking to Greer, Hamilton wrote to establish a special bond with Fayed, forged through common tribulation and the promise of redemption: 'As someone who has been the victim of serious libels myself, I can well understand the distress and inconvenience caused to you. I am very concerned at the low standards to be found in the news media in this country and I think it is important that those individuals who have the misfortune to be victims should take resolute action to defend themselves and secure punishment for the perpetrators.'

A moody Fayed found these expressions of sympathy 'totally useless'. But he was reassured by Greer: 'You have in fact achieved a very considerable success . . . Two MPs have already made contact with the Secretary of State's office in an endeavour to get him to once again look at the role of the independent directors.' Now the next phase of Greer's plan, as he explained to his paymaster, was to cement the little parliamentary group in place. They comprised between them – and not by accident – the three officers of the backbench trade and industry committee: chairman Grylls, vice-chairman Smith and secretary Hamilton. The Trade Secretary would surely pay attention to such a group if they appeared in his office on the top floor at Victoria Street. Greer counselled Fayed to lunch his new team generously at Harrods, then to despatch them on a delegation to the minister. The MPs were given their instructions for the lunch. To Grylls and Hamilton: 'You should plan for a car picking you up at 12.30 pm at the Members' Entrance.' To the Bertie Wooster-esque Tim Smith, a slightly more tentative: 'I have accepted this date and hope it is convenient to you. Can you let me know?'

The lunch, on 10 March, was the first time that Fayed met his newly-acquired stable of Conservative MPs as a group. One can imagine that he was all charm up in the fifth-floor chairman's office above the swarming shoppers, handing out

Harrods teddy bears and inviting his tame politicians in their business suits to inspect the famous cornucopia of goods in the store. Greer too, would have been in hand-rubbing mode. 'Today's lunch went very well indeed,' he cooed to Fayed after it had been cleared away.

One stimulating piece of lunch-time gossip for the politicians was the relationship between their new enemy, Rowland, and Edward du Cann. Du Cann, chairman of the 1922 committee of Conservative backbenchers, and simultaneously an extravagantly-paid director of Lonrho, was Rowland's chief representative at Westminster. That relationship was impossible to conceal. But it is worth remembering that not one but both sides in the Lonrho-Harrods dispute were paying British politicians throughout the saga of their quarrel.

The most significant outcome of the lunch was that Grylls, Hamilton and Smith agreed to go in a deputation to the new Trade Secretary, Paul Channon, and complain about Rowland. Greer promised: 'I will keep tabs on them and make arrangements ... to brief them thoroughly before they meet the Secretary of State.' However, the meeting did not materialise. Indeed, Channon wrote unsympathetically to Fayed refusing to assist with his complaints against Rowland and the *Observer*: 'I cannot agree that the personal matters in dispute ... provide grounds on which it would be right to order an investigation of the *Observer* Ltd.'

Ever resourceful, Greer moved to Plan B. In April 1986, he told Fayed's lawyer: 'You will be pleased to know that Tim Smith has been persuaded to go ahead and try for an adjournment debate' – one which allowed a backbencher to make a late-night speech for fifteen minutes on a vote for 'the adjournment'. He added to Fayed himself: 'Tim Smith has at last agreed.' How exactly had Tim Smith been persuaded to agree? A sum of cash did the trick. Smith now admits he was paid to arrange the adjournment debate. It may have come from Greer's slush fund. Fayed, on his own account, had handed over a total of £10,000 by this point to Greer for miscellaneous bribes.

Greer and another of Fayed's lawyers, Royston Webb, discreetly briefed Smith the night before the debate on what he was supposed to say. Greer assured Fayed the debate was a 'magnificent opportunity' to abuse Rowland and the *Observer* from behind the shield of parliamentary privilege. Anything Tim Smith said, no matter how libellous, could be reported freely in the papers. The power of parliamentary privilege is important in a country where the oppressive libel laws give rich men virtual immunity from insults. It is a power, however, that is supposed to protect MPs acting in what they believe is the public interest. Tim Smith was abusing it.

Hansard records that the Honourable Member for Beacons-field rose at 11.17 pm on 18 June 1986 and denounced the *Observer* for running stories that were 'fabrications' and 'for-geries' against the Fayeds. His concern was with the *Observer*'s independence, he said: 'Perhaps it would be fairer to readers to print under the newspaper's masthead, the slogan: "Owned by Lonrho and censored by the unions".' It might have been fairer to parliament and to Smith's constituents also to print on Tim Smith's forehead in large letters: 'Bought by Harrods'.

Three of the team – Grylls, Smith and Peter Hordern – helped to promote another of Greer's anti-Lonrho stunts in the summer of 1986. Each dutifully wrote to Paul Channon urging the minister to block Rowland's proposed purchase of *Today* newspaper, Eddie Shah's loss-making venture. Michael Grylls' drafts of his parliamentary correspondence – 'written in his capacity as chairman of the backbench trade and industry committee', as Greer put it – were copied in advance to Greer Associates. From his public position, he pronounced: 'It would in my opinion be appalling if Rowland were given control of yet another newspaper.' Prior to writing this letter, on 14 May 1986, Grylls had received money from Greer.

A fourth long-standing contact of Greer – Andrew Bowden, MP for the marginal seat of Brighton Kemptown – agreed to join the letter-writing campaign. 'I have known him for 20 years and can depend on him,' Greer was to boast. Bowden had provided a Greer employee, Anthony Mayes, with a research assistant's Commons pass in 1984 and was in due course to become another beneficiary of Greer favours in return for his help. Graham Bright, a fifth MP, who was to get help from Greer staff during his election campaign, also wrote to minister Channon at Greer's request.

Throughout this phase, Neil Hamilton took a back seat. He

was working on his pending 'Panorama' libel case, and was subsequently rescued from the political wilderness: David Mitchell, Transport Minister, in October offered him a post as unpaid PPS – a first step on the ladder to promotion.

Hamilton also specifically refused to help with the *Today* newspaper campaign for reasons that caused him some embarrassment. A second batch of politicians had been contacted by letters in Mohammed al-Fayed's name and asked to approach the Department of Trade and Industry over the summer, while Greer was off sailing in the Caribbean ('I will be contactable through a ship-to-shore radio'). Hamilton was in this second-tier group. But he had a problem. Eddie Shah was one of his constituents, and Hamilton plainly did not want to be seen acting against his interests by trying to block the sale. But his letter of refusal was distinctly odd: 'Dear Mr al-Fayed . . . As you know, I have the greatest sympathy with you and your family over the disgraceful way you have been treated by the *Observer* newspaper. However, it is impossible for me to do what you have asked on this occasion for reasons which I have explained to Charles St George at Ian Greer Associates, and which he will communicate to you. I am sorry to be so cryptic, but Charles St George will explain my difficulties.' It is hard to see why the Cheshire MP felt the need to be 'cryptic', and to use Greer's firm as a channel for an unwritten message. The situation is explained, however, if he had been covertly paid via Greer and needed a good excuse for not delivering the usual service.

The battle between the two tycoons raged inconclusively throughout the remainder of 1986. Greer's small platoon of parliamentary troops failed to prevent Rowland buying *Today* newspaper. But Fayed scored one PR success, when the *Observer*'s lawyers admitted they could not prove the Mark Thatcher allegations. Dozens of letters were sent to MPs and peers by Greer in Fayed's name, boasting of this tactical victory. Another little public relations coup was the appearance in the *Sunday Times* in June 1986 of an account of an obscure court case in Denver, Colorado, concerning skulduggery at a Zambian amethyst mine. It was alleged that the minority shareholders in two Lonrho companies had been cheated. Two of the 'stable'

– Grylls and Hordern – followed up the article with letters to the Trade Secretary accusing Lonrho of business malpractice. Channon promised to look into it.

But as Christmas approached, a dramatic riposte from Lonrho landed not only on Channon's desk, but in the pigeon-holes of all 650 MPs. Rowland, whose lawyers and investigators had been scouring Bombay, Haiti and Alexandria to unearth Fayed's history, had discovered that the merchant bankers Kleinwort Benson had made very few, if any, independent checks on the Fayeds' wealth, before guaranteeing their 1984 purchase of Harrods and the House of Fraser. 'The Department of Trade and Kleinwort Benson have been accessories to passing off a fraudulent Public Offer,' Rowland now wrote menacingly to Channon.

> Kleinwort Benson's own sketchy and damaging list of Fayed assets makes nonsense of the claim of fabulous wealth. It was scandalous ... They flung aside the rules for a cheat ... It was a corruption of the Department of Trade to push it through, and a disgrace to the minister involved ... Mohammed al-Fayed has used inside methods to circumvent the Department of Trade and benefit himself, and has had political help to do so, from Mrs Thatcher and Norman Tebbit.

Rowland repeated that he wanted a DTI investigation. And he made clear he would go to law to compel Channon to make a fresh decision on the matter.

To defend his beleaguered client, Greer fired back another salvo of planted PQs about alleged Lonrho arms deals: Peter Hordern tabled them in exchange for payment. Greer set up another MPs lunch at Harrods. As well as the loyalists – Hordern, Grylls and Smith – he managed to inveigle along to this meal both Rob Hayward, the PPS to junior Corporate Affairs Minister Michael Howard, and David Atkinson, the PPS to Channon himself. But, with or without lunch, the situation was becoming ominous for Fayed. Just how ominous was revealed to him in January 1987, from an most unexpected source.

Carla Powell, the Italian-born wife of Mrs Thatcher's Foreign Affairs adviser, Charles Powell, is a colourful character. She owns 200 pairs of shoes. And she loves gossip. She once caused a major scene by buttonholing Tory newspaper magnate Conrad Black and informing him that his political editor on the staunchly Conservative *Telegraph* was a supporter of the Labour party. Nobody had elected Charles Powell. He was a civil servant, seconded from the Foreign Office. Nevertheless, thanks to Mrs Thatcher's preference for loyal and industrious individuals, he was an intimate of the Premier and such a power in the land that people called him the Deputy Prime Minister. Nobody had elected Carla Powell either, although she had an unrivalled seat at a variety of top tables, and was an enthusiastic supporter of Mrs Thatcher.

There is a story that Powell came home one day and told his wife, who was deep in vivacious shopping-related conversation on the phone: 'You'll have to get off the line – I'm expecting a call from the boss.'

'But Charles,' said Carla, 'I'm talking to her already.'

Fayed, as the Sultan of Brunei's *pro tem* financial adviser, had helped Powell out during negotiations to keep the Sultan's funds in sterling accounts and away from the Americans. Both Charles (who spoke Finnish) and Carla Powell had remained on good terms with Fayed's Finnish wife, Heini. And with Fayed too. She was 'a dear friend', says Fayed. He goes on to tell how Carla left a message that January saying: 'Mohammed, watch out!' Fayed received the impression she had gleaned from one of her innumerable contacts that a DTI inquiry into Fayed's background would be announced – in three months' time. The recommendation to launch the investigation was supported by Corporate Affairs Minister Michael Howard, she believed. Carla Powell and Charles Powell, while conceding that Carla had a friendly relationship with Fayed, both deny that such a tip-off occurred. Charles Powell points out that he himself was given no advance knowledge of the DTI inquiry.

At the beginning of 1987, the priority for ministers in Mrs Thatcher's Government was a looming general election, which she was planning to call in five months' time. No politician in their right mind would want a tycoon on the loose in the pre-election period who possessed Tiny Rowland's awesome capacity for anti-Government invective and an apparently bottomless pocket. After his fanciful story about Mark Thatcher and Fayed, what on earth might Tiny publish next on Britain's first family? The setting-up of a lengthy DTI inquiry into Fayed's problematic background might well have been seen as the right device to shut Tiny up and see the Tories safely past polling-day. Fayed, however, believed he had heard words that showed Michael Howard was hostile to him.

Ian Greer pulled out all the lobbying stops. His client was in danger. More accusations were made by letter to Channon against Rowland and his security man, ex-detective Kenneth Etheridge. Fayed's men demanded a DTI inquiry, not into them, but into Lonrho. To follow this through, Neil Hamilton was successfully re-activated. He tabled two PQs to Howard, pressing for answers to the Fayed letters, with their wide-ranging accusations. Hamilton also tabled a motion, organised by Greer, defending Harrods against union criticism of their labour relations. 'This House applauds the agreement reached ... between Harrods Ltd and the staff ... [and] abhors the personal attacks made under parliamentary privilege on the owners of Harrods Ltd.'

Greer and Fayed tried to persuade Tim Smith to become a permanent paid 'adviser' to Harrods. But although Smith took cash from Fayed, he was unwilling to go so far – perhaps because such a continuing post would be difficult not to declare in the Register of Members' Interests. So Greer began to fish for new supporters. 'I have just seen Andrew Bowden MP over lunch. At last we have a campaigner!' he enthused to Fayed, ever-sunny about the way things were going. 'I have known Andrew for 20 years and can depend on him. He is without doubt the right person. We can use Tim Smith in other ways.'

In the spring, the lobbyist set out to organise a discreet 'freebie' on Fayed's behalf for Hamilton and other potential Fayed friends – Smith, Grylls, the new recruit Bowden, and a possible new supporter, William Clark. They were confidentially offered a weekend in Paris, staying at the sumptuous Ritz Hotel in the Place Vendôme. 'This is in every way a private invitation and I would therefore be grateful for it being kept as such.' It was an attractive little trip for any MP and his wife to look forward to. But on 8 April, Neil Hamilton and Christine heard a piece of personal bad news. Their long-standing associate and fellow litigant, the anti-immigration MP Harvey Proctor, was charged by police with gross indecency after spanking rent boys. Proctor, who had wisely dropped out of their joint libel action against the BBC before it came to trial, was eventually convicted and ejected in disgrace from his seat.

More bad news followed the next day in a Westminster council of war held by Fayed himself and the two MPs, Grylls and Smith. Channon, as Secretary of State, had just notified them formally that his Department of Trade and Industry would, after all, appoint inspectors to inquire into the purchase of House of Fraser plc. Fayed's mind went back to what he had believed to be Carla's warnings. How was it that, after two secretaries of state, Norman Tebbit and Leon Brittan, decided there were no grounds for an inquiry into his takeover of House of Fraser, Michael Howard's Corporate Affairs department now suddenly changed its mind in the spring of 1987 and put DTI inspectors in? Fayed researched the junior minister's background in all the detail that a rich man was able to command, and developed the darkest suspicions about Howard's judgement. He became preoccupied that Howard might have a conflict of interest because a businessman cousin, Harry Landy, had once had connections with Lonrho. And ten years on, it is still Howard, rightly or wrongly, on whom Fayed thirsts for revenge.

Meanwhile, Greer hastily postponed the projected 'private' free weekend in Paris for his stable of MPs. With Fayed now the object of an official investigation, he said, it might be 'misconstrued'. Bribery worked well at Westminster only if it did not look too obviously like bribery.

It was the eve of the general election campaign, on 13 May 1987, when the 'gang of four' Fayed MPs presented themselves in the Secretary of State's office at the DTI, for the opening shots in a desperate battle of political pressure. If Fayed lost the battle, he was liable to lose Harrods. The agenda for the Channon meeting had already been orchestrated by Greer: 'I am anxious to see a delegation . . . seek an interview with Paul Channon. This should be sought during the course of the next few days. It is important for us to be very clear what we want to come out of such a meeting. Are we asking for a change in the appointment of inspectors? Are we trying to persuade the Secretary of State to set a time-limit on the inquiry? We may find it difficult . . . Consideration should be given to pressing for Lonrho to be the subject of a full-scale inquiry . . . Andrew Bowden and the other MPs can continue to table questions on other relevant matters.'

That very day, parliament was dissolved and the general election campaign began. In the minister's office, Sir Peter Hordern and the three backbench trade and industry committee officers, Hamilton, Grylls and Smith, duly complained on Fayed's behalf. They said he was entitled to know more about why the inquiry had been set up, and upon what information Channon had acted. They again urged the minister to investigate Lonrho instead. Smith had already put down a blizzard of irritating PQs to Michael Howard about Lonrho. The team had a success: they had made a chorus of complaints that one of the two inspectors, Philip Heslop QC, had a conflict of interest because he had represented businessman Ernest Saunders of Guinness, an associate of Tiny Rowland. Heslop resigned.

As parliament broke up for the three-week election campaign, Greer now made urgent solicitations to Fayed for money. He needed extra cash to give politicians, he told the Harrods proprietor. But the paperwork for the new transactions was obscure and inadequate. Fayed handed over a cheque for £12,000. Then Fayed's brother Ali (who acted for Mohammed in his absence) handed over a second for £6,000. This was supported by a letter from Greer saying he needed it for the election expenses of 'one or two Conservative candidates'. Fayed believed he was simply being asked to pay more bribes to Government politicians. He also handed over his main election contribution – much larger, secret sums – direct to Alistair McAlpine, the Conservative party treasurer. Fayed says those donations amounted to £250,000. Lord McAlpine concedes that Fayed made several payments to him for party funds between 1985 and 1987, although he is unwilling to specify the amounts. The Conservative party offers secrecy to donors – British citizens and foreigners alike.

A second tranche of money – £11,000, as Central Office eventually conceded – was obtained by Greer from Dave

Allen, boss of the DHL courier firm. Although Ian Greer Associates was a limited company, and thus theoretically liable to disclose all political payments, it was able to use a 'small company' loophole, recently legislated by the Conservative Government, to avoid declaring the destination of any of this money.

It has, however, proved possible to discover what happened to the Fayed/Allen cash. Conservative Central Office files reveal that it went 'to the fighting funds of individual MPs for their local campaigns . . . 21 Conservative MPs to whom the money . . . was given in amounts ranging from £500 to £5,000'.

The full tally of those who have now admitted receipt of 1987 election cash from Greer includes not only 21 Tories, but several Labour and Liberal names as well. Some of the money looks as though it should have been declared on the Register of MPs' Interests under existing rules. In fact, none of the MPs who were subsidised by Greer, whether they were required by the existing rules or not, ever chose to make the fact public. Every one of them, with the possible exception of Greer's personal constituency MP, knew that they were getting campaign funds not from a local supporter, but from a political lobbyist.

Eventual disclosure of Greer's use of the money turned out to be something of a surprise for the generous Mohammed al-Fayed himself. For Greer, it seems, did not tell him the full truth in 1987. Far from paying off 'one or two Conservative MPs' in marginal seats who might help Fayed, the money was clearly scattered around where Greer thought it might do the lobbyist himself the widest range of good in the future, as well as paying off old debts. Greer never made good his promises to supply the Fayeds with a breakdown of where their money went. The one payment that was unmistakably Fayed-related was also the most disgraceful. Sir Andrew Bowden, fighting a marginal seat in Brighton Kemptown, got the biggest contribution to his campaign 'fighting fund' from Greer: it was in excess of £5,319. This was more than the sum declared on Bowden's election returns for his total campaign expenditure. Bowden declared £4,660. Moreover, it was more than the legal maximum allowed for an individual's total expenditure to contest that seat: £5,135. And thirdly, having had election expenses (and more) paid for by a third party, Bowden was under an obligation to declare himself in the next Register of MPs' Interests. Mr Bowden has said he did not know the money came from al-Fayed.

There was a second contribution to campaign funds which, on the face of it, should also have been declared on the register. This was £2,000 given to the campaign of Norman Lamont in Kingston, Surrey. Lamont, Greer's constituency MP, also had the use of Greer's house during the campaign. He should have declared any contribution over 25 per cent of total election expenses – approximately £1,500 – as 'sponsorship'. Although Conservatives are customarily hot on Labour MPs declaring their trade union 'sponsorships', it was a different matter when their own sponsorship by lobbyists was involved. There were three other names on Greer's list whose existence was later to give Conservative Central Office particular cause for concern, because they were considered 'prominent' figures: Michael Portillo, Gerry Malone and Michael Hirst.

Portillo, at the time a Government Whip, got £500. He was to rise to a key Cabinet position by 1996, as Defence Secretary and a possible future contender for the Conservative leadership. His response to the eventual disclosure of the Greer payment in 1996 was to snap to journalists: 'So what?' But Portillo's network of connections and potential obligations was of the utmost importance. Although there is no evidence he took part in any Fayed campaigns, once he became Defence Secretary Portillo was involved in the award of contracts worth billions. Some of the contenders were Greer clients – the American firm ITT, for example, promoting their Bowman radio system. He was a personal associate of one of Greer's stable of paid MPs, Michael Brown, who says they went on holiday together. 'I would call myself a friend of his,' Brown says, 'although I don't know whether he would call himself a friend of mine.' Portillo was also a political associate of another Greer MP, Neil Hamilton, in the Thatcherite No Turning Back group which Michael Brown organised. And Portillo was on the payroll of British Airways as a parliamentary 'consultant' until he joined the Government in 1985. BA were another Greer client.

The second 'prominent' name on the list was Gerald Malone, the 'able young man' who had agreed to meet the troubled Fayed and offered such helpful advice on behalf of his boss, Leon Brittan. He got £1,000 from Greer. It was not enough to save his marginal seat of Aberdeen South, but Malone returned to parliament in 1992 for another constituency. By 1996 he was Health Minister, and holding meetings with the chiefs of hospitals which could easily have been – like the Royal Marsden in 1992 and Royal Brompton in 1993 – Greer clients. In 1987, Malone wrote a fulsome thank-you letter to Greer for the money, signed 'Yours aye'.

The third 'prominent' person on the party list was Michael Hirst, MP for Strathkelvin and Bearsden. As one of the party's very few Scottish MPs, he was prominent only in the sense that a tree stands out in an empty landscape. It is not obvious why Central Office felt nervous about his being named, or why Greer singled him out for cash. He got £500.

Lynda Chalker, then a Foreign Office Minister, was given some money in her Wallasey constituency, out of Greer's election fund. A donation of more than £500 went on printing artwork for campaign literature: this followed an earlier donation of more than £1,200 for computer equipment in the constituency office. Again, Chalker's seat was marginal, and in such cases, a very economical injection of money brought a big relative return of goodwill from an individual MP.

The then Party Chairman, Norman Tebbit, got £1,000 for his campaign, as did junior minister David Trippier (secretary of the all-party parliamentary footwear committee, 1979–83) in Rossendale. A close contact of Greer, the then Social Services Secretary, John Moore, got £1,000 and some help with literature in Croydon Central. Colin Moynihan, another junior minister, had the services of a temporary secretary paid for in Lewisham East. The other Tories who received £500 (with their constituencies) included: Kenneth Warren, chairman of the Select Committee on Trade and Industry, and MP for Hastings; Robert Atkins (South Ribble); Sir Gerald Vaughan (Reading East); David Mellor (Putney); Malcolm Thornton (Crosby); Neil Thorne (Ilford); Gerald Bowden (Dulwich); John Lee (Pendle); Tony Durant (Reading West); David Shaw (Dover); Nirj Deva (Hammersmith, now MP for

Brentford); John Punnyer (Lewisham and Deptford) who received £250 only.

Greer also made some investments in Labour MPs. The most notable was Doug Hoyle, the MP for Warrington North, now Labour party Chairman, and subsequently influential as a member of the Privileges Committee which inquired into 'cash-for-questions' in 1994. As far back as 1984, Hoyle had been in receipt of contributions from Greer and went to his drinks parties. The Labour MP had already volunteered his services to Greer in the Fayed campaign: ('Doug Hoyle ... is also keen to be helpful ... we can use him in other ways'). He got £500. A small payment of £250 also went to Stan Crowther (Rotherham) and payments of £500 to the Liberals' Alan Beith (Berwick) and Richard Holme (Cheltenham). Ian Wrigglesworth of the Social Democratic party got £500 for his unsuccessful fight in Stockton South.

There was a curious absence from Greer's donation lists. Although he was scattering election funding like confetti, none apparently went to his most trusted parliamentary lieutenants: Grylls, Smith and Hamilton. But Grylls had already had a total of £27,000 from Greer in the 12 months prior to the election, so he was awash with money. Smith was getting cash direct from Fayed. And in Hamilton's case too, there may be an explanation.

Following the start of the election campaign, Fayed's phone records show Hamilton ringing to confirm he would visit Fayed at 11.15 am in London on Tuesday 2 June – only nine days before polling – when Hamilton's constituency campaigning was at its height in the north of England. Only something compelling could have torn Hamilton away from his constituency at such a time. And it was the first time the two men had met alone. Fayed says the explanation is simple: he gave the MP an envelope full of £2,500 in banknotes.

The election the Conservatives fought in 1987 was heavily funded with secret money. Cash also came from Wafic Said, the Syrian front man for the Saudi rulers, who two years earlier had clinched the gigantic al-Yamamah arms deal with Mrs Thatcher; money came from Greek and Asian shipping millionaires with tax haven status in London; money came from a Swedish businessman, Octav Botnar, who later left the country owing millions to the Inland Revenue. In a panic a few days before polling, Lord Young, then working as Mrs Thatcher's special campaign manager, grabbed Party Chairman Tebbit by the lapels and shouted: 'Norman, we're going to lose this fucking election! You're going to go, we're all going to go! The whole thing is going to go!' He ordered full-page advertisements in all the newspapers up to polling day, regardless of expense. Turkish tycoon Asil Nadir of the Polly Peck company financed the media blitz, with secret off-shore cheques paid to the 'Conservative Industrial Fund'.

Restored to a more self-confident mood, Mrs Thatcher's final meeting was a 'family rally' at Wembley arena, more sophisticated and stage-managed than Kenny Everett's banalities in 1983. This time, the pop group Hot Chocolate came on to sing a silky version of (curiously) John Lennon's 'Imagine' ('Imagine no possessions, I wonder if you can . . .'). Then the lights dimmed, gradually, towards darkness. As they did so, the close air was filled by a thunderous, electronically synthesised rendering of Edward Elgar's 'Jerusalem' and a burst of wild, criss-crossing laser-beams flashed across the darkness. An arrangement of video screens showed a succession of hypnotically-edited scenes with Mrs Thatcher greeting world leaders and giving speeches, and the crowd began to chant in the bewitching alternation of darkness and blinding light: 'MAGGIE, MAGGIE, MAGGIE'. As the music reached its climax, the lasers and screens suddenly disappeared and a spotlight was trained on the mouth of a blue velvet tunnel, similar to those from which gladiators appeared in a Roman arena. She appeared, dressed in a suit of identical blue, walking determinedly and waving. The crowd, the core of Britain's rising lower middle class, greeted her with a deafening furore, which took several minutes to subside.

The 1987 election was, as before, comfortably won by the Conservatives. Mrs Thatcher had 146 more MPs than the Labour party. Those MPs included once again the hacks from the lobbyist's stable – Hamilton, Brown, Bowden, Smith and Grylls. With such a heart-warming result, Ian Greer Associates too, were safely back in the lobbying game.

**Margaret (now Baroness) Thatcher, Prime Minister 1979-90,
whose eye was caught by the up-and-coming Neil Hamilton**

7

The Spoils of Victory

**'Get thee glass eyes, and like a scurvy politician,
seem to see the things thou dost not.'**

Shakespeare, King Lear

For the lobbyist Greer, as he stroked Humphrey the brown poodle in his Westminster office in June 1987, the fulfilled prospect of a lucrative, third Thatcher administration was one which justified a display of high spirits. A little jig down Catherine Place outside, perhaps, or a pair of mother-of-pearl opera-glasses from Asprey as a special present for himself. For by now he had more than thirty politicians within his ambit, most of them from the ruling party. Some, like John Moore and Norman Lamont, were very senior; others, like Hamilton and Portillo, were coming men.

The horizon did, however, reveal both good and bad news. The good news was that cash from the renewed annual contract with the owner of Harrods was flowing regularly into Greer Associates' account at the Hill Samuel bank in St James's Square. The bad news was that the Fayed campaign was starting to look like a losing battle. The DTI inquiry was a target at which Lonrho's global squads of lawyers could fire off all their toxic discoveries about the Fayed family history. The coiffeured Greer needed to get the DTI inspectors off Fayed's back, or at least give the impression to his Egyptian paymaster that no efforts were being spared in the employment of political influence to do so.

The purchased positions of what Greer called 'our group' of MPs were to change. Bowden – his marginal seat safely won with Fayed's cash – faded into the background. Tim Smith would eventually be identified by a furious Tiny Rowland as a Greer hireling and neutralised; Grylls was to remain steady and Neil Hamilton became a dedicated soldier for Fayed. Like all soldiers, he tended to march on his stomach.

According to Fayed, the first Harrods 'brown envelope' had been handed over directly to Hamilton in June, during the general election campaign. It was the two men's first meeting alone. Before that, Hamilton had done a limited amount of Fayed's parliamentary work at Greer's request: he had tabled questions and motions, written letters and helped make up a deputation. But if he had needed cash to persuade him to act, it would previously have had to come from Greer's pocket, not Fayed's – from the £5,000 wad which Fayed says he was handing over to the lobbyist every quarter for his 'slush fund'. From now on, however, Hamilton was to see much more of Fayed – whom he starts to refer to familiarly as 'Mohammed' – and to accept money and treats from him directly. Why should Fayed change tactics and start paying Hamilton direct in this way? Fayed says: 'He came to me and complained that he wasn't getting enough from Greer alone.'

There was a second *tête-à-tête* meeting between Hamilton and Fayed only a week after polling day, on 18 June. Fayed's office message pads record Christine Hamilton ringing up from the Commons prior to the 5 pm encounter. Three weeks later, on 8 July, Hamilton had another private meeting at Harrods at 4.15 pm. Hamilton himself had phoned the previous day to confirm it. Fayed says that at these meetings he gave Hamilton more money.

The MP certainly started to behave as though he had suddenly received a stimulating injection in the wallet. He turned up at Harrods for an MPs group meeting on 15 July, which Greer had been attempting to set up ever since the election. There he agreed with Bowden, Grylls and Smith to form a fresh deputation to the new Trade Secretary, Lord Young. Young was the re-shuffled replacement for Paul Channon, who had authorised the DTI inquiry into Fayed in the first place. A new minister might be persuaded to take a different attitude.

Before that meeting, Hamilton set out to push the latest stunt from the Fayed camp – an assault on Lonrho for the allegedly misleading nature of his company's accounts, about which complaints had been laid with the Stock Exchange.

Clipping another *Times* article on the subject written by Kenneth Fleet, the MP sent it off with a stiff letter on his Commons notepaper to the Stock Exchange chairman, Sir Nicholas Goodison.

Hamilton pressed his own demand for a speedy Stock Exchange inquiry, and explained in the usual way that his keen interest in the 'very serious issues' at stake was 'as vice-chairman of the Conservative trade and industry committee, I have taken a close interest in the long-running feud between Lonrho and house of Fraser'. Hamilton stuck a copy of this officious letter in an envelope and sent it over directly to Fayed at 60 Park Lane on 23 July, addressing him warmly as 'Dear Mohammed':

> Enclosed is a copy of my letter to the chairman of the Stock Exchange ... I have now been elected secretary of the Conservative finance committee and vice-chairman of the trade and industry committee, all of which gives me a better position from which to act on your behalf. Previously, as a PPS it was less easy. I will be writing shortly to Francis Maude, the new minister at the DTI. Yours ever, Neil.

About a week later, Hamilton presented himself at 4 pm with Tim Smith and Peter Hordern at the Trade Ministry offices in Victoria Street. The MPs made Greer-inspired pleas to the new Trade Secretary that his ill-intentioned department should leave the proprietor of Harrods alone. They tried to persuade Young to make the inspectors wrap up their inquiry quickly. They demanded again that the DTI start a Lonrho investigation instead, both into their allegations of financial skulduggery at a Lonrho amethyst mine in Zambia, and also into the presentation of the Lonrho company accounts. More quantities of paper were dutifully pushed from desk to desk in Victoria Street, as these latest representations of the 'trade and industry committee officers' were minuted by officials and circulated for comment, analysis, and analysis of the analysis – all, as usual, at the taxpayers' expense.

With the break-up of parliament for the summer, the politicians, lawyers, accountants and civil servants then left London in droves for Italy and the south of France. The tycoons too,

departed for their yachts. Like eighteenth-century siege war-
fare, this kind of metropolitan intrigue was essentially seasonal
in character, and would not resume in earnest until the party
conferences of October and the re-opening of parliament
thereafter.

Neil and Christine Hamilton shared the same migratory
instincts as their Westminster colleagues: the beginning of
September found them in holiday mood, driving across
France. They were heading for Paris. It was, however, a
holiday they did not intend to pay for. They had asked Fayed
(or 'Mohammed'), whether the previous spring's 'private in
every way' invitation was still open to stay at the Paris Ritz and
visit the late Duke of Windsor's restored premises in the Bois
de Boulogne – a further feat of renovation on which Fayed had
spent more of the millions he could so plainly afford to throw
away. This beautiful house occupied a special but curious
place in English history: it was the mansion to which the Duke
retreated with Mrs Wallis Simpson after his abdication as
King Edward VIII. The Egyptian had meticulously brought it
back to life.

Of all the instances of bad judgement in Neil Hamilton's
political career – from the Hitler imitations to the ginger
biscuit he was later jokingly to offer to declare as a gift – none
was to prove as disastrous as this free holiday. It was done so
greedily that it stuck in the memory of his paymaster, and
rankled.

The entrance in the Place Vendôme to the Ritz, which used
to be a fine eighteenth-century private mansion, is understated. There was nothing understated, however, about Neil
Hamilton's conduct there. Braking to a halt on 8 September
near the Tuileries Gardens in the heart of fashionable Paris,
the Hamiltons were courteously relieved of their car and asked
by Frank Klein, the manager, how long they would be staying.
'Five nights,' said Hamilton. It turned out to be six. But either
way, this was a big-ticket request. The room bill alone would
have been worth £2,500–£3,000 had it been charged to them.
The 'extras' they took – the breakfasts, dinners, dry-cleaning,
afternoon tea every day, parking, the raids on the minibar –
totalled an impressive £2,121. Hamilton signed the 'extras'
bill, left it for Fayed, had his car fetched round to the Place

Vendôme kerbside, and drove away with his wife, *en route* for Strasbourg and the rest of their holiday.

But that six-day beanfeast of champagne, raspberry cakes and 'Fillet-of-Challans-Duck-cooked-pink-and-served-in-a-salamis-sauce-garnished-with-soufflé-potatoes' had not been enough for them. The MP telephoned Fayed as part of the preparations for his return voyage, asking for another free stay. 'I instructed the hotel to indicate to Mr Hamilton that there was no accommodation available,' Fayed said later. 'I felt that he was abusing my hospitality.' Hamilton did not declare the holiday in the Register of Members' Interests.

No sooner was he back in England for the Blackpool party conference than Hamilton was pursuing another money-making scheme. One of the lavish receptions Ian Greer Associates was throwing nightly in the conference hotel was for constituents of Hamilton – the National Nuclear Corporation (NNC). They were a consortium, subsequently taken over by GEC, of the engineering firms who designed nuclear power stations.

Following the announcement in March of the controversial intention to build a new nuclear plant at Sizewell, the Cheshire-based NNC had, on Neil Hamilton's recommendation, signed up Greer in April 1987 to lobby for them at Westminster and help make sure the construction decision went through. The firm were discreetly paying Greer £40,000 a year: a total of £60,000 in all, from March 1987 to September 1988, plus £6,500 expenses. As soon as the lobbying contract with Greer was signed, Hamilton started making effusive parliamentary speeches in praise of nuclear power. Just as he had previously urged the nation to keep lead in its petrol fumes, so he now told them they should have nuclear power stations in their backyard. Following the successful lobbying party for politicians at Blackpool, the NNC agreed to hand over some money directly to Hamilton as well. The firm paid him £7,500, expressed as a one-year 'consultancy'. Hamilton declared this on the form for the MPs' register which came round the following month, without revealing the amount. It was later to be claimed by Greer that he had also paid Hamilton an undeclared 'introduction fee' for the NNC business, starting in the following year, 1988.

The grotesque situation thus arose that the company were paying for political support not just once, when Hamilton got to his feet to make Commons speeches praising NNC as constituents, and urging the growth of nuclear power. They were paying three times. They were paying Hamilton personally; they were paying Greer on Hamilton's recommendation; and they were, unknown to them, paying Hamilton again via the 'commission' Greer was secretly handing over to the MP. NNC were actually entitled to Hamilton's political support and assistance without paying for it at all, as a firm in his own constituency. The taxpayer was meeting Hamilton's parliamentary salary already. To that objection, presumably, Hamilton would have replied: 'Don't be naive.'

He found time too, to earn his nickname, 'the Cheshire contra'. While many people thought the contras, the CIA-backed rebels in Nicaragua, were murderous terrorists, Hamilton spoke up for the UK visit of a contra leader, calling him a 'freedom fighter'. He insisted, however, that the African National Congress in South Africa was a 'typical terrorist organisation'. Sentiments like that were shortly to earn him another free trip, alongside his ex-Monday Club colleague, Michael Brown, on a winter tour in the South African sunshine paid for by the apartheid regime in Pretoria.

While Hamilton busied himself with these opportunities, Greer began to organise yet another delegation to protest to the Trade Secretary at the continuing DTI inquiries into the Fayeds' wealth. Fayed was called before the inspectors in October, for his first session of questioning. The Lonrho camp were now asking for two months' grace to unearth further evidence against him. Greer drummed up a preliminary meeting of what he called 'our group' prior to the Young delegation in November. To help the plan along, he gave Michael Grylls MP some more money as part of an 'introduction fee'. But, so soon after the Paris binge, Hamilton cried off the Lord Young delegation, writing to Fayed: 'I have to be at a meeting of the Treasury Select Committee of which I have recently been appointed a member. I am very sorry about this and I have asked Peter Hordern to tell Lord Young that I entirely support his representations.'

His absence from the meeting scarcely mattered. For, in

concert with Peter Hordern and Tim Smith, Hamilton had already penned a vituperative three-page letter to the Trade Secretary. It was so over-the-top that anyone who had been familiar with Hamilton's semi-comic rantings to the Italian neo-fascists when young would have wondered whether his penchant for play-acting had not surfaced once again:

> We have witnessed the creation of a twentieth-century Spanish Inquisition. I can hardly believe that these events are taking place under a Conservative Government which has announced its dedication to non-intervention ... a monstrous injustice that private individuals should be subjected to such treatment ... Having had experience of what it is like to be hounded by determined, powerful and unscrupulous organisations, I have the greatest sympathy for the Fayeds ... Those who meekly co-operate and are open-handed with the authorities are rewarded only with expense and contumely ... I have taken the opportunity to sift through the avalanche of paper ... Foremost in this nasty campaign is the *Observer* newspaper, supposedly a high-minded organ ... of greater concern to very rich men, the need to expend vast reserves of energy and waste months of time ... There can be little justification for protracting this inquiry further.

The sole pay-back from this tirade in terms of value to his paymaster was that Francis Maude, Under-Secretary for Corporate and Consumer Affairs (and yet another member of the No Turning Back group) wrote back on Young's behalf: 'I have asked officials to remind the inspectors of the need to complete this inquiry as soon as possible.' Greer dropped another of his airy progress notes to Fayed:

> Parliament goes back today and my main considerations are: (1) to keep the group together – I think we ought to have a meeting towards the end of this month. (2) To keep pressure on Tim for an adjournment debate ... The debate could be a major step forward because from conversations with him, he is prepared to say many things about Rowland that have never been said before, with the protection of parliamentary privilege ...

The Harrods team of MPs turned up for a planning session with Fayed on 15 January 1988. But Lonrho's investigators had unearthed evidence damaging to the Fayeds' version of events and Mohammed al-Fayed's mood had plunged. The bullying streak in Tiny Rowland, never far from the surface, would have been gratified to see how downhearted his opponent had become. Angry and depressed, Fayed was still waiting for all these politicians he had bought and paid for actually to do something. Tim Smith rang up to hear demands for another pro-Fayed adjournment debate. Greer later claimed that Fayed had starting shouting at him: 'I want processions in parliament!' Greer had a private talk with Royston Webb, Fayed's lawyer. The lobbyist tried to persuade Webb that Fayed should reconcile himself to being flayed in the forthcoming DTI report; he should 'take a deep breath, put everything behind him, and concentrate on running Harrods and forging new relationships with the government'.

Webb replied that it was unlikely Fayed would look at it that way. He warned the lobbyist to prevent Tim Smith staging another pro-Fayed adjournment debate, whatever Fayed currently said: the way the evidence was piling up before the DTI inspectors, debate might make matters even worse for his boss. They were reaching their own conclusion that the rock-solid family wealth that Fayed had deployed in the Harrods purchase did not exist.

The Hamiltons also rang up Fayed to console him. Christine invited him to dinner in the House of Commons. Fayed replied that rather than come to dinner, he wanted Hamilton to do something concrete for his money. He wanted new evidence about Lonrho and their dealings in emeralds put before the Trade Secretary. And he wanted Hamilton to write him a personal letter of support.

Both MPs, Smith and Hamilton, reported back to Greer, who hastily faxed Fayed: 'Neil Hamilton is writing to David Young on the emeralds issue. He is also writing to you as requested.' Hamilton certainly did his best to oblige, in style:

Dear Mohammed . . . It is quite incredible that after all this time there is still no indication of how long it will be before the inspector will report. I greatly sympathise with you for having to endure this trial to which so much publicity has been given by those in the Lonrho interest, like the *Observer* newspaper. In particular, I consider it a distasteful and unwarranted intrusion into your private life and that of your family, that the inspector should be seeking details of your ancestry, income and assets . . . quite apart from the privacy to which you should be entitled . . . This investigation has nothing whatever to do with competition, which is supposed to be the essence of Government policy . . . Everyone knows the Fayeds to be among the world's most significant businessmen. I have no doubt that were it not for the paranoid and personal vendetta pursued against you by Tiny Rowland, you would not now be enduring the indignity of this inquiry. We must raise in the House of Commons the propriety of such investigations. Having myself suffered invasions of privacy and campaigns of lies in my successful battle with the BBC in 1984–85, I have the greatest possible sympathy for you . . . It seems to me to add insult to injury and to be quite outside the legitimate scope of the inquiry for your private life to be crawled over and examined in respect of years which can have no conceivable direct relevance to the Lonrho accusations. Yours ever, Neil.

Enclosed with this sycophantic document was the text of an equally cynical letter to the Trade Secretary. Hamilton spoke of his long-standing interest in the Fayed affair 'along with the other officers of the backbench trade and industry committee'. He demanded that Lord Young act on Lonrho's 'many nefarious dealings' including the 'amethyst fraud' and 'Lonrho's failure to disclose to its shareholders certain dealings in emeralds'. The letter continued: 'Rowland and Lonrho were long ago described as the unacceptable face of capitalism. The record gets worse with the years and still nothing is done.' Greer was mightily relieved at the way Hamilton's massage of the Harrods proprietor had been done (naturally, Hamilton copied the correspondence to him). 'I think the letters are excellent', wrote Greer. 'Well done!' One paymaster appeased, Hamilton turned to another: the next week, on 2

February 1988, he went off with Michael Brown and three other MPs on his free trip to South Africa.

The crisis came for Fayed in March 1988, when the DTI inspectors called him in again and cross-questioned him for three days. Fayed refused to co-operate with their questions about his origins, thus guaranteeing that the report would be adverse. In the run-up to this encounter, both Smith and Hamilton successively trooped into Fayed's offices. Smith, who had continued to put down PQs for Fayed, admits generally that Fayed gave him cash; Hamilton, it is alleged, received another wad of notes direct from Fayed the following day, 18 February. Hordern, of course, continued openly to receive his pay from Harrods. Grylls received more than £9,500 in assorted 'commissions' from Greer in the year up to June 1988. Everyone was getting paid.

Before Fayed's DTI session, his lawyer sent Greer a lengthy background statement on the case 'which might serve as a useful *aide-mémoire* for our friends'. One of those parliamentary 'friends', Neil Hamilton, had to fit in his background reading between another free trip – this time paid for by the Government of New Zealand – and his hired parliamentary work on behalf of Greer and the National Nuclear Corporation. On 7 March 1988, *Hansard* records an intervention by the Hon. Member for Nuclear Power: 'NNC has a first-class record ... it is vital for the future of the nuclear industry that power stations continue to be built in a cost-effective way, and the best way to achieve that is to have an independent contractor constructing these stations after privatisation.'

Just as Fayed's relationship with the DTI inspectors reached a tense climax, parliament announced an inquiry into the burgeoning lobbying business. The Select Committee on Members' Interests said that they would conduct the study, in the wake of publicity and controversy about the impact of lobbyists on decisions such as the siting of the Channel tunnel, and the way British Airways had been allowed to swallow up British Caledonian. This last had been a vintage Greer/Grylls operation, complete with lashings of free trips for MPs. The inquiry, however, was to prove a slow and feeble affair, easily lobbied – not to say nobbled.

The committee existed to oversee the entries of commercial interests in the MPs' register, which were uninformative, deficient, and sometimes downright dishonest. The inquiry into lobbying was widely seen as a diversion to avoid tackling these abuses. Like all select committees, it had a majority from the governing party. Its chairman, Sir Geoffrey Johnson-Smith, was a Conservative who – as a leaked memo by Tory Whip David Willetts later showed – was highly susceptible to Government pressure, for all the Westminster pomposity about the 700-year-old sovereignty of parliament. Nevertheless, it would have been reckless of Greer, under the shadow of such an inquiry, to carry on throwing bundles of cash at MPs. After the announcement of the parliamentary hearings, Greer started to encourage Hamilton a different way – by discreet gifts.

Encouragement was needed. On 12 April 1988, the DTI inspectors notified Fayed how bad their Harrods report was going to be, sending him their 500-page 'provisional conclusions' for comment. The brothers had, they said: 'dishonestly misrepresented their origins, their wealth, their business interests'. Fayed's lawyers stalled on a response as long as they could, needing to find out whether the report had a final delivery date. Later that month, Hamilton and Greer met for a talk.

Subsequently, on Friday 29 April, the Hamiltons drove down to Cornwall, went to an antique dealers, Tony Sanders, in Penzance and chose two watercolours of the Newlyn School, plus a painting called 'Scamper' by Mark Lemon, which they put in the back of the car. They may have gone on to spend the weekend visiting Christine Hamilton's retired father, who lived in the nearby village of Manaccan.

The bill for the paintings – £700 – was sent to Ian Greer, who paid it as part of what he was later to describe as 'commission'. Greer subsequently referred to the pictures as part-payment of an 'introduction fee' he owed Hamilton for the National Nuclear Corporation lobbying contract. This does not seem a very satisfactory explanation of the transaction. Hamilton was already being given money – £7,500 – by NNC. By that point NNC had also paid a year's fees to Greer – £40,000. On what Greer said was his normal basis for commission, ten per cent of the first year's fees, he could be said to have owed Hamilton £4,000 if one ignored the fact that Hamilton was already receiving a pay-off from the firm. But if so, why did he not pay his debt at once? Why keep Hamilton dangling? And why pay him with pictures, in such a round-about way? Part of the explanation is that – as he eventually claimed to the select committee inquiry – the payments were 'spasmodic' presents. What he meant is that they would not incur income tax for the recipient, if the Inland Revenue accepted they were genuine gifts. (If the Revenue did so accept, of course, they were being deceived.)

The other part of the explanation, however, may be that the existence of the pictures was easier to conceal from a nosy parliamentary committee than the existence of a large cheque. The bill for the pictures was paid in Greer's name, although they hung on the Hamiltons' wall. Neil Hamilton did not declare receipt of the pictures on the Register of MPs' Interests, as he should have done whether they were gifts, commission, or wages. And the final element of the explanation may well be that the pictures were not needed to encourage Hamilton to work for NNC at all – but were to encourage him to work for other, more secret Greer clients – in particular the frustrated Fayed.

Returning to London with his pictures, Hamilton called Fayed and arranged to have tea with him at Harrods. On 27 May, a fax to Fayed from Ian Greer Associates confirmed that Hamilton had, as newly-arranged, put down two PQs for priority written answer, designed to smoke out the DTI report's delivery date and imply it was a waste of money:

1. *'To ask the Chancellor of the Duchy of Lancaster what is the estimated cost to public funds so far of the current inquiry into House of Fraser.'*
2. *'To ask the Chancellor of the Duchy of Lancaster when inspectors were appointed to carry out the current inquiry into House of Fraser PLC; and what is the earliest date on which he expects to receive their report.'*

Greer's firm then faxed over to Fayed the answers their man had obtained: the investigation had so far cost more than

£1 million, and 'I am unable to say when a report will be received.' Hamilton may have been in the habit of fulminating over the waste of the taxpayers' money by the DTI inspectors – but answering each of these PQs, of course, increased the cost of the investigation.

By now, Hamilton was working like an energetic retriever, fetching in further juicy pieces of business for Greer. That spring of 1988, he and his MP colleague, Michael Brown, signed up US Tobacco Inc to Ian Greer Associates. It was a big contract, worth £120,000 a year, plus expenses. Both MPs, Brown and Hamilton, were paid after they brought in US Tobacco as a customer. Brown got a £1,500 cheque (which he never declared in the MPs' register). Hamilton's immediate reward was once again more discreet. Hamilton could look at it as an 'introduction fee' for US Tobacco if he liked. But the context makes it appear more from Greer's point of view like a scheme also to push forward the pressing Fayed project by means of one more judicious bribe. Hamilton's previous parliamentary attempt had failed to identify a date by which the DTI report had to be delivered. Fayed's lawyers continued to stall. The inspectors' deadline of 10 June for their response came and went. The lawyers' game-plan was to seek public sympathy, while at the same time giving the inspectors little time to try to rebut their final pleas on Fayed's behalf, which would be delivered as late in the day as possible. A parliamentary motion was drawn up, condemning Tiny Rowland's 'barrage of vicious propaganda' and urging the DTI to complete the report 'without delay'. Hamilton had to be recruited to put the motion.

His reward was another trip to the shops. On 7 July, the Hamiltons went to Peter Jones, the department store in Sloane Square, and headed for the furniture floor. They picked out some wrought-iron furniture for their garden – a table, a parasol, and six chairs. On 12 July, apparently not yet satisfied they had reached their budgetary limit, Christine Hamilton returned and got four more chairs. The total bill was almost £1,000. On the same day, 12 July, Greer triumphantly faxed Fayed: 'Have seen Neil and others. Expect motion to go down tonight. Am drafting series of questions to be put to Trade and

Industry next week and a further very strong anti-Rowland motion before parliament rises for the summer. Will be in touch tomorrow. We have got them on the move.'

Hamilton, replete with garden furniture, fulfilled his task. The next day, the horticulturally-minded MP called Fayed himself, to tell him about his good work. Greer reported: 'We're getting more signatures. Everything's going smoothly.' The only bump on the track was a problem, not with Hamilton, but with the lobbyist's second tame MP, Tim Smith.

Tiny Rowland, for all his expensive hired investigators, never grasped that Neil Hamilton was a bought man. But he did discover who was behind Tim Smith and the PQs from him about the old Lonrho amethyst mine. He hinted broadly at bribery in a press release: 'It was worrying to us ... that a Member of Parliament should make public complaints in a repeated and surprising way without approaching our substantial British company to check the facts ... It has become clear that Mr Tim Smith is an associate of the public relations expert and parliamentary lobbyist Mr Ian Greer, who in turn is connected with the corrupt and corrupting Mohammed al-Fayed.'

Nothing came of this defamatory barb from Rowland. It certainly did not frighten Hamilton. A week after tabling his motion on Fayed's behalf, he could have been seen in Knightsbridge going in to lunch with the Egyptian at Harrods. He came away, according to Fayed, with yet another wad of £50 notes.

Having laid down the best Westminster artillery barrage they could, Fayed's lawyers finally delivered a stack of lengthy rebuttals to the DTI inspectors as late as they dared, on 15 July. There were 571 pages of argument and new evidence. The inspectors refused to be deterred, and handed over a completed report to Lord Young a week later, on 23 July. It was as devastatingly rude as they had warned, condemning Fayed even for deceit about his true date of birth.

Fayed's lawyers counter-attacked. So predictably did the MPs Hordern and Grylls, who besieged Lord Young's office once again. Grylls said of the Fayed lawyers' letter: 'It certainly raises matters which cause me, and many of my colleagues, concern. I hope very much that the points raised will be given serious consideration by you.' Mohammed al-Fayed, he intoned, was 'deeply concerned . . . He informs me the inspectors have not conducted their inquiry in a way he finds satisfactory. Indeed he questions their integrity.'

Greer faxed to Fayed: 'I am seeing Michael [Grylls] today and will discuss with him other tactics. I am also enclosing a draft of Neil Hamilton's letter which we are holding until the end of the month . . . Will organise [Tim Smith] to write, but give us the letter to hold until the end of the month.' And again: 'I have spoken to Tim Smith who has agreed to write a letter along the lines we wish.' Smith's four-page letter was memorable. Greer said when he was shown the final text: 'It is quite splendid.' Royston Webb, Fayed's lawyer, said he was 'thrilled'. The letter said:

There was no justification for the appointment of inspectors . . . I believe that Norman [Tebbit] and Leon Brittan acted entirely correctly throughout . . . I was particularly concerned at the suggestion made by Neil Hamilton that Lonrho's representatives may have prompted suggestions and questions to the inspectors . . . Both Peter Hordern and Neil Hamilton make the key point that references to the MMC [Monopolies and Mergers Commission] of takeovers are to be made principally on grounds of competition . . . What does it matter whether the money was inherited or made by this generation? In any case, I thought we rather approved of self-made men . . . I hope that you will . . . announce that you propose to take no further action and that this matter is now closed.

Neil Hamilton also surpassed himself. Before he and the other politicians peeled off for the summer holidays, the MP delivered to Lord Young his personal twenty-three-paragraph rant against the DTI inspectors. It was put together with assistance. Greer faxed Fayed: 'We have agreed the text of the letter and it is strong.' It read:

There appears to have been an obsession with the family background of the Fayeds and the sources of their wealth – inquiries which would be relevant to an application for membership of a gentleman's club, but which do not seem to me to have any relevance whatever to the Government's interest in a merger or a takeover . . . It is quite understandable that the Fayeds feel they have not been fairly treated, that justice is not being seen to be done and that our legal system is being turned into a tool of Tiny Rowland's vendetta . . . the Fayeds have suffered injustice and oppression . . . We should never tolerate an abuse such as this again.

Straining at the leash, it seemed, Hamilton wrote personally to Fayed the minute he got back from his summer jaunt on 1 September 1988: 'Dear Mohammed, I have now returned from the USA . . . I am glad to learn from Ian Greer that meetings are taking place with the DTI . . . Perhaps it might be useful if the three of us got together shortly. I am now back in this country and will be dividing my time between Cheshire and London.' One reason for Hamilton's zest may have been that his and Christine's concluded summer trip to the 1988 Republican Convention in New Orleans – which nominated George Bush – and on to the fashionable Rocky Mountains resort of Aspen, Colorado, to see friends, was financed by another Greer sweetener. Following his provision of the pictures and garden furniture, Greer had now discreetly paid for the Hamiltons' plane tickets – more than £1,500. It was no wonder, perhaps, under those circumstances, that Hamilton's letter to Lord Young, on the eve of catching his taxi to Heathrow airport, had been so full of indignant public spirit.

The lobbyists' defensive tactics seemed to work. They congratulated themselves shortly afterwards on snatching victory from the jaws of apparent defeat. Despite the DTI inspectors' private denunciation of Fayed as the biggest liar since the fairy-tales of Baron Munchausen, the proprietor of Harrods got the last laugh – or at least, the next to the last laugh. Young, wading through the text of the report on a long plane trip back from New Zealand, decided to suppress it, just as the four MPs had urged. He would not publish it, and he would take no immediate steps against Fayed. The report was shuffled off to various investigative bodies – the Serious Fraud Office, the Office of Fair Trading, the Stock Exchange –

which served to push the issue of eventual publication and executive action far into the indefinite future.

This did not mean that the battlefield fell quiet. Far from it. For peace of mind at Harrods, the lid had to stay indefinitely on the report and its contents. The Fayed camp had a desperate need for intelligence about the Secretary of State's intentions; the discrediting of Lonrho and ministerial arch-enemy Michael Howard remained a priority. Greer approached a new Tory backbencher in the hope of milking him for information about the Government's stance, telling Fayed: 'As promised I saw Sir Dennis Walters this morning, and urged him on ... He is seeing David Young quite regularly. I have asked him to have a word with him to try and assess what the current position is.' Tiny Rowland himself had no intention of keeping quiet while the DTI report – his baby – was suppressed. He, above all, had a shrewd idea of what it contained. Rowland's calls with anti-Fayed 'news' to the beleaguered staff of the *Observer* increased in intensity and intrusiveness. One of the news desk staff wearily passed the phone to home editor Magnus Linklater one day, saying 'It's your tiny friend again.'

The voice on the line said, with menace: 'I heard that. I am not tiny. And I am most certainly *not* your friend.'

Greer brazenly testified to the October 1988 opening sessions of the parliamentary inquiry into lobbying that he 'would not dare' offer inducements to MPs. 'It does not happen, as far I am aware.' Meanwhile, he was paying-off certain politicians as usual. Only the previous month he had put more money in Michael Grylls' pocket. He was due to pay Michael Brown the balance of his US Tobacco money – more than £2,000 – before Christmas, and another hefty wedge would go to Grylls in the New Year. Hamilton was pocketing Greer's valuable 'gifts'. The MP also continued to ring up Fayed, go round to see him, and come away – especially before Christmas – with bundles of banknotes, Harrods ties, whisky bottles and Harrods hampers worth £185. Alan B'stard MP would have been proud of him.

Only Tim Smith fell off the gravy train. He stopped taking money from Fayed after receipt of a distinctly threatening letter. Rowland was circulating to thousands of people the glossy brochure called *A Hero from Zero*. In it, he laid out all the evidence about the Fayeds' true origins which he knew must be in the unpublished DTI report. As a propagandist, Smith for his own safety should perhaps have confined himself to the discreet methods of Michael Grylls, who misled a constituent privately: 'I must say that I do not consider *A Hero from Zero* to be anything other than a work of fiction and therefore I do not think you should base your conclusions on it,' he told an inquiring John Jillings, from Bagshot. He did not tell Mr Jillings that a little more than a fortnight before, he himself had received an £8,000 cheque from the Hero from Zero's personal lobbyist.

Smith felt obliged to mislead the nation more publicly, tabling this PQ on 28 January 1989: 'Does the Solicitor General have any additional information about the book, *A Hero From Zero* . . . Will he be recommending it for the Booker prize for fiction?' Tiny Rowland decided that he had been, as he put it 'insulted beyond reason'. Constitutionally speaking, Tiny Rowland was a constituent of the Beaconsfield MP who was attacking him. Smith had chosen once before to ignore the warning Tiny had given him. This time the threat had to be unmistakable:

Dear Mr Smith, For some little time I have been puzzling over why you should want to make supportive remarks in parliament about the Fayed brothers, and offensive ones about Lonrho, but I don't think I have to puzzle any longer. As usual with the Fayeds, it's just a case of how much, and in what way . . . If you shy away from repeating your remarks outside the protection of the House of Commons, we will all have confirmation of what you are . . . In the absence of that report – the sad proof of just how far into the machinery of politics and administration the Fayeds managed to penetrate – ours is the official record . . .

The stop on publication is consistent with the nature of the contents of the inspectors' report – that is, that the Fayed brothers corruptly obtained favour at the highest levels. Those who could say 'Yes' to publication are the very men who will say 'Ouch'. But dear Mr Smith, do take a bit of comfort from your constituent – me – halfway through this letter. Whatever you may have taken, and no doubt it seemed all right at the time, don't cry. It's all right. With all the judges and justices involved, the words of Lord Denning ought to mean something. 'Be you never so high,' he said, 'the Law is above you.' But in your case, 'be you never so low', Mohammed al-Fayed is beneath you.

Smith could not but have got the message – 'I'll see you in jail if you don't stop.'

Greer withdrew him from the front line. Neil Hamilton however, unmarked by Rowland's eye, still kept up the attack. With an appointment in his diary to go round and see Fayed the following day, he shot to his feet in the Commons on the afternoon of 15 February, at the mention of the name of an *Observer* writer. Labour MP Tam Dalyell asked a question based on a book about the Westland affair, one of whose authors was David Leigh (one of the authors of the present book). Hamilton leapt up and said in the chamber, under parliamentary privilege: 'David Leigh is an embittered left-wing propagandist employed by Mr Tiny Rowland.' This was a puzzling attack. David Leigh was actually among the journalists who had criticised Rowland's use of the *Observer* for his private anti-Fayed vendettas, and he was shortly to resign from the paper in protest. He remained bewildered for the next seven years by Hamilton's parliamentary outburst, until Fayed revealed that the day after Hamilton spoke, 16 February, the MP visited Mohammed al-Fayed by appointment at 6 pm, and obtained another £2,500 roll of banknotes. Clearly, that day's published *Hansard* helped to show that Hamilton was giving good value by his assaults on Lonrho.

At Drones restaurant in Pont Street on 21 March 1989, the Hamiltons, Neil and Christine, gathered with Ian Greer for a good lunch – something all of them always enjoyed. They had no idea that an unpleasant surprise for Fayed's supporters was looming. Instead, they believed there was something lucrative to celebrate: Greer and Hamilton had both been in touch with Mohammed al-Fayed already that morning, to discuss their latest ingenious lobbying scheme. Tiny Rowland's annual meeting at Lonrho was coming up in nine days, and the Fayed camp had some spicy new material to disrupt it.

Tiny Rowland could be linked with Colonel Gaddaffi, the pariah ruler of Libya, it seemed, through allegations of illicit arms dealing. That day, Fayed's lawyer had already written some letters to ministers, sent to Greer's office to be typed up on Hamilton's own Commons notepaper – all they needed was his signature and they could be kept available and despatched at the right moment – to be produced with a disconcerting flourish at the Lonrho AGM.

The draft letter from Hamilton to Foreign Secretary Douglas Hurd said on the top: 'NOT TO BE RELEASED UNDER ANY CIRCUMSTANCES WITHOUT THE PERMISSION OF IAN GREER.' This was presumably a warning to Greer's office staff.

Hamilton duly signed the drafts, and off they went. To Hurd, the letter under his name said:

> I am deeply concerned ... the press allegations of illicit arms dealing must warrant the closest examination ... My attention has been drawn to the regular use by Lonrho of the company jet to and from Libya ... I strongly believe that an urgent investigation should be conducted into Mr Tiny Rowland's associations with Colonel Gaddaffi, together with any links which he or his subsidiary companies may have with the regime.

To Defence Secretary George Younger, he was gravely patriotic: 'There are, quite apart from the security implications relevant to Mr Tiny Rowland's links with Colonel Gaddaffi and the Libyan regime, serious defence implications. I thought I should draw your attention to them.'

Greer organised by remote control from Cannes that Easter a further set of more or less defamatory PQs Hamilton was publicly to put down, which could be fed back into the newspapers and printed under parliamentary privilege. They dealt with Rowland's business associate, the Egyptian Ashraf Marwan, his alleged diplomatic passport, and his alleged links to Libya. 'Agreed with Neil Hamilton four questions,' faxed

Greer busily from the south of France. 'Also believe letter possible from Neil to chairman of Civil Aviation Authority about Marwan flights and facilities.'

Hamilton's PQs asked the Foreign Secretary whether Marwan was an accredited diplomat. (Answer: No.) They asked the Defence Secretary about: 'Lonrho's attempts to frustrate British arms sales to Kenya' (yet another newspaper story placed in circulation); they asked the Home Secretary about the use and abuse of diplomatic passports; and they asked the Trade Minister what it was hoped would be a quotable question: 'What information he has on the volume of arms export business with Libya conducted by Lonrho or its subsidiary, Tradewinds plc.'

This last question had been pre-heated by a letter to Alan Clark, the Trade Minister, a couple of days earlier, enclosing Hamilton's allegations to date and adding: 'As I understand the alleged illicit export of arms is your responsibility, I would very much appreciate your comments on my letter to Douglas Hurd.' Although Clark's reply to the PQ was uninformative, his private letter was warmer: 'I am ... seriously concerned about any attempt to export arms illegally from the UK.' He was passing the information to Customs, he said.

Hamilton's final push on Libya was to table an Early Day Motion which could be quoted by the press (sent by Greer to Fayed and his lawyer beforehand): 'This House notes with concern the close links between Lonrho, its subsidiary Tradewinds, Dr Ashraf Marwan, a close friend of Col Gaddaffi and the Libyan regime. It takes account of the serious security implications and calls for an immediate investigation into the company's operations.'

However, the Fayed camp did not have time to congratulate themselves on the mischief they were causing Tiny Rowland before a thunderbolt struck. Rowland, ruthless millionaire that he was, got hold of a leaked copy of the whole DTI report. He published it, in full, in a special mid-week edition of the Sunday *Observer*, which he commandeered for the purpose on the day of Lonrho's annual meeting. Rowland may have failed to prise Harrods away from his rivals. But he got the last laugh, as shareholders at the AGM in London, and the whole world besides, goggled over the inspectors' denunciations of Fayed's origins: 'The lies of Mohammed Fayed and his success in gagging the press created a new fact: that lies were the truth and that the truth was a lie.'

This bombshell did not lead Neil Hamilton to alter his stance one bit. The fact that his paymaster, Fayed, was officially pronounced a liar and a cheat did not, it seemed, trouble his mind. Why should it? He was being paid. Hamilton's nonchalance led him to some strange bedfellows, as the Labour party became Fayed's chargers for a brief while. In the openly anti-Lonrho camp by now were some of the *Observer* journalists Hamilton had been so abusive of, and Dale Campbell-Savours, the Labour MP for Workington in the Lake District. Campbell-Savours – lanky, ascetic, dogged questioner on the Members' Interests Committee – was a diametric opposite to the pudgily profligate Hamilton. He did not take money. 'Not even a cup of coffee,' as Fayed said, in wonder.

Campbell-Savours had originally taken an anti-Fayed position, repelled by the smell of collusion between Thatcher, Tebbit and the Egyptian. But by now, the reports reaching him from disenchanted *Observer* staff made him recoil even more from Tiny Rowland. The Fayed camp hoped to persuade Campbell-Savours to spearhead an attack on Fayed's chief bugbear, the man to whom he attributed all his embarrassment: Michael Howard. Greer told Fayed on 11 April, nearly a fortnight after the DTI report had been printed:

Neil Hamilton and I are talking further tomorrow about the questions/motions that will be tabled in the House by Dale Campbell-Savours relating to Lonrho and the ownership of the *Observer* ... Questions relating to MH [Michael Howard] are also likely to be made public this week, again by Dale Campbell-Savours. Kinnock's [Neil Kinnock, the Labour leader] personal attention has been drawn to the issues and he has expressed interest. We are keeping him up to date with information. This must be entirely confidential as it could be embarrassing if Conservative members knew of our plans regarding MH.

Nothing surfaced about Michael Howard in the end.

Campbell-Savours was insufficiently manipulable. But Hamilton's name appeared together with Campbell-Savours' on a motion condemning – again – the independent directors of the *Observer* 'for failing to prevent any of the recent abuses of this once great newspaper', and on a second Campbell-Savours motion condemning as a 'fabrication' the latest Rowland-inspired story to appear in the paper, which had led to uproar among *Observer* journalists and internal complaints to the directors. Other supporters of the Labour man were Hamilton's closest personal friend, the far-right Gerald Howarth, and – recovering his nerve a little – the venal Tim Smith.

The Campbell-Savours motion to which Hamilton – most inconsistently – signed his name was No 993, attacking the *Observer*'s old 'Mark Thatcher in Brunei' story. This story, dictated by Rowland, 'was rigorously opposed by ... the two members of the *Observer*'s investigative unit, David Leigh and Paul Lashmar', the motion said. The journalist being praised for standing up to Rowland was the same David Leigh who Hamilton had previously abused in parliament as a lackey of Rowland. It was a striking demonstration of Hamilton's cynicism.

On 27 July, Hamilton had already just had a sizeable secret cheque from Ian Greer, and at 2.30 pm he went to see his other benefactor, Fayed. He came away with another envelope of cash, Fayed says, and the invitation for the Hamiltons to stay that September at Fayed's Balnagown Castle in Scotland. Hamilton later downplayed the accommodation by saying it was only in a flat over a converted stables in the grounds. This did Balnagown a little less than justice – owned by Fayed since 1972, the castle pictured in its proprietor's colour brochure is an enormous Highlands pile built in Easter Ross in 1375 but improved by Fayed into a sumptuous stately home, set in a private wooded valley with nineteenth-century Italian gardens, a trout stream and magnificent deer stalking.

The MP Michael Grylls was also called back into Fayed's service. His assignment was to write to the Attorney General demanding to know what was being done to track down and prosecute the 'mole' who had so embarrassed Fayed by leaking the DTI report. The Attorney General promised him 'a full investigation'.

But Fayed's problems were far from being the only ones on Greer's books at this point. Greer had other paying clients who needed parliamentary care and attention. Fayed also had to compete for the time of MPs like Hamilton and Grylls, while they worked on other, equally lucrative projects.

On 27 July, Hamilton stood up in parliament and delivered a long oration on behalf of Sir James Goldsmith, a man among those, he said, who had 'most popularised the concept of free enterprise in its modern form'. The tycoon was trying to mount a hostile takeover of the cigarette company British American Tobacco. Hamilton said: 'I begin my speech . . . by declaring that I have no financial interest of any kind.' A similar speech was made by Hamilton's closest personal friend, Gerald Howarth. They had been selected and briefed by Goldsmith's lobbyists, the firm of GJW. Both were privately indebted to Sir James for guaranteeing their costs during their 1986 libel poker game against the BBC. Many would have thought they should have declared this financial interest.

July had been a busy month altogether. Hamilton and Grylls jointly put their shoulders to the wheel on behalf of the big beer monopolists. The major brewers were running a campaign of extraordinary shamelessness which soon succeeded in blocking proposals by the Monopolies Commission for the sell-off of captive 'tied' pubs, and rendered Lord Young, the Trade Secretary, politically impotent on the issue. Hamilton, who said when it suited him that he believed in the ideology of 'competition', was now vigorously campaigning for the retention of a monopoly. On 9 May 1989, he signed a parliamentary motion backing the brewers. They were paying Hamilton a regular £2,000 a year via the Brewers' Society.

The unpopular minister, Lord Young, received a mauling at a hostile meeting of the backbench trade and industry committee (chairman: Michael Grylls). Grylls and Greer were making money out of the situation in the usual way. Whitbread, one of the biggest brewers, had paid the Conservative party £30,000 the previous year. Now they signed Greer up for £100,000 a year, and Greer in turn handed over hefty 'commission' payments to Michael Grylls in return for the 'introduction'. On Greer's standard calculation, Grylls' 'commission' for the Whitbread contract was worth £10,000. As with all these deals, the 'introductions' and 'introduction fees' functioned as a roundabout way of channelling cash from companies to MPs who would assist them, without the accompanying vulgarities of the 'brown envelope'. If a company wanted political support from an MP, they were made to pay.

The beer campaign was so successful that Greer was to include it in his selection of boastful 'case histories' sent out to potential clients. One of the keys was local pressure on Tory MPs, whose Conservative clubs got cheap beer. The campaign was a vindication of Greer's insistence that it was worth paying good money to influence backbenchers. Lord Young mournfully records in his memoirs how he was eventually told to forget his ministerial decision: 'It was nothing to do with public opinion, which was uniformly for the proposals. It had nothing to do with the merits, which were rarely discussed . . . I had a meeting with the Chief Whips of both the Lords and the Commons. I was told quite firmly that they could not get my proposals through.'

As the brewers returned peacefully to their monopoly, Greer and Grylls got a fresh piece of business. A group of Hong Kong businessmen paid £65,000 to put on pressure, in the hope of holding the British Government to its promise to provide 50,000 passports for Hong Kong inhabitants after Communist China took over the colony in 1997. It was called the 'Honour Hong Kong' campaign and began at the end of 1989. Under the standard Greer system, Grylls was in line to collect £6,500.

With much profitable business coming in from brewers, tobacco barons and Chinese entrepreneurs, Greer could take the inevitable prospect philosophically: that Mohammed al-Fayed of Harrods would now want to bale out, and no longer pay large regular sums for his service. It was Neil Hamilton, typically, who wrote the last paid-for letter in the Fayed saga.

Hamilton was as cocky as ever. The applause was still ringing in his ears from a lunch-sozzled audience at the London Savoy in November, when the right-wing *Spectator* magazine had dubbed him 'Parliamentary Wit of the Year 1989' for barracking Labour – and leader Neil Kinnock in particular – and making a comical defence of the honours system in parliament. That speech had showed quite a wit indeed, for someone who had taken so much money under the counter: 'The worst corruption we have seen in this country in recent years has been the corruption that comes from social-ism, whereby the government of the day bribe the electorate with their own money.'

The MP began his letter to David Waddington, Home Secretary, in December 1989, attempting to throw vengeful suspicion on two Fraud Squad police officers for leaking the DTI report to Tiny Rowland: 'As vice-chairman of the back-bench trade and industry committee, I have taken a keen interest in the controversy.' He went on to speak of the 'very serious allegations' and demanded the answers to a series of questions about an inspector and a sergeant in the squad (who were eventually to be cleared by an inquiry): 'Were all copies of the inspector's report assigned to individual members and marked in such a way as to be identified individually? Was the copy leaked to the *Observer* numbered 26? Was this copy entrusted to the Fraud Squad officers investigating the case?'

Nowhere, as usual, does Hamilton mention in this letter his connection with those who had been paying him. But it was a parting shot from the Members for Harrods. The campaign was over. That winter, the Fayeds ended the regular contract with Ian Greer Associates as 'political advisers', except for future special assignments. If any comfort for the Egyptian brothers was to be found, it was in the DTI report's conclu-sion that they had taken a concerned and enthusiastic interest in their new acquisition and that management of the House of Fraser had since been 'law-abiding, proper and regular'. Mohammed al-Fayed had the shop – and the Government were going to let him keep it.

The lobbyists had been promoting the cause of the owner of Harrods for four years. They had taken £100,000 from him officially, plus expenses – and another £100,000 or so, on Fayed's account, for assorted cash bribes and election expen-ses. Plus, for Tim Smith, extra payments adding up to around

£6,000. Plus, of course, more than £25,000 in cash and hotel stays for the Hamiltons. Plus, on Fayed's account, £250,000 cash down to the Conservative party for the 1987 election. That made a total of around £500,000 which Fayed had felt required to pay to influence a corrupt political process. And all for what? Fayed had got to keep his store. But he had paid too high a price for his own comfort.

**Slobodan Milosevic, President of Serbia
and mastermind of the Balkan wars**

8

Selling Death

'I have become greatly concerned at the way in which governments can be bounced into taking decisions which are highly adverse to many, as a result of the pressures that are put on them by flashy lobbies.'

Neil Hamilton, House of Commons, 4 December 1984,
arguing against the removal of lead from petrol

'I don't give a fuck. These people are paying your wages.'

Ian Greer on the Serbian Government, 1992

Ensconced in his Catherine Place office – with its Asprey silverware and a Division Bell in the hall, the team of person-able young men, and the poodles on the sofa – Ian Greer had become an emblem of British political life in the 1980s.

If you wanted political wires pulled, Greer was the new way in which to do it. In an age infested by people who 'promote', 'package', 'market' and 'consult', Ian Greer belonged in the pantheon of political PR, along with the Conservative party's famous salesmen, Tim Bell, Maurice Saatchi and Gordon Reece. But he was much more discreet. Greer always tried to give the impression that what he did was a public service – oiling the transmission-belt in the democratic machine. He liked to talk about 'the right to be heard'. He compared himself to a barrister, taking on all kinds of clients and pleading their cause. But unlike the work of a barrister, what Greer did with his tame MPs was secret, and unregulated by any code of professional discipline. In fact, there were strong arguments that what Greer was doing at the end of the 1980s was gravely corrupting the democratic process for money. At the zenith, he was to take £300,000 a year out of his lobbying business, and was to claim he had made his firm worth millions. The Fayed contract was only one of many with which he worked in the shadows to build up those millions.

Evidence has now surfaced of the way Greer ran two other major campaigns around the same time as Fayed's, in which he paid politicians to advance a client's cause. One of those clients was a foreign regime, and one was a foreign corporation. Both accounts, had they not been hidden from view, would have been regarded by most people as disgusting. Some might even think that secret lobbying of such a kind ought to be outlawed. The contracts in question were for the Government of Serbia, during the bloody break-up of Yugoslavia; and for US Tobacco Inc, makers of the carcinogenic chewing tobacco, Skoal Bandits.

Blood Money

In the spring of 1992, the Serbian regime of Slobodan Milosevic unleashed a hurricane of violence across the still-born Balkan republic of Bosnia-Herzegovina, the most ferocious carnage to blight Europe since the Third Reich. Behind the scenes, the Serbs had also been busy within British politics, and it was Ian Greer Associates who acted as promoters of their interests. President Milosevic paid Greer almost £100,000 for his help.

For half a decade, Milosevic had been preparing for war in pursuit of a 'Greater Serbia' in which other ethnic groups and any trace of their history would be obliterated. For the latter part of 1991, Milosevic's troops had fought a war against the hastily cobbled-together army of emergent Croatia. There, his artillery had battered the lovely city of Vukovar, on the banks of the Danube, into the dust of its own stone. Upon the surrender of the town, the Serbs massacred a crowd of patients and prisoners in the hospital. But all this was merely a prelude.

Now, Milosevic and his Bosnian Serb acolytes – Radovan Karadzic and General Ratko Mladic – unleashed a terrifying rag-bag of death squads, freebooting paramilitary units, artillery batteries and regular troops against the astonished Bosnian Muslim citizenry.

Serbian units moved across the Drina river, the border between Serbia and Bosnia, to begin a pogrom that became known as 'ethnic cleansing', rounding up Muslims and killing them, deporting them or incarcerating them in camps and prisons. The historic Drina bridges at Visegrad and Foca were turned into human abattoirs as corpses turned the turquoise water red with blood. Women were held in special rape camps, and serially violated until either released – pregnant and therefore undesirable – or murdered. Many were like the 18-year-old counter girl from a video shop in Visegrad called Jasmina, who spent four nights locked up with a soldier called 'The Wolf' and was about to be passed over to one of his mates when she decided to embrace death as a mercy by jumping from a third-floor window.

Meanwhile, Serbian guns were pounding the Bosnian capital of Sarajevo senseless, and in the north west, a gulag of concentration camps had been established whose names would become stains upon our century: Trnopolje, Brcko-Luka, Omarska. There was a familiar ring to the murder and torture: in most of these communities, the intellectuals, businessmen or professionals tended to be Muslim, resented and hated by the Serbs. It was against this industrious, educated stratum of society that the Serbs turned first, with a barbarian loathing that echoed another, more cataclysmic, persecution of this century. It was also a pogrom marked by its macabre intimacy: neighbour turned suddenly against neighbour; people knew their jailers and torturers. Another feature of the violence was its recreational nature. Guards in Omarska would make home-videos of their handiwork. Sexual mutilation was common: one man in Omarska was forced to bite off the testicles of a fellow inmate, who, once castrated, had a live dove rammed into his mouth, forced to eat the bird. The deportment of the guards was, said one witness, 'as though at a sports match'.

The justification of such a programme in the corridors of Western power had to be carefully managed by the Serbs. Central to the project in Bosnia was the need to obfuscate what The Hague War Crimes Tribunal labels 'genocide' with talk, rather, of 'inevitable civil war' – to create some impression of comparable rival claims, an equation between perpetrator and victim, and thereby stall robust international action. To exert this kind of influence, the Serbs needed to locate the fulcrum of the international stage, and to lobby there. And one of the main focal points, it would emerge, was Britain. Britain had long-standing relations with Serbia – political, economic and sentimental – and applied the skills of an accomplished and respected diplomatic machine to preserving them.

One senior American diplomat at the United Nations described Britain as having forged 'the lowest common denominator' at the UN Plaza in New York – taking and selling the line of least resistance to the Serbs. Thus, for three bloody years, the British stifled, filibustered and sabotaged initiatives by elements in the US administration and elsewhere for tough action and a quick peace, to a point which drove American diplomats to distraction.

One senior official in the State Department who had tried to get his Government to intervene more robustly said: 'I learned to treat Britain as a hostile power, out to block anything, everything. They were prepared to go to the wall against us on Bosnia. I came to think of the British as like having the Russians around the State Department. Or maybe the Serbs themselves. Usually your guys were refined and subtle diplomats. But over this they were going crazy. I got one pre-emptive visit from a Brit about a memo I hadn't even finished writing! Dammit, someone came up to me in goddam Safeway on a Saturday morning and collared me about the arms embargo!'

Britain's apparent debt to Serbia was one of the remarkable themes of the Bosnian war. American sources posited a number of possible explanations. There was a harking back to the second world war with a contemporary twist: Belgrade had been a 'mine of information on the Soviet bloc', says one former US intelligence officer, 'discussed exclusively with the British by grateful Yugoslavs', to American annoyance. There was also the fact that British intelligence needed Belgrade as an established listening post for the orient.

There was an underground link: Belgrade was a hub for shady dealing with Arabs and the Third World, notably in arms. During the Iraqi 'Supergun' scandal of 1990, sanctions-busting British parts for Saddam Hussein's gun were exported to Belgrade, then on to Baghdad. Then there was the British diplomatic formula, dating from the nineteenth century and the 1930s, that in a fluid situation, the bully, however foul, was the best guarantor of 'stability'.

But there was also political pressure, bought for cash. The Serbs were paying lobbyists to reinforce this latent sympathy – or at least tolerance – of their carnage through personal contacts at the highest levels in Westminster. And one of the central figures working to establish those contacts was Ian Greer. Greer knew full well what kind of creature he had taken on – or at least he behaved as though he did. He announced the Serbian contract – one of his biggest to date – to his own staff by saying that the new client was 'a group of Serbian Yugoslav industrialists' – a lie to his own directors. Throughout the entire campaign, he continued to refer to Milosevic's regime as 'industrialists' during discussion with the staff, and even at board meetings. When he was asked what the names of these companies were, Greer was evasive, and mumbled the question into touch. The two staff members assigned the contract were spun the same line, although they had their suspicions that the client was the regime, and not a commercial enterprise. They were told not to discuss the contract with anyone. But even the idea of promoting 'Serbian industrialists' was too much for many staff, when they got home from work to watch the Serbs' handiwork on the television news. Employees talked about the company being 'riven down the middle' and some complained to Greer. The response to one employee was: 'I don't give a fuck. These people are paying your wages.'

Greer did his job the way he knows best: he hosted a series of receptions and parties held in the Palace of Westminster at which leading Serbian apologists and supporters could rub shoulders with MPs and foreign policy committee members. He worked though backbench committees, like the all-party Yugoslav affairs committee, seeking to set in motion the ousting of anti-Milosevic politicians and replacing them with witting or unwitting stooges for the Belgrade regime. With a politician of Yugoslav origins, John Kennedy, sitting on a Conservative policy group, Greer secured a direct route to the ear of the then Defence Secretary, Malcolm Rifkind. This was one of Greer's more subtly-waged campaigns, in which the weapons were not so much the brazen bung, but more the whisper in the ear, the twist of language, the defiling of history and truth.

To the outside world, the British appeared to move in early, sabotaging pressure from American advocates of aerial bombardment to intervene in the bloody spring of 1992. Spy-satellite image analysts at the US National Security Agency, who had advised the air force in the 1991 Gulf War, now unveiled photographs showing Serbian artillery around Sarajevo to be completely unprotected. Their prescription, delivered to diplomats at a secret briefing, was that 95 per cent of the guns could be eliminated in one day. Secretary of State James Baker converted to air strikes. In early August, the world was dismayed and confused by the revelation of the concentration camps. Other nations looked set to intervene in Bosnia, but Britain held them back, by calling and managing the London Conference of August 1992. By that time, Greer's contract with Milosevic had just been completed: the crucial groundwork had successfully been done.

'The temperature was rising,' says a diplomat on the US team that went to London. 'We went hoping that there was going to be a turn for the better.' 'We had difficulty finding out what London was trying to do,' recalls Victor Jackovitch, who became America's first Ambassador to Sarajevo, now in Slovenia. 'It was hard to get information about the agenda. When we got there we realised what was happening: the British were opening a valve to get the pressure down. Allow the Serbs to make promises and accept them knowing perfectly well that they had no intention of keeping them. Brilliant by the Brits: here was the start of the policy of doing nothing.'

It would be absurd, over-generous, to credit Ian Greer with having formulated British non-policy on Bosnia. This was the work of mightier figures – Foreign Secretary Douglas Hurd and his civil service lieutenant in the Foreign Office, the former intelligence supremo Pauline Neville-Jones, who at the end of the war picked up highly lucrative executive posts at National Westminster Bank, and promptly fixed a handsome deal after a spot of 'working breakfast' with Milosevic, privatising Serbia's telephones. But beneath them was a pyramid of politics and committees, and these were days of confusion, and of particular cluelessness on the part of most politicians, on uncharted terrain. Among these politicians, who found it hard to work out how the siege of Sarajevo might affect their constituency electorate, there was a vacuum of opinion. This was the lobbyist's dream come true. These were days in which the power of nuance, of whispering the right poison in the right ear, became important.

With Croatia in ruins, and as ethnic cleansing reached its bloody climax in Bosnia in the spring of 1992, the flow of Serbian Government money to Ian Greer Associates was well under way. Greer denied to his staff that the money was coming from the Government of Serbia, rather than from some Balkan 'businessmen', and has denied it publicly since. In the *Sunday Times* in 1995, he said he had been 'approached ... to promote the cause of Yugoslav industrialists in Britain'. But he was lying. The Serbian regime paid Greer £55,000 between 5 December 1991 and 31 March 1992, while Milosevic was taking the surrender of Vukovar and arming his people for the onslaught in Bosnia. Then, in April 1992, as the death squads cut a swath along the Drina valley, Ian Greer swallowed another flow of cash from Belgrade – £41,250 to secure his services until 30 June. The total was £96,250 in what was – if the term has any meaning at all – blood money.

Before banking Milosevic's thousands, Greer had to make some necessary payments to a third party: a British Conservative candidate with a bizarrely colourful background who was operating energetically on the Serbs' behalf. He went by the name of John Kennedy, but called himself a Yugoslav from Montenegro, the statelet that had placed itself at the miserable service of Serbia, and whose rocky soil had also spawned Radovan Karadzic, the Bosnian Serb 'President' currently under indictment by the Hague War Crimes Tribunal for genocide.

Kennedy was born John Gvozdenovic in Belgrade, to an English academic mother and a father from a minor Montenegrin aristocratic family (they had met at Zagreb University). He says the family came to Britain when he was one year old.

In a profile published by the nationalist Serbian magazine *Intervju* in 1995 a few weeks before the Srebrenica massacres, Kennedy deployed this aristocratic descent to claim a link to the Montenegrin royal family, by way of his paternal grandmother. It is a claim which helped him find a niche in English high society as private secretary to Prince Michael of Kent, cousin to the Queen (he secured the post late in 1993, while his Serbian chums were engaged in their bloodiest excesses around Sarajevo and Gorazde). *Intervju* further said: 'to some of his Belgrade friends, Kennedy has shown a monograph about his family, with a photograph of his Scottish castle where his mother lives today.' There was no Scottish castle.

After leaving the nondescript Royal Russell public school in Surrey, Gvozdenovic/Kennedy became interested in the politics of the swivel-eyed Monday Club. He also joined the more level-headed Bow Group, and came into contact with mainstream Thatcherite John (now Lord) Moore, son of a Brighton publican and then a Cabinet minister. Moore had received election campaign funds from Greer in the past. He gave Kennedy a researcher's photo-pass to the House of Commons.

Kennedy made sure to be seen at Ascot and around the better dining clubs in London. He wore hunting and shooting outfits, despite his suburban roots. He sought to court a string of high-society belles, and spun yarns to his fellow Tories about commuting by helicopter to London from his Surrey heli-pad. One colleague, Garret Smyth, went to check, and found 'a three-bedroomed 1930s semi' in Carshalton. Kennedy put Moore's Commons number on his business cards for a consultancy called 'Kennedy Associates'. One of his early business coups was to procure £110,000 from Prince Idris of the exiled Libyan royal family, after which 41 MPs signed a June 1990 Commons motion seeking affirmation of Idris's family as rightful heirs to the Libyan throne, in opposition to a rival clan. Another of his political contacts was Neil Hamilton himself, the foot-soldier of sleaze. Hamilton registered receiving occasional 'consultancy payments' from a PR company, Pinpoint International. This was the pro-Idris Kennedy operation, set up with Conservative MP Tim Janman. And in 1989, under the invaluable patronage of Moore,

Kennedy became prospective Tory parliamentary candidate for, appropriately, Barking.

Gvozdenovic/Kennedy also made a start on influencing British policy in the Balkans. In the summer of 1991, the not-quite-dapper 29-year-old 'aristocrat' started to visit the militaristic Serbian regime, and subsequently set up British connections for them. He became secretary of a Tory group, the Conservative Council for Eastern Europe. In August 1991, as the columns of tanks advanced into Croatia, Kennedy wrote to the *Guardian* in a huff at the suggestion that he might be sympathetic to the brutish Serbian cause, saying sanctimoniously: 'The fact that I spent two hours in talks with the Serbian President last week as joint secretary [of the Conservative Council for Eastern Europe] should not imply that I was representing any other interests.'

By the end of 1991, the Croatian war was frozen into stalemate. A third of Croatia was under Serbian occupation. There had been one especially memorable episode, in September 1991: the Red Cross had tried to evacuate a psychiatric hospital in Pakrac, central Croatia, under bombardment by the Serbs. They had been given unofficial word of a cease-fire. But the patients' convoy was attacked by snipers and mortars, and many of these unfortunates were killed or wounded. All this unfolded before the eyes of the mass media.

Ian Greer might have noticed these events. Vukovar surrendered in December 1991, upon which the Serbs had executed the inmates of the hospital, a war crime for which the perpetrators are wanted at The Hague. The towns of Osijek, Vinkovci and Sibenik had been subject to ferocious bombardment, and the Croats of Glina, Drnis, Petrinja, Slunj and elsewhere either put to flight or killed. Dubrovnik, medieval jewel of the Adriatic coast, had been heavily shelled. It was all on television.

Kennedy's political associate, John Moore, introduced him to Greer, and the Government of Serbia signed a contract with the lobbyist to promote their cause in Britain. The kickback from Greer to Kennedy for the Serb lobbying contract was 50 per cent of the Serbian cash. Greer and Kennedy threw at least four receptions for MPs with the Serbian cause in mind, during the second half of 1991 and early 1992 – for the Yugoslav affairs all-party committee or the Conservative Council for Eastern Europe. They would invite people who showed an interest, and forged a circle of anti-interventionist MPs, including the Conservative David Faber and Labour's Bob Wareing. Like many tired, old-style leftists, Wareing was susceptible to the anti-American Serb point of view, and would subsequently become an especially valuable contact, chairman of the Yugoslav affairs committee, and make visits to the Serbian side during the fighting. Faber also visited Serbia and joined the committee. Part of the Kennedy/Greer campaign was to entice MPs into visiting Serbia, with Kennedy making the introductions on the ground.

The Council for Eastern Europe was under the sway of Henry Bellingham MP, who happened to be Parliamentary Private Secretary to the then Defence Minister, Malcolm Rifkind. Rifkind's own spineless performance on Bosnia, and opposition to any tough action against the Serbs, would be one of the dominant themes in Britain's non-handling of the war. Subsequently, in the spring of 1992, while Greer and Kennedy were on Belgrade's payroll, Lady Thatcher – now out of office – made a famous plea for intervention against the Serbs, accusing the West of 'moral cowardice'. It was Rifkind who led the counter-charge of grey-suited men shouting: 'Emotional nonsense!'

The former gossip columnist Lady Olga Maitland saw a good deal of Greer during this period: she was running for a Conservative seat at Sutton for the first time, and Greer paid her 'commissions' of several thousand pounds for various forms of help and advice in January and February during the currency of the Serb contract. (One payment was for help in recovering money owed him by Kuwait.) Lady Olga, who had a Yugoslav mother and strong anti-Milosevic views, watched Greer's lobbying process closely at the time, and observed: 'They knew that they had a route to Rifkind. It's not that they instructed Rifkind, but they confirmed his views. Kennedy always put himself forward as the great expert.'

The champagne – £3,600-worth – flowed lavishly at the National Portrait Gallery in Trafalgar Square that February, amid the hubbub of 600 smart guests, mostly politicians and industrialists. Greer had hired the art gallery for the biggest bash of his career: the firm's tenth anniversary. The guest of honour was the Prime Minister himself, Greer's acquaintance for a quarter of a century. The lobbyist would not have been sorry when the newspapers got hold of a charming anecdote to point up the fact that John Major came to his parties: it seemed that, suddenly remembering the point, Greer sent to The Chandos, the pub nearby, and presented to the PM on a silver salver the drink his intimates knew he really liked – not bubbly, but a weak gin and tonic. What the diary columns did not go on to say was that Mr Major's gin and tonic, the 300 bottles of bubbly, and many others, came from a secret river of cash being provided by the butcher of the Balkans, Slobodan Milosevic.

In 1992, while his secret lobbyists in Britain pressed his cause, Milosevic turned his attention to Bosnia. In April, the war began. Television cameras were filming masked Serbian para-militaries loading Muslim corpses on to trucks in Zvornik.

But it was springtime in London for Ian Greer – and general election time. He was banking the second generous tranche of Serbian money – and spending it in style. His fellow hireling, Kennedy, ran as the Tory candidate in Barking. His managing director, Andrew Smith, was showing the flag in another Labour seat, at Cynon Valley. There were more champagne parties to celebrate the return of John Major to office – lunches at Greens in Mayfair in April, dinners with fellow Tories at the Carlton Club . . .

By late spring, the Muslims had vanished from the Drina valley. The gulag of camps was established, hundreds of thousands of people had been blasted out of their homes and those lucky enough to survive and bribe a way out were being herded over the mountains at gunpoint to be dumped in the minefields or in no-man's-land. Sarajevo had become a nightmare. May was an especially bloody month in Bosnia: people queuing for scarce supplies of bread in a narrow Sarajevo street were blown to pieces by a carefully aimed Serbian mortar, for the world's television cameras to behold. During the last week of the month, an orgy of killing began inside the camps. The first reports were leaking out of a mass grave at

Brcko, and Muslims thrown into an abattoir furnace.

Ian Greer Associates, fat on Serbian money, had an important social event to buy into in London that month: the
Commons versus Lords Tug o' War. This is an annual
tradition on Abingdon Green, outside parliament, where politicians usually strut in search of television cameras. It is a
charity do – a bumptious expression of their compassion for
the suffering, held in order to raise money for cancer sufferers.
For Greer, the event must have had as much to do with
commercial opportunity as with cancer relief. He shelled out
£4,200 for seventy places – seven tables of ten – to the
organising committee, which included three of Greer's staff
and his 'good and close friend', Sir Michael Grylls. Alongside
them were his Chancellor contact Norman Lamont, Michael
Howard, and a galaxy of aristocratic ladies: the Lady Mackay
of Clashfern, the Countess of Caithness, the Viscountess
Montgomery of Alamein, the Duchess of Roxburghe, the
Countess Ferrers. The 'Captain of the Commons' was listed
as John Bowis OBE (who had just had a Greer worker seconded to him throughout his election campaign). The
committee was in turn appointed by the two chairmen, one of
whom was Lady Grylls. The event was sponsored by a construction company which was a Greer client, Taylor
Woodrow: their logo of men pulling a rope appeared on T-
shirts worn by the contestants.

And how Greer must have loved this boisterous occasion.
There was an undercurrent of schoolboy jinks about it – a
suggestion of Billy Bunter and steamy showers after rugger. The
team of men wore shorts and packed against one another along
the rope, heaving and grunting, while the ladies looked on.
There were copious drinks at a pre-tug reception on College
Green, followed by a binge dinner for 400 in a marquee
specially erected in College Gardens. The function raised
£80,000 for the Macmillan Cancer Relief Fund, but those
Greer invited to the affair must also have felt they were on an
impressive inside track: Greer would plainly have had so many
friends among the 400 to whom he could nod and wave.

Greer was targeting as many MP contacts as he could,
writing to them and putting forward the Serbs' position. The
contract ran until the end of June 1992. Greer said subse-

quently in 1995 that 'when the UN imposed sanctions [on Yugoslavia], we thought it would be inappropriate to continue our association with Mr Kennedy'. On this, Greer wins half a point. The debate on the arms embargo and sanctions against Serbia began at the United Nations in September 1991, and had been in the public domain for several months beforehand as the war in Croatia proceeded. But the final imposition of mandatory sanctions on Yugoslavia came on 30 May 1992. Greer's contract finished at the end of June.

After that, John Kennedy continued to go it alone, so the fruits of the work with MPs outlived Greer's contract with Belgrade. Kennedy arranged more trips for MPs; he escorted Radovan Karadzic, the Bosnian Serb leader currently charged with war crimes, round London; and he sought to organise extensive Serb donations to the Conservative party. He was also selected as Tory candidate at the next election for the winnable Midlands seat of Halesowen and Rowley Regis. But if Kennedy was the continuing Serb apologist, Greer too was unmistakably and lucratively in at the start of a job well done.

At its most creative, Kennedy's and Greer's work involved injecting the language of obfuscation into the British debate; language that came to be deployed so effectively by diplomats, by Defence Secretary Rifkind and Foreign Secretary Hurd. Language like: 'There is little any outside group can do to arrest this civil war', as Kennedy was to argue in a letter to the *Independent* on the very day – 6 August 1992 – that a *Guardian* reporter entered the vile camp at Omarska and discovered some of the atrocities and the evil that had been going on. The lobbyists perpetrated the old trick of urging neutrality between bully and victim; it had worked well in the 1930s with Hitler, and it was working well in the bridge that was built between Whitehall and the butchers of the Balkans. Greer took money from murderers – and his conscience never apparently tormented him so far as to want to give any of it back.

Welcome to Chewing Country

The fictional spirit of Alan B'stard MP was most uncannily imitated by Neil Hamilton MP one fine day in New York in 1988, when he strode into the lobby of the top-of-the-range Essex House Hotel, accompanied by his wife Christine.

Hamilton was luxuriating in a piece of behaviour so shameless that even his own Conservative colleagues spluttered in disgust when it came out. He was taking a handsome amount of cash, with a few perks thrown in, from a foreign firm in exchange for promoting an addictive drug that the British Government was trying to ban on the grounds it was likely to give the nation's teenagers mouth cancer. The story of Skoal Bandits, re-designed 'teabags' – small pouches of moistened, powdered chewing tobacco – was so outrageous that Alan B'stard's own scriptwriters might have hesitated before penning it. 'It was monstrous that US Tobacco were free to peddle a noxious substance like this,' says the Conservative Health Minister at the time, David Mellor. But thanks to the endeavours of Neil Hamilton, orchestrated as usual by Ian Greer, the firm's operations were not closed down for five years.

The Essex House in New York, into which Hamilton marched in 1988, is one of the city's finest hotels, on the south side of Central Park. Flanking it is Fifth Avenue to the east, the finest shopping mall in the world, and to the west the mighty Avenue of the Americas, with its great towers of glass and steel. Neil and Christine in the Big Apple: how much better could life get? They had visited the Paris Ritz the previous year: these were the sort of top spots to which Hamilton the MP was becoming accustomed. The sort of things that he and Christine ('We Do Things Together') were doing together involved good food and fine wine in grand surroundings – and not at their own expense. This time US Tobacco (UST), the manufacturers of Skoal Bandits, were delighted to pick up the tab.

He and Christine had visited the tobacco firm's Connecticut headquarters and were now staying in a $500-a-night suite at the Essex House. The couple had barely spent a dime during the whole trip. Everything had been paid for by their hosts. They were in the private apartment the company kept at the hotel. It had a large drawing room, two bedrooms, a marble bathroom and kitchen and a fridge stocked with drinks. If the Hamiltons wanted anything else brought up, room service was waiting for the muted trill of their phone call.

The Hamiltons were there because US Tobacco had a problem in Britain and wanted results from this British politician, who they planned (in Greer's parlance as reported by Fayed) to 'rent' like 'a London taxi'.

They had first introduced Skoal Bandits in the United States in 1983. With the campaign against smoking cigarettes gaining momentum, US Tobacco thought they had hit upon a commercial way of tapping into the old Deep South practice of lodging pellets of shredded tobacco leaves between the lower lip and the gum. The oral snuff habit was mainly confined to people over 50, especially women. But two years of market research suggested that reformed smokers and young men were the likely new customers. Despite – or perhaps because of – pressure from health groups in the United States about the safety of the product, US Tobacco decided to market it overseas. In 1985 they set up their European base in the UK. The company received a £193,000 Government grant to build a distribution centre at East Kilbride in Scotland. One of the Scottish Office ministers responsible for authorising the grant was Allan Stewart, another member of the right-wing No Turning Back group of MPs. The grant would have increased to £1 million if, as planned, the warehouse had expanded.

US Tobacco aggressively marketed their new 'smokeless' product. In the United States students were recruited to hand out free samples to their colleagues. Although not explicitly advertised as such, Skoal Bandits were made to look like a safe form of tobacco consumption. The company sponsored the 1984 Winter Olympics and often used famous baseball players in their advertising in the US. The subliminal message given to the public was that the product was a healthy, even athletic, substitute for smoking.

They planned a similar campaign in the UK. Students were employed at £30 a month to push the tobacco teabags on campus. Financial help was also offered to college sports teams.

In the early 1980s, public health authorities worldwide found that the use of smokeless tobacco increased the risk of oral disease, including cancer. They also found that the products were highly addictive and increased the likelihood of young people taking up smoking. In Britain, the Department of Health had been consulted before the grant was given to build the factory, but had apparently put up no effective resistance.

Almost immediately, ASH Scotland, the anti-smoking group, became aware of the existence of the factory and the product. Anti-tobacco groups, described by Neil Hamilton as 'health fascists', began a campaign to get the product banned and the factory closed down. Within weeks they had per-suaded the Independent Broadcasting Authority to ban Skoal Bandit advertising from British television and radio, and newspapers shortly afterwards agreed to a voluntary advertis-ing ban. The American tobacco giants had been fighting health groups for years and were accustomed to their protests. But in Britain they were coming under sustained political fire in parliament. They were on the defensive.

A small chorus of MPs, most notably the Scottish Labour MP John Home Robertson, began asking questions in the House about Skoal Bandits and its possible dangers to chil-dren. Even the MP for East Kilbride, Morris Miller, was opposed to the UST warehouse, although any job in the area was precious. UST fought back. Their first move was to send a circular to selected MPs, particularly in Scotland, pledging that Skoal Bandits could bring jobs to Scotland. In fact the distribution plant employed fewer than half a dozen people.

In December 1985, Michael Brown MP began to ask his first supportive parliamentary questions about Skoal Bandits. US Tobacco had someone to fight its corner in the Commons. For a man who claimed 'I can honestly say that I never had one puff of a cigarette', he put up a good defence for the tobacco trade, but that was not the only mystery about Michael Brown's intervention. The overtly gay MP for Brigg and Cleethorpes, former member of the Monday Club and asso-ciate of the Hamiltons and Harvey Proctor, had no apparent constituency interest, and no connections with Scotland, where UST's base was located. But Brown did have an interest in the lobbying game. He had worked briefly with Michael Forsyth, the abrasive Thatcherite, in his lobbying firm, Michael Forsyth Associates.

Forsyth was now a Scottish MP, for Stirling, soon to be

appointed to a ministerial post in the Scottish Office. Like Brown and Hamilton, Forsyth and Allan Stewart (the Scottish Office Minister in charge of the original grant to UST), were members of the Thatcherite No Turning Back group, apparently the hub of the pro-tobacco movement. Hamilton, Brown and Forsyth were three of a number of No Turning Back Tories who signed a parliamentary motion in 1986 welcoming research which asserted that passive smoking was not dangerous.

In January 1986, John Home Robertson, the Scottish Labour MP, began to pilot a private member's bill through parliament – the Tobacco Products (Sales Restrictions) Bill, later to become the Protection of Children (Tobacco) Bill, aimed at Skoal Bandits. It had cross-party support to make the sale of Skoal Bandits to minors illegal. This is where Neil Hamilton, Michael Brown's associate, joined the parliamentary fray, exchanging letters with the junior Health Minister, Ray Whitney. No financial links seem to have been made with Greer, at first. The minister reassured Hamilton that 'it would be anomalous to take action solely directed at Skoal Bandits while other tobacco products are sold legally in the UK'. By the end of that year, Hamilton and Brown were US Tobacco's most vociferous supporters in parliament. Brown asked parliamentary questions while Hamilton worked behind the scenes, writing letters and lobbying support. In September 1986, Brown was flown by US Tobacco to their headquarters in Connecticut to be briefed by the company, and enjoy their hospitality. He recorded the free trip in the MPs' register: this was the only declaration Brown ever made in relation to US Tobacco. Andrew Roth's *Parliamentary Profiles* describes Brown succinctly as 'an assiduous free tripper who repays his hosts'.

By the end of 1986, Home Robertson's Bill had become law, and the Government's medical advisory group on cancer – the Committee on Carcinogenicity – privately recommended banning Skoal Bandits. The World Health Organisation joined a small but growing clamour of domestic and international concern. The Government began to consider imposing a UK ban. This would have been disastrous for US Tobacco. A nationwide ban in the UK would almost certainly have extended across the European Union. A year later, in February 1988, Edwina Currie, junior Health Minister with strong views on the subject, announced flatly that she planned to ban 'oral snuff', as the product was known. There would be a three-month time limit to hear representations.

The stage was set for a classic Greer/Hamilton campaign. In America, US Tobacco enlisted top-drawer support. They had donated large sums of money to the Republican party over the years. In a ploy similar to those the tobacco firms used to pry open recalcitrant Far East markets, they steered the debate away from the language of health and towards that of free trade. They wrote to the US Trade Representative in Washington, complaining that such a British ban would breach the GATT and other free trade agreements. Consequent pressure from Washington did delay Currie's ban. Once more, a threat had been postponed. But the threat had been enough to convince UST that they needed more committed political help.

Hamilton and Brown were on hand. If Hamilton's interest in the company's fortunes had previously been ideological, as he would claim, it indisputably now became a means to a few quick dollars. Buttons were pressed. Brown and Hamilton arranged for Greer to meet Ted Kravotil, senior vice-president of UST, in charge of worldwide government relations.

Greer would have given Kravotil his usual optimistic repertoire of sales talk – the 'carefully prepared programme of meetings', the name-dropping of ministers and influential backbench MPs, and the promise of an *à la carte* menu of parliamentary questions and Early Day Motions. Kravotil must have left feeling that if Greer could not save Skoal Bandits nobody could: he signed him up. The cost to US Tobacco of hiring IGA was £120,000 – small change to the tobacco giant if Greer could postpone the ban. The fee was to buy a year's-worth of influence-peddling. Some of the money found its way back, in the usual fashion, to the two MPs, Hamilton and Brown, who were doing the political work at Westminster. But there was a problem. According to Greer staff, Hamilton and Brown were both demanding their cut from Greer of the commission from the contract. This usually meant paying an MP ten per cent of the first year's fee, in this case £12,000. But Greer was not going to give them £12,000 each. 'They're not getting 20 per cent,' he was heard to exclaim, 'they'll have to split the commission between them and take five per cent each.' Neither Hamilton nor Brown declared the tobacco money in the MPs' register. They may not, of course, have regarded Skoal Bandits as a very voter-friendly product. Rather like Philip Morris, makers of Marlboro (another Greer client), US Tobacco liked to keep their lobbying low key and secretive. Other US Tobacco payments went to a third Conservative MP, Sir William Clark, also one of Greer's contacts. (He had been a candidate for the aborted group trip to Paris to stay at Fayed's Ritz the previous year.) Clark was to declare unspecified sums received as a consultant to US Tobacco in a subsequent register – to the outrage of some constituents. Croydon Council, in his con-stituency, had been among those campaigning most strenuously to ban the tobacco 'teabags' from sale.

Greer's first move was to form a select contact team of right-wing libertarian MPs who would be briefed by US Tobacco. Its members included Hamilton and Brown, Wil-liam Clark and other No Turning Back Tories. Naturally, Greer found his old friend Grylls available to put his name to a parliamentary question he wanted planted, asking what scientific or medical research had been done in the UK regarding oral tobacco. Hamilton and Brown claim that the commission payments placed them under no obligation to Greer or US Tobacco, and that the payments were uncon-nected to their position as MPs. But both immediately became the prime movers on the US Tobacco account for Greer. According to IGA executives, the two MPs became IGA's 'eyes and ears and voice' in the Commons. Once more Brown asked the parliamentary questions while Hamilton worked closely with Greer behind the scenes.

The tobacco company were pleased with Ian Greer Asso-ciates. Was their subsequent invitation to Hamilton a reward for past services or an incentive for the future? Kravotil extended the invitation through Greer Associates for Neil and Christine Hamilton to travel to the US, supposedly so the company could brief the backbencher. It looks as though it was essentially a free holiday, on the same lines as the one enjoyed (and declared) by Michael Brown in 1986. US Tobacco arranged a subsequent meeting in London which they were keen for Hamilton to attend. Unfortunately for UST the meeting was on a Friday, a day Hamilton usually spent in his constituency. Despite the fact Hamilton had a flat in London, he agreed to attend on condition the company paid for his accommodation at the St James Court Hotel in London. Situated at Buckingham Gate, the hotel is a lavish one.

The lobbying campaign gathered momentum, and the ban on Skoal Bandits had yet to be confirmed. Hamilton and Brown embarked on a series of meetings with ministers, MPs and civil servants to try to keep it that way. Edwina Currie angrily showed them colour photos of face cancer victims. So instead they approached her boss Kenneth Clarke, then Health Secretary, who saw them politely but without much enthusiasm. David Mellor, who succeeded Currie as Health Minister in December 1988, was an obvious target. When Hamilton and Brown approached him on 9 May 1989, they claimed to be supporting Skoal Bandits purely on right-wing libertarian grounds. They omitted to mention that they were each earning £6,000 from Ian Greer and (in Hamilton's case) had taken an undeclared trip to the US. Mellor was surprised and repelled to be lobbied by the two rightist politicians: 'It was monstrous that US Tobacco were free to peddle a noxious substance like this – teabags full of tobacco to chew in the mouth – within this country. I was astonished when I received representations from certain members appealing on civil liberties grounds for the right of people to damage themselves consuming this appalling substance.'

Mellor did not know of the MPs' links with Greer. Malcolm Rifkind, at this point Minister of State for Scotland, was also approached by Brown. Rifkind's junior Minister in the Scottish Office was none other than Michael Forsyth, for whose lobbying company Brown had worked years earlier, and who was a trusted friend of Hamilton and Brown from the No Turning Back group.

Despite the brush-off from Mellor, Hamilton continued to ply his US Tobacco trade in the Commons, even going so far as to propose an amendment to the Finance Bill of 1989 which would have benefited oral tobacco. But the signs were looking ominous for Skoal Bandits. Finally, on 13 December 1989, the Oral Snuff (Safety) Regulations were tabled, setting a timetable for the banning of Skoal Bandits in the UK. As a last throw of the dice, Hamilton put down an Early Day Motion calling for the safety regulations to be annulled. It was to no avail. Five years after being given a Government grant to set up their noxious trade, the manufacturers of Skoal Bandits were finally sent packing. But at every stage of the game, Ian Greer or some of his circle of Westminster politicians had been there to hinder those who cared for the state of the nation's health.

Neil Hamilton MP

9

The Yes Minister

'When the Prime Minister appointed me, he told
me to make myself the most unpopular member of
the Government. In fact the Prime Minister urged
me to behave like an absolute bastard ... It is a
task I perform with relish.'

Neil Hamilton, Conservative Party Conference,
Blackpool 1993

The riverside terrace of the House of Commons is one of the
more attractive spots in the Palace of Westminster complex at
which to sit and chat. It provides a superb view of the Thames
as it flows regally beneath the arches of Westminster Bridge,
and it was hereabouts, of course, that Wordsworth
enthused:

> *Earth hath not anything to show more fair.*
> *Dull would he be of soul, who could pass by*
> *A sight so touching in its majesty.*

Another advantage, not mentioned by the poet, is that one
cannot easily be overheard. Seated at one of the wooden
outdoor tables on 26 June 1989, a distinguished figure could
be seen instinctively smoothing his white hair with a hand, as
he flicked through a computer print-out. The carefully-styled
silver mane of Michael Grylls MP contrasted with the grizzled
black beard of his interlocutor, Andrew Roth. Roth was a
formidable New Yorker who had made a profession of
researching the background of British MPs like Grylls, and for
the first time Roth had got the drop on him. The print-out, of
a proposed entry in Roth's forthcoming directory of MPs,
read:

GRYLLS. Linked to Ian Greer ... warned of conse-
quence of GEC takeover of Plessey (his friend Ian Greer
was its lobbyist) July 86 ... urged speedy takeover of
BCAL by British Airways (to whom he recommended his
friend Ian Greer as its lobbyist) July 87 ... allowed
unprecedented presence of lobbyist Ian Greer at meeting
of Tories' trade and industry committee April 89 ...
Beneficiary of Ian Greer Associates in connection with
Unitary Tax Campaign for which he had until April 89 a
'research assistant' and a percentage (five per cent? ten
per cent?) of business recommended.

Roth recalls how he found out: 'I met someone who used to
work for Greer and now worked for a friend of mine. He told
me Greer was paying Michael Grylls "introduction fees" –
and what particularly shocked him was that he suspected
Grylls was taking money for referring his own constituents to
the lobbyist.'

The informant was correct. Grylls took commissions from
Greer for introducing Charles Church, who ran a property
development firm headquartered in Camberley, in Grylls'
own heart-of-suburban-Surrey constituency. Church's firm
were on record at the time complaining about the difficulty of
getting planning consents in the crowded south east of England: so that may have been their problem.

Grylls had been taking a steady stream of money, referring
to the lobbyists at least five clients. As well as Charles Church,
there was the disposable lighter company, Biro Bic; the substantial British Airways account; Whitbreads, the giant
brewery; and the 'Honour Hong Kong' campaign. Grylls did
not disclose his connections with any of these firms on the
Register of MPs' Interests. Nor, indeed, apart from a passing
and cryptic reference to being on the payroll of the 'Unitary
Tax Campaign (Ian Greer Associates)', had he genuinely
disclosed his links with the lobbyist.

When, in 1989, Roth began to prepare Volume 'E to K' of
Parliamentary Profiles – his massive reference book on MPs –
the profiler was determined to see Grylls exposed. He always
showed a print-out of the entry he proposed to publish to each
MP beforehand, for their consent: it was the only way to avoid

the oppressive British libel laws putting him out of business. That was how in June of that year he had found himself sitting anxiously on the terrace with the man he had described as having 'the looks of a 1930s matinée idol'.

'I'd slipped in the entry that said he'd taken five per cent or ten per cent commission from Greer, although I didn't have any proof. Grylls accepted it without demur! So I went back happy to the office and sent off the entry to be printed.'

Grylls may have appeared impassive on the subject of Greer while in Roth's presence. But as soon as the now-confident investigator left the terrace with his print-out, there followed a burst of activity by Ian Greer and all his stable of MPs. They knew that trouble was likely to ensue when Roth's volume appeared in the bookshops in the autumn. But by then, the books were to be wiped clean of all outstanding payments to politicians.

Grylls was given a total of £10,000 cash by Greer. The MP Michael Brown was made a £2,000 'final payment'. And accounts were squared with Neil Hamilton by another 'final payment' to him of more than £6,000. This 1989 money set the seal on Hamilton's parliamentary corruption. It consisted, unequivocally, of a large cheque from Greer Associates, which the MP did not declare but promptly paid into his bank.

With this clearing of the books, the prospect of a halt to the Westminster sleaze machine might now seem to loom. But it would have been naive to think so. The sleazers were merely re-grouping.

In October 1989, Roth's book came out, revealing that Grylls had been taking commissions from lobbyists. Although the sleaze merchants were fond of complaining about persecution by the press, this was in fact the first time for five years that any serious attention began to be paid to the corruption building up at Westminster. Investigator Mark Hollingsworth, from the Granada Television programme 'World in Action', was already on the case. And a Labour member of the Members' Interests Committee, Dale Campbell-Savours, was also alerted. He recalled that Greer had privately denied paying MPs, the previous year, when the committee had begun hearings into the mushrooming lobbying game.

At those hearings, the well-groomed lobbyist had shown

great sang-froid considering that he had recently funded two dozen MPs' election expenses, was handing over cash to Brown and Grylls, and was paying the bills for Hamilton's paintings, garden furniture and plane tickets. In a blandly untruthful performance, the lobbyist had denied 'sweetening' MPs. He assented to the question: 'You are completely dissociated from them?' agreeing: 'We have no need to . . . I have enough friends in the House.'

Campbell-Savours now made a fuss about the contents of Roth's book. Greer deflected his renewed enquiries. All the Labour MP achieved was that the committee registrar was told to circulate in December to all MPs, alongside their annual declaration form, a new instruction that they *must* register one-off commission or 'introduction' payments received in the course of the past year – not that there had ever actually been any doubt about the matter.

Grylls himself had already rushed to register in the immediate wake of Roth's publication, no doubt hoping to head off trouble. But it is a measure of the extraordinary bravado of Neil Hamilton that, despite this specific instruction from the registrar, he refused to register the July cheque he had received from Greer. Instead, that December Hamilton sent off another letter to the Home Secretary on Mohammed al-Fayed's behalf, accusing two police officers of leaking the hostile DTI report to Rowland. It was in December, too, that Hamilton personally tabled a parliamentary motion for Greer's client, US Tobacco, opposing the proposed ban on their carcinogenic tobacco chews. Hamilton clearly felt no need to rein back as his heroine, Mrs Thatcher, celebrated a decade in power. His venomous parliamentary barracking of Labour leader Neil Kinnock was attracting the leaderine's attention. Furthermore, the outside cash was starting to mount. A mark of this good fortune was that in April 1990 the Hamiltons sold Laburnum Cottage in the constituency, and bought the grandiose Rectory at Alderley Edge for £400,000. The wrought-iron garden furniture and the watercolours they had acquired from Greer certainly did help furnish a home. The couple took out a mortgage of £200,000: the repayments alone would have swallowed up Hamilton's official parliamentary salary.

But pay-offs met the shortfall. He was getting a nominal retainer of £2,000 a year from the Brewers' Society, to continue boosting the cause of the monopolistic big brewers against the small independents. The MP also got £10,000 in 1989 from the petrol giant Mobil. He described his relationship with them in the MPs' register as 'taxation consultant', and Mobil say one of their companies had an arcane dispute with the Inland Revenue over US/UK taxation, about which they regarded Hamilton as an expert. This seems a rather unlikely concept: whenever they wanted, the oil majors could hire tax experts who knew far more than Hamilton, who had never earned a serious living as a tax lawyer at the Bar. One clue as to the reality of the relationship is that Mobil also simultaneously became a substantial paying client of Ian Greer Associates. The firm wanted parliamentary clout because the big oil companies were undergoing a Monopolies and Mergers Commission (MMC) investigation into their high petrol prices. They also wanted to block a housing development near their Coryton, Essex, refinery. The money from Mobil was to prove in the end to be one of the contributory causes of Hamilton's downfall, but in 1990 it was meeting nearly half his new mortgage payments.

Hamilton was in demand, probably because he was not too fussy about where his money came from. He was hoping to draw £10,000 a year from January 1990 as the new non-executive director of Plateau, a mining exploration company then in the process of raising £16 million from credulous stock market investors. Plateau's was associated with a Welsh mining consultancy, Robertson Research, who said they had potentially valuable interests in gold and platinum in Zimbabwe, Ecuador and Cyprus. No doubt the advertised presence of an MP on the board was reassuring.

Hamilton was brought in by Colin Bird, the managing director, who previously ran mines in South Africa for the giant Anglo American Corporation. Bird knew the MP through the National Association of Licensed Open-cast Operators, where Hamilton had had yet another paid consultancy from 1981. 'He understood the mining business,' Bird says. With the help of Clive Smith, a Midlands entrepreneur, who had given advice to Robertson Research on floating several natural resource companies, Plateau's arrival at the Stock Exchange was full of promise. The directors' report for the year complimented Hamilton 'for his contribution to the development of the company'. Within eighteen months the share price of 90p collapsed to 13p and the investors lost their money.

Hamilton also acquired a fourth – and even more questionable – source of income, as a lobbyist for apartheid South Africa. Interestingly, this was a regime with which Ian Greer had always refused to do business, he said for ethical reasons. He took the lobbying account of their deadly enemies instead, the underground resistance party, the African National Congress. Neil Hamilton, however, took free trips to South Africa in the company of Michael Brown; he berated the ANC as a 'typical terrorist organisation'; and he attacked the BBC for broadcasting a concert in aid of Mandela.

In 1990, an obscure organisation called Strategy Network International appeared in London. It lobbied for the apartheid regime's causes, including their puppets in Namibia and the Unita rebels in Angola. Their representative was a bizarre figure in the circumstances, a good-looking protégé of Michael Brown, who referred to him as 'little Derek'. Derek Laud was black: he had first surfaced at the age of 21 in the early 1980s, with Brown as his mentor, making unlikely speeches on behalf of the Monday Club and Harvey Proctor's Immigration Committee. It must have been a high camp experience for the Monday Clubbers of the time to see a black man calling in cultured tones for the repatriation of black immigrants. Laud subsequently ran as a token Conservative candidate against black Labour MP Bernie Grant in Tottenham. Laud's skin colour now undoubtedly made him a useful front man for Strategy Network International. He recruited Hamilton as a parliamentary 'consultant' in June 1990, offering him another £8,000 a year. Hamilton, of course, omitted to register this controversial new source of income.

For all Hamilton's good fortune, in the New Year of 1990 the prospect of exposure for Greer's team edged a little closer. Hollingsworth's 'World in Action' programme came out, and accused Grylls of taking money for introducing the monopolistic British Airways to Greer and his lobbyists. The sleaze count in the atmosphere rose further with the publication of the Members' Interests Committee finding in February that another Conservative MP, John Browne, had been taking money and not declaring it, from the Saudi Arabians and from a Lebanese middleman seeking construction contracts. Browne, who was eventually suspended and de-selected, put up a truculent performance which clearly alienated even the committee's Tory majority. They had pronounced themselves willing to hear the case, even though a libel action by the MP was theoretically pending (a robust stance which was not to survive pressure from Government Whips the next time the issue arose).

Thanks to the nagging of Dale Campbell-Savours, while Hamilton started to pay off his mortgage on the Rectory with his ill-gotten gains, official Members' Interests Committee hearings began, at last, on the charge detonated by Andrew Roth's book – that MPs were getting undeclared money from Ian Greer Associates. The inquiry was a failure. Greer was allowed to make complete fools of the MPs on the committee.

The transcripts of evidence suggest that the Conservatives used their built-in majority to squash any serious investigation. For Greer was allowed to withhold the identities of the MPs he was paying, the amounts of cash they got, and the companies on whose behalf they received their supposed 'introduction fees'. This made it impossible to discover what parliamentary action the MPs might have been taking for their money.

Both Greer and Grylls were untruthful. Greer, no doubt anxious to present a picture of 'one-off' payments which did not impose any continuing obligation, said that MP 'A' (recognised as Grylls), had received payments for introductions three times – in 1985, 1986 and 1990. Grylls had in fact got at least ten payments during the period, and received money from Greer in 1985, 1986, 1987, 1988, 1989 and 1990. He had introduced at least five companies, not three, and had received stage payments for the various 'introduction fees'.

Greer said that MP 'B' (who no-one at the time knew to be Hamilton) had received two payments, in 1986 and 1988. In fact, the true total number of his recorded payments received from Greer appears to have been five, not two, spread over four years between 1986 and 1989.

And finally, Greer listed MP 'C' (who no-one knew to be Michael Brown). He said this anonymous MP had received a single payment, in 1988. It was a half-truth. In fact, Brown had received two stage payments, in 1988 and 1989.

Grylls himself continued to mislead the committee when he testified to an accompanying inquiry into his personal declarations on the Register of MPs' Interests. Apparently unable to keep his and Greer's stories straight, he said his third payment came in October 1988 (Greer claimed to the committee that it came in 1990). Grylls repeated that he had only had three payments, from introductions effected to 'three company chairmen who are friends of mine'.

For his misdemeanours, MP 'A' (alias Michael Grylls) was thrashed with a feather. The committee feebly found that he had not registered his Greer interests in 'sufficient detail'. No penalty was envisaged. 'There was 'no evidence' Grylls had done parliamentary work for those firms he introduced to Greer, they said, although as the committee never identified who the firms were, there was little danger they would ever find any evidence about anything. It was a shameful performance, judged by any judicial standards. Judged by the party-political factors which really drove the committee, the verdict was to be expected.

However, Greer's refusal publicly to name either Hamilton or Michael Brown to the inquiry was double-edged for the two MPs. The lobbyist had protected them. But they had never registered the money and gifts they got from him. Given that Greer possessed delicate information which the two politicians were plainly unwilling to see exposed, he could perhaps be thought from now on to have a continuing hold over them.

This was a significant point. For very soon, Hamilton was promoted. That July, Mrs Thatcher made him an assistant Whip. Following his dream, Neil Hamilton – former ranter and raver of Aberystwyth's lunatic Monday Club – was appointed Minister of the Crown. The Whips are the prefects in the parliamentary public school – they make sure backbenchers turn up for votes, spy on them and occasionally bail them out of financial or sexual scrapes. Hamilton, who was witty in an offensive sort of way, thrived in this gossipy male atmosphere. However, the promotion did not do much for his financial position. All his new 'outside interests', paying more than £30,000 a year, now had to be resigned. But his overall income as a politician fell dramatically (£20,000 'reduced' MP's salary, plus £16,000 Whip's salary, added up to £36,000. His previous MP's full wage of £26,000, plus the 'outside interests', was running at an annual £56,000.) Hamilton was to describe his ministerial pay as 'peanuts'.

Just as Hamilton flourished at Westminster, so did Ian Greer and his lobbying firm. Greer was raising £3.5 million a year from a gushing stream of new clients. One excellent source of business was from the utilities. Their directors acquired grotesquely large 'fat cat' salaries and executive share options from successful privatisations. Under these circumstances, lobbyists could help push privatisations through Westminster, press for advantageous terms, and fend off political criticism when the size of the pay-offs was discovered. Among Greer's most notable new clients was Thames Water, one of the most criticised privatisations.

Another surprising – but lucrative – source of lobbying business was the new hospital trusts in the marketised National Health Service. London had too many hospitals, campaigning to survive ministerial threats of closure. These organisations were also trying to get the political go-ahead for building schemes in partnership with private developers. It was a logical extension of the market thinking which the Government sought to promote that hospitals should start to spend their funds, not on treating sick people, but on buying political influence.

The Royal Brompton, the Royal Marsden cancer hospital, Queen Mary's Roehampton and Hammersmith Hospital, all hired Greer to lobby successfully against closure or amalgamation. At least one of the Conservative MPs who asked parliamentary questions on the Royal Marsden's behalf, Lady Olga Maitland, had a financial link with Greer: she and her barrister husband both benefited from Greer commissions. The Royal Brompton, with a market-minded Canadian chief executive, went on to re-hire Greer to lobby for a scheme under the Government's 'Private Finance Initiative' to swap prime land in Chelsea with a private developer, Robert McAlpine plc, in return for their constructing a £30 million clinic for the hospital.

Another group who found Greer's discreet services helpful were the arms contractors. In 1993, the lobbying firm hired Defence Secretary Malcolm Rifkind's former political adviser, Perry Miller, boasting of his usefulness in 'a behind-the-scenes role'. Greer claimed that he secured a big British army truck contract from the Ministry of Defence for Leyland-DAF. He lobbied for the vastly-expensive Eurofighter project to go ahead, on behalf of Lucas Industries. He proposed that airships from Airship Industries should float above the Northern Irish border watching for terrorists crossing. Greer took money from Shorts of Belfast to promote the arms manufacturer's privatisation, and sales of their Starburst missile system to the Malaysian regime. Greer's firm tried to push for Ferranti's dipping sonar to be specified on Westland's new anti-submarine helicopter, the EH101; and promoted the privatisation of Royal Ordnance, which ended up in British Aerospace's hands.

Greer also took money from foreign defence firms to help swing British military contracts their way. Boeing paid him to persuade Rifkind to order massive Chinook transport helicopters for the RAF: the minister eventually bought fourteen in April 1995, worth £240 million. Lockheed, another giant, paid the firm to promote a US alternative to the Nimrod plane radar surveillance system. And ITT hired Greer to persuade ministers to order the US firm's personal radios to re-equip the entire British army, in an enormous contract worth £2 billion. ITT are favourites to be awarded the deal, which was still in 1996 in the hands of the Defence Secretary, Michael Portillo – a recipient of a Greer contribution towards his 1987 election expenses.

As might be expected, other aggressive purchasers of Greer's backstairs influence included the tobacco industry, its sales constantly threatened by health campaigners. Philip Morris (Marlboro cigarettes) hired Ian Greer Associates for £120,000 a year to head off the continuous threat of advertising bans. Wining and dining MPs such as Dame Angela Rumbold and John Whittingdale went alongside the distribution of money to health charities, both to spread favours and improve the tobacco company's image. Minutes of a 1993 meeting between Greer's staff and an executive from Philip Morris spell out the odious tasks expected of the lobbyists: 'It would be . . . helpful to know if the Rt Hon. Virginia Bottomley (Health Secretary) and the Rt Hon. Kenneth Clarke QC, MP (Chancellor) had any pet charities which Philip Morris could usefully assist.'

Philip Morris also wanted John Bowis, Conservative minister responsible for the homeless (and a Greer contact), to attend a ceremony at which a £25,000 cheque would be handed over to the charity Crisis at Christmas. Discreetly, the money would be in the name of Phillip Morris' more innocuous-sounding subsidiary, Kraft Foods. In similarly deceptive vein, the meeting discussed plans to develop links with Labour politicians and to set up a 'smokers' rights' group headed by a Labour MP. Political donations to the campaign funds of individual politicians from all three parties were planned, and receptions at the party conferences: 'Given the stated policies of the Lib Dems and the Labour party, it might well be that their receptions would be held by Kraft Foods.'

Of all the confidential clients out of whom Greer was making money, none were more controversial, however, than those who were foreign governments. If it seems strange that a lobbyist can sell political influence to a foreign company, it seems doubly strange that they should be allowed to do so on behalf of a foreign state. In the US, such lobbyists are required to register as the agents of a foreign power – and not without good reason. Is it really in the national interest for foreign policy to be secretly modified by a lobbyist? Greer may have found apartheid South Africa too much to stomach. But he was perfectly prepared to lobby, not only for the brutal government in Serbia, but for Taiwan, Pakistan, Brazil, and for Mohammed Mahathir's regime in Malaysia, which came under fire over allegations of corruption and misuse of aid money supplied for the building of the Pergau Dam.

Greer may have thought that that 1992 election – which the

Tories were considered likely to lose – would spell the end of his best lobbying days. He sharply cut the secret election money he paid to individual MPs' 'fighting funds', compared to the lavishness of 1987. Only a handful got money, and it was only a token £250. Also, he divided what cash he did invest more equally among Labour, Liberal Democrat and Conservative. The payments went to three Tories – Linda Chalker (who had also been a 1987 beneficiary), Robert Atkins in South Ribble and Vivian Bendall in Ilford North; and three Labour – Doug Hoyle again in Warrington, Gwyneth Dunwoody in Crewe and Nantwich, and Chris Smith in Islington South. Once again the Liberal Alan Beith got help in Berwick. The declaration required by the Companies Act in the directors' report of Ian Greer Associates concealed the recipients of these modest subsidies: it merely said £2,750 had been donated to 'various political parties'.

Members of Greer's staff were also seconded to campaign for three politicians: John Bowis, who became a Health Minister; John Major's PPS, Graham Bright ; and the London MP Sir John Wheeler. Greer's aide, Andrew Smith, now promoted in the company brochures to 'former researcher to Neil Hamilton', himself ran as a candidate for the Conservatives in the hopeless Welsh Labour seat of Cynon Valley. Neil Hamilton went out of his way to speak for him there.

Major did win the 1992 election, to the astonishment of many. Unexpectedly, good times for lobbyists were here again. Greer rapidly re-positioned himself and put his hand in his pocket. He handed over £5,000 to publish Major's dull election speeches and save them for posterity.

In the slipstream of the election victory, Major promoted Neil Hamilton. Balancing left- and right-wing factions in his party, Major made Hamilton one of Michael Heseltine's team of six ministers at the Department of Trade and Industry, with a special brief for deregulation – tearing up what the Conservatives called 'red tape', but what some called the fabric of society. Hamilton the attention-seeker was thrilled at his new job. He told a journalist: 'I have the essential streak of vanity. It's surprising how many people seem to wander into this profession wholly unequipped. They don't like the limelight.' To applause at the party conference, he showily ripped up yards of supposed red tape 'regulations' (the stunt was bogus – it was sheaves of blank computer paper). Eerily conjuring up once again the spirit of Alan B'stard MP, Hamilton boasted: 'The Prime Minister urged me to behave like an absolute bastard.' As the Minister for Corporate Affairs, he was a gatekeeper of immense interest and value to his old mentor and paymaster, Ian Greer. Hamilton was not only in charge of the 'deregulation unit', but also competition policy (which included monopolies inquiries); the insurance industry; company law; the insolvency service, which handled firms that went bankrupt; and investigations into fraudulent or failed companies. It was a position which called for even more detachment and integrity than most Government jobs.

On taking office, Hamilton was handed a copy of the ministerial rule book, *Questions of Procedure*. It told him: 'Ministers will want to order their affairs so that no conflict arises or is thought to arise between their private interests and their public duties.' This scarcely seemed to be the case as far as Hamilton's continuing relations with Ian Greer were concerned. The lobbyist had so many confidential clients with interests at the DTI or directly in Hamilton's own corporate affairs section that it was hard to see how the minister could turn round without bumping into one or more of them. Greer himself was frequently running in and out of the DTI.

The new minister had his supporters among the senior civil servants, for all his claims of being an 'absolute bastard'. One source close to him remarked: 'He was clearly on the right of the right-wing group. He is somebody who speaks his mind, doesn't hide his feelings. Quite refreshing really. He didn't hesitate to debate his views with those he didn't agree with, which was not a hallmark of the Thatcher administration.'

The secret financial connection to Greer was a factor of which the minister's own civil servants and his ministerial chief, Michael Heseltine, were unaware. Hamilton experienced at least six specific conflicts of interest as a Government minister. There is no way of telling whether Hamilton showed favour to these clients of Greer or not. That is the point about conflicts of interest. As the ministerial rule book rightly said, no such situation should be allowed to arise in the first place.

Contact with the affairs of the first Greer client came within weeks of the minister's arrival at the DTI's Victoria Street headquarters. Lloyds Bank launched a hostile takeover bid for their ailing high street rival, the Midland. The Midland Bank hired a lobbyist – Ian Greer, who else? – in April 1992, for political influence to help fight off the Lloyds bid.

According to the bank, Greer's job was 'to make sure that ministers and backbenchers were aware of Midland Bank's opposition'. The key political aim was to push the Department of Trade and Industry and the relevant ministers, Hamilton and his boss Michael Heseltine, to follow the recommendation of the Office of Fair Trading, and refer the bid to the Monopolies Commission. If a reference was made, with the consequent delay, it was likely that the unwelcome bid would collapse.

In early May, Hamilton the new minister was interviewed by Sarah Whitebloom of the *Observer* and the hot topic of the Midland came up. 'While of course emphasising that his lips are sealed regarding the Midland situation, Hamilton states that competition policy has been at the heart of the Government's economic and industrial policy since 1979. "I've been an enthusiastic advocate of greater competition." ' On the final authority of his boss Michael Heseltine, Hamilton's department subsequently did refer the bid to the MMC, and it duly collapsed. Greer marked another tick on his lobbyist's tally.

One of the central achievements of the Conserative governments was the creation of the 'fat-cat' triangle of privatised utility companies – water, electricity and gas. At a time when the newly-elected Prime Minister was demanding that the citizenry tighten its belt and scrimp for the sake of the nation, the Government established a clan of bloated executives who could charge as much as they liked for heat, light and dish-water, meanwhile composing their own wildly generous packages of salaries, perks and shareholdings. The poor consumers' domestic bills soared to bewildering heights – with no competition to turn to – but at least people could see clearly where their money was going.

The fattest cats of all were at British Gas, whose stranglehold over its consumers was so tight that it aroused the MMC's keen curiosity. The commission was about to recommend that British Gas be broken up and its monopoly dismantled, and this became the second biggest competition issue to cross minister Hamilton's desk upon his arrival at the DTI. Despite their fabulous lifestyles and giddy salaries, British Gas still managed to find some £500,000 of consumers' money to spend on buying up almost every lobbyist in town to hold on to their lucrative new ransom. (That was about a year's salary for chief executive Cedric Brown and chairman Richard Giordano *before* their perks and shares.) The main hireling in this noble cause was, inevitably, the minister's friend and former paymaster Ian Greer. The investment paid off. For all the guff about competition and free enterprise, Hamilton's department gratified the lobbyists and did no more than trim British Gas's colossal monopoly at the outer edges. As with all these big monopoly issues, Hamilton's boss Heseltine took the final decision. But Hamilton was nominally in charge and always involved.

There were other Greer clients whose business crossed Hamilton's path while he was a minister. Trafalgar House, the construction giant, were paying Ian Greer handsomely. Trafalgar wanted Greer to secure them planning permission for a huge development near Paddington station in London. This bung to Greer coincided with another Trafalgar House matter arriving on Hamilton's desk. In November 1992, former shareholders in a company taken over by Trafalgar – the Davy Corporation – protested at the takeover and demanded that the DTI hold an inquiry into it. They were seen off.

Another old favourite client of Greer's was a flashy entrepreneur called Michael Ashcroft, who had a Florida-based (and Bermuda-registered) car-auction firm, ADT. In 1990, IGA had run a campaign to help Ashcroft bid for a slice of the British Airports Authority (BAA). In a rather feeble attempt at a joke, the campaign was codenamed 'Project Sheep', because of the initials BAA. At the time Hamilton was a minister in 1992, Ashcroft was still paying Greer while one of his close business associates, Tony Berry, was being investigated by the DTI. The investigators' reports were going via Hamilton. Berry had a recruitment agency called Blue Arrow, which had collapsed, and the DTI was considering disqualifying him as a director. Ashcroft submitted pleas to the DTI on behalf of his friend. The proceedings against Berry were dropped in October 1994. The DTI says of the Berry case: 'These matters passed through Neil Hamilton's office, although they were decided by Michael Heseltine.'

A striking conflict of interest involved the insurance giant, Prudential. The knotty portfolio of insurance was an important part of Hamilton's ministerial brief. And during his term of office, the Pru hired Ian Greer Associates for more than £100,000 as part of a campaign for greater deregulation of the business. Prudential got the introduction they needed. On 7 September 1992, there was a lunch to discuss the matter. Present were: the Pru's chief executive Mick Newmarch, Greer's deputy director Andrew Smith and minister Neil Hamilton. In 1994, the Pru were busy again, this time campaigning against the planned finance regulator, the Personal Investment Authority. On 2 February 1994, Newmarch got himself another meeting with Hamilton. 'Hamilton was the minister for deregulation,' says Newmarch, 'and I had a meeting in his office to talk to him about it.'

Greer's business was now set to become not so much 'cash for questions', as it had been for Fayed, but 'cash for ministerial access'. And there was nothing more astonishing in all of Hamilton's ministerial dealings than those with a large group of City accountants who had banded together as 'The Big Eight'. Greer pitched for the contract which the consortium wanted to forge with the right lobbyist, and for whom the accountants had set aside £120,000. His sales line was that the Corporate Affairs Minister would be 'sympathetic' to their clients. A briefing document sent to one of the accounting firms involved said: 'One highly unusual outcome of this soundings exercise has been the sympathetic comments that have come from the minister.'

The accountancy firms wanted to end their traditional principle of unlimited liability because of 'Armageddon claims' of up to £8 billion against auditors following company crashes such as the Bank of Credit & Commerce International, Polly Peck, Barlow Clowes and Maxwell Communications. The 1993–4 lobbying campaign was led by Price Waterhouse and its senior partner, Ian Brindle, with Coopers & Lybrand, Ernst & Young, Grant Thornton, BDO

Binder Hamlyn, Touche Ross, Arthur Andersen, and KPMG Peat Marwick. Greer's firm won the lucrative business only after a contest with other lobbyists, especially the firm of GJW. It is clear that Greer explicitly used Hamilton's name to get the business.

Then, within days of recruiting the new clients in May 1993, Andrew Smith, Greer's deputy managing director, boasted he held an 'off the record' meeting with Hamilton to give him a detailed briefing on his clients' case. A formal meeting was further arranged with Hamilton in July 1993. It was again attended by Andrew Smith, with representatives from 'The Big Eight' alongside senior civil servants.

DTI civil servants were accustomed to Greer and his lieutenants scurrying about. 'Lobbying,' said one source 'was a service one understood. It existed, and one accepted it. I came across Greer a number of times. It's better to have these contacts. They put their case, and we're all perfectly capable of bearing in mind the opposite point of view.' But this seems naive. The department did not know the true nature of the relationships.

In fact, there was only one client of Greer to whom the minister ended up giving the cold shoulder: Mohammed al-Fayed. Hamilton may have felt that the way events had turned out left him with little alternative. But to the owner of Harrods, his conduct must have looked like the blackest ingratitude. As soon as Hamilton got the Corporate Affairs job, Fayed fired off an effusive letter of congratulation. It read: 'Well, I suppose they can't keep a good man down for ever! Congratulations on your appointment. Long overdue ... I shall be expecting you to contribute to my Trade and Industry by popping in with your orders ...'

Fayed went on to draw the new minister's attention to the lawsuit he was bringing at the European Court of Human Rights in Strasbourg against the DTI itself, disputing the inspectors' report on his House of Fraser takeover. This reminder of smelly dealings in the past must have been about as welcome to Hamilton in his important new office as would be a box of old fish chucked out of the back door of Harrods' food hall. The letter was headed 'Private and Confidential', but it was sent quite openly to Hamilton at the ministry, where it was opened by civil servants. What Fayed had not quite grasped was that he was technically in litigation with Hamilton himself as the minister, because of his dogged and continuing attempts to overturn the DTI inspectors' report. The civil servants disapproved of Fayed. They considered a direct approach to the minister in this way to be reprehensible. But Hamilton did not immediately declare his past interest in Fayed's affairs and excuse himself. He blithely carried on dealing with Lonhro and Fayed matters for some time. On 13 May 1992, for example, he officially answered a parliamentary question from Alex Carlisle about the DTI inquiry. He told Carlisle the inquiry had been 'independent . . . a carefully considered and thorough investigation'.

This reply, drafted by his officials and signed off by the minister, was a cynical, diametric opposite to Hamilton's previous claims as a backbencher that the inspectors' behaviour had been 'such a monstrous injustice' that it amounted to the work of 'a twentieth-century Spanish Inquisition'. Fayed must have gasped in astonishment at his former lackey's shameless U-turn. Only in June, when Hamilton started to receive highly confidential reports on the progress of Fayed's Euro-case, did he think it prudent to explicitly rule himself out. His declaration (no mention of cash, the Ritz, or Greer) led to an internal DTI inquiry into the extent of Hamilton's previous lobbying, that led in turn to a discussion in which Hamilton agreed that it would look better if he played no further part not only in the Fayed affair but also in Lonhro's concerns. This agreement was not reached until 29 June – two months after he took office. One source close to the Government recalls: 'We were told there had been an association in the past, and we respected him for that. We have to take people on trust. Ministers are serious people, and you have to rely on them to declare their interests. We don't do a judicial inquest into them.'

Hamilton, keeping his nose clean, did not even give Fayed the courtesy of a reply. The munificent Egyptian was affronted to get a phone call instead in which it was explained that Hamilton felt it best to 'distance himself' from the owner of Harrods from now on. One can detect a cultural difference here: in some circles it might have been considered a point of honour that, once bribed, you stayed bribed. For Hamilton, however, no sense of obligation apparently remained. This was Fayed's return for all the gourmet dinners, the bottles of fizz, the gift vouchers, the paintings, the plane tickets, the wrought-iron garden furniture, and the rolls of banknotes – the brush-off. Of course, Mohammed al-Fayed, unfortunate as it was eventually to prove for the welfare of the whole Major government, was unlikely to take that sort of cynicism lying down.

The Government now embarked on a moral crusade under the watchword 'Back to Basics' – extolling family values, social discipline and clean living. But simultaneously, the administration of which Neil Hamilton was an ornament gave a new term to the history books: 'sleaze'. The word had the honour of an official definition from a judge in the end – Lord Nolan in 1995, looking into the collapse of public standards of which Hamilton was to become a symbol. Sleaze was, said the judge, 'a pervasive atmosphere ... in which sexual, financial and governmental misconduct were indifferently linked'.

Elsewhere in Europe, Italy had been nominally managed for half a century by that country's Christian Democrat party. There, the political system had become an edifice of corrupt patronage, based on kickbacks. Britain's politicians were minnows in this game by comparison. But Britain's Conservatives had been in power while a whole generation of infants grew up to adulthood, and were beginning to act as though they had caught the knack of permanent power. Along with political permanence, the laws of history seemed to say, went sleaze. An earlier generation would have called it moral corruption.

There was a lot of steamy sex involved: British tabloid newspapers tended to enjoy rooting that out much more than trying to unstitch dry financial situations. Conservative MP Alan Amos in March 1992 was found 'acting indecently' with another man on Hampstead Heath. The National Heritage Minister, David Mellor, was taken in adultery with a model, Antonia de Sancha, and – more seriously regarded – in September 1992 was discovered to have had a free holiday with Mona Bauwens, a Palestinian. Mellor resigned, although the

Transport Minister, Steven Norris, survived intact despite the revelation on the eve of the 1993 Tory conference of five extra-marital affairs. A Miss Julia Stent bobbed up shortly afterwards to say she was pregnant with the illegitimate child of Environment Minister Tim Yeo. The wife of David Ashby, Tory MP for Leicestershire North West, said that his homosexual relationship with a doctor had wrecked their marriage. Gary Waller, Tory MP for Keighley, admitted fathering an illegitimate child. Lord Caithness resigned as a minister after the suicide of his wife, attributed to an affair of his. Stephen Milligan, Conservative MP for Eastleigh in Hampshire, and PPS to Jonathan Aitken, Defence Procurement Minister, was found dead on his kitchen table, wearing ladies' underwear, after inadvertently asphyxiating himself. Hartley Booth, PPS to Douglas Hogg at the Foreign Office, and MP for Finchley, was found to be having an affair with his research assistant, Emily Barr. Former Trade Minister Alan Clark, it transpired, had slept with the wife of a South African judge, and the judge's two daughters as well. Richard Spring was obliged to resign as PPS to Northern Ireland Secretary Sir Patrick Mayhew after a three-in-a-bed situation involving a Sunday school teacher. And in an incident which struck closer to home for the sleaze party, Hamilton's and Greer's friend Michael Brown, the MP for Cleethorpes, stepped down as a Government Whip after being 'outed' for homosexual relations with a 20-year-old.

While sexual antics monopolised the front pages, more characteristic of the financial looseness of the perpetual governors at Westminster was the departure of Northern Ireland Minister Michael Mates: he left the Government over the revelation of his gift of a watch to Asil Nadir, the Turkish fugitive from justice who had been generous in his donations to the Conservative party. Mates was then further obliged to depart from the chairmanship of the Defence Committee after the disclosure of undeclared military consultancies. The back-bencher who succeeded Neil Hamilton as 'consultant' to the Pretoria-backed Strategy Network International lobbying organisation was Michael Colvin, Conservative MP for Romsey. He too omitted to declare it in the Register of Members' Interests, saying this was an 'oversight'. Colvin then actually went on the board of Ludgate Laud, another lobbying company set up by the egregious black Monday Clubber Derek Laud: hiring oneself out in this blatant way was eventually banned, but only after the publication in 1995 of Lord Nolan's report condemning such practices.

All in all, the political machine operated by the ruling party in John Major's time was not characterised by excessive fastidiousness. Yet it did gave the impression that its participants expected it to go on, untroubled, into an indefinite future. Neil Hamilton, the minister in charge of corporate probity, was not alone in his lack of scruple. Why should he expect to be found out? And if found out, why should he expect to be punished?

**Neil Hamilton brandishes a ginger biscuit,
assuring an admiring crowd that he would declare it
on the MP's Registry of Interests**

10

End Game

'A lot of shit's going to come out.'
Mohammed al-Fayed, September 1994

The Thames-side terrace of the House of Commons hosted a special Conservative event in 1993. In the spring sunlight there were no indications of the political downpour that lay ahead. The slurping and chattering of the 140 politicians and guests at the river's edge on 19 May was a sound that almost carried up on to Westminster Bridge, where the Japanese and American tourists were videoing each other against the famous backdrop they believed to be impressive, and even in a way sacred: Big Ben and the Mother of Parliaments.

Tippling behind an awning were John Major, the Prime Minister; the Chancellor of the Exchequer, Norman Lamont; and half the Cabinet. They were paying attention to various rich individuals, who had just become slightly the poorer by four-figure sums: – the price they had paid to Conservative Central Office for their invitation to this opportunity to mingle and – who knows? – maybe even press their personal concerns on a top politician. This was how fund raising was done in the modern Conservative party.

The fund-raising reception was presided over by the lobbyist's friend – the silver-haired MP, Michael Grylls. Ian Greer's long-standing associate was now running an operation which presented itself as an exclusive club for political insiders, but was essentially a money-making scheme. Grylls chaired the donation-chasing Conservative Industrial Fund. He had the acquisitive Tim Smith MP in tow, who had also risen in esteem and was now a Central Office deputy treasurer.

Four years earlier, on this same riverside terrace, Grylls had endured his tricky meeting with the political investigator

Andrew Roth, and had been forced to concede that Greer was paying him 'cash for introductions'. But that small awkwardness had been long since smoothed away. In the modern Conservative party, as in the Christian church, it seemed all sins were forgiven.

For the lobbyists and their lieutenants had continued to rise and prosper. Grylls' 'usual fee' from Greer was currently running at a steady annual £10,000 – although that was not a figure he chose to advertise. Both he and Smith had rewards for their fund-raising efforts from a grateful party – for Smith, a foot at last on the very bottom rung of the ministerial ladder – a junior post in Northern Ireland (in 1994); and for Grylls, a knighthood in 1992.

These men were getting money from businessmen and funnelling it discreetly to the party. Grylls' cryptically-named Industrial Fund had once been the receptacle for the best part of the secret £440,000 that Turkish tycoon Asil Nadir had handed over to help finance the Conservatives' 1987 election publicity campaign. Nadir, later wanted for fraud, wrote the undeclared cheques from off-shore accounts in Jersey of his British Polly Peck trading company, which later collapsed.

This riverside fund-raising scene is bathed in a further hazy light by Greer's later admission that he himself had been personally responsible for raising £750,000 and putting it into the Tories' pockets during his lobbying career. Secret party donations, private payments to politicians and the broking of political favours – all seem to blend and merge in the merry clink of glasses on the Commons terrace in the spring of 1993 into a complacent picture.

One wealthy man, however, was about to swing a hammer and crack the glass. In Knightsbridge, the owner of Harrods was still smarting, four years on, at the way ministers had consigned him to a DTI investigation whose leaked report doused him publicly with its dirty water, despite all his payments to lobbyists, politicians and party funds. It rankled that Hamilton, since he became a minister, had refused to speak to Fayed. He often said: 'The Government have shat on me.' Feeling that way was why Mohammed al-Fayed had decided to take his case to the European Court of Human Rights in

Strasbourg. It was to prove a doomed venture, but it was a decision which brought him into contact for the first time that spring with Peter Preston, then editor of the *Guardian*.

An unlikely – and dangerous – liaison began almost by accident. By then Peter Preston had been editor of the paper for 18 years. Preston's journalists were chasing the growing scandal of secret party donations, and that summer the *Guardian* led its front page with allegations (which it was later unable to substantiate) that the Saudi ruling family had joined the motley parade, handing over cash to a Cabinet minister for the 1992 election. Preston had vetted that story before publication, talked to the reporters on the case and been consulted at home late in the evening to hear that checks he wanted had been made. He knew it was going to cause a stink.

Next morning there was a call from Hugo Young, the *Guardian*'s chief political columnist and chairman of the Scott Trust which owns and guards the paper. He had been contacted by Anthony Lester QC (Lord Lester of Herne Hill), the Liberal peer who specialises in European Human Rights. Lester had the Strasbourg case for Mohammed al-Fayed on the stocks. The owner of Harrods, said Young, seemed pretty excited about the Saudi tale. 'If you want any help, he's ready to talk.' Help, as the day wore on, became wanted. One strand of the Saudi story led back to an excited Labour party; but Labour, having blown hot, suddenly blew very cold indeed. Conservatives queued up in the House for their moment of denunciation. Preston, tracking back on a variety of the sources, already knew the paper was going to have a tough time.

Twenty-four hours later, the editor was on the Harrods escalator, up five floors through milling shoppers and into the modest glass hole in the wall called the Chairman's Office. He had read, of course, all about the Fayed brothers from Alexandria – especially Mohammed, Tiny Rowland's adversary, fulminating star of one of the most lurid Department of Trade inquiries in history. But Lonrho's bitter, bruising battle for the House of Fraser was four years gone. Tiny himself was heading towards involuntary retirement, his Lonrho company no longer in his hands. And Fayed was the clear, continuing winner. Preston had never met him, or written about him directly. He put on the biggest pair of kid gloves he could find, and carried a very long spoon.

Fayed's office is small but heavily ornate, rather like one of the antechambers of Versailles. Fayed himself seemed ornate to Preston, a vivid, mobile Egyptian face stuffed into a striped shirt and glistening grey suit. He was indeed ready to talk – a torrent of words in a thick, initially bemusing accent. For half an hour, Preston struggled to get to grips with a saga of the 1980s full of Mark Thatcher, Margaret Thatcher, arms contracts, a baffling array of Saudi princes, and undeleted expletives in every sentence.

How, Preston asked, did this all fit with the latest Saudi storm? So Fayed paused and told him about Tim Smith, the MP for Beaconsfield and Deputy Treasurer of the Conservative party. 'He came to me before the election, pleading for money. I gave him a flea in the ear. "You're getting no more money out of me. Why don't you go and ask your Saudi friends?" And he said, "That's a good idea," and he left.' Preston could have steered the conversation back to the Saudis. But he knew a little about Tim Smith. A friend of a friend had once worked for him. So instead he said: 'How did you come to know Smith?' Thus Fayed, in full flow, began to talk about something entirely different. There was Ian Greer, the political lobbyist. 'He came to me when Rowland and Du Cann were shitting on me and said he could help. He brought me Tim Smith and Neil Hamilton.' They had asked questions in parliament for him, and they had been richly paid to do so. Thousands of pounds in envelopes, cash in hand. And Hamilton, now the DTI minister in charge – among other things – of corporate probity? He was a 'greedy bastard' Fayed said to Preston. He and his wife had stopped for a week at his Ritz Hotel in Paris, running up bills for thousands of pounds. They had eaten every night in its restaurant. They had drunk hugely expensive bottles of wine. They were . . .

But by this time there was a paper to produce and a Saudi crisis to try to deal with. Preston said he would like to meet again and returned to the *Guardian*. It was not the story he had gone to find. But it was, by any standards, a story which ought to be checked and, if possible, told. Not a one-off, an individual MP on the take – more of an orchestrated industry. And perhaps no wild allegation either: why should the man who paid the bribes put himself in peril by admitting as much to a journalist? Over the next few days, the editor pulled aside David Hencke, the *Guardian*'s Westminster investigator. Working with reporter John Mullin, he was to find out how many questions Tim Smith and Neil Hamilton had asked on Fayed's behalf, and whether money had been declared in the Registers of Members' Interests. They were to get a clearer picture of Ian Greer Associates. But they were also to go gently and cautiously. What Mohammed al-Fayed said was no more than highly interesting. It was not even the beginning of proof.

Hencke and Mullin set up shop in a pocket-handkerchief office hidden from the *Guardian* newsroom. They soon discovered Greer was the biggest and best-connected of the parliamentary lobbyists, but had few admirers in his trade. They unearthed his 1990 admission that he had paid money to anonymous MPs 'A', 'B' and 'C'. Greer had found £5,000 to publish a book of John Major's speeches and could, it seemed, occasionally get the Prime Minister along to dinners for his clients. At election times, his cars and his staff were available to help selected candidates. Such feats, however, were proof of nothing except his lobbying skill. What about Neil Hamilton's 1987 stay at the Ritz? Twice, in early July, Preston returned to Harrods after shopping hours, puffing up five floors when the escalators stopped. Mohammed al-Fayed was as helpful as before, but no longer alone. Either Michael Cole, his press spokesman (and a former BBC Royal Family correspondent) or Mark Griffiths, his young aide-de-camp, were there for meetings now. The Hamiltons, to be sure, had signed the Paris bill when they left. That bill had been located. Preston was allowed to examine it and take notes. But he could hear the sound of brakes beginning to be applied.

Fayed was proud of Harrods. He was prouder still of the refurbished Ritz. He – and his alerted advisers – were clearly anxious about harm to those businesses. The *Guardian* could be told what had happened: but it could not take a copy of the bill away. Hencke and Mullin had been ploughing away for nearly three weeks. On 22 July, they asked to see Tim Smith and Neil Hamilton in swift succession. They had a list of parliamentary questions that Smith had asked on behalf of

Harrods. The two reporters met him alone in a Commons committee room. They put it to him that he had been covertly paid. They reported back to Preston that the MP had been shaken to the roots, stammering and quavering: but he had denied everything. The only thing he had ever taken from Mohammed was a teddy bear. There had been a general invitation to the Tory backbench trade and industry committee to stay at the Ritz, promulgated through Ian Greer. But Smith had stayed clear of that.

Neil Hamilton knew Hencke quite well and was initially more welcoming when they met on the Commons terrace later that afternoon. The smiles faded quickly when the questions on cash for questions started, however. Hamilton, too, denied everything. But what about the Ritz stay? He might, he said, have spent a night there. Not a week? The reporters gave the details from the bill. The Minister's memory gradually revived. They thought they had caught him dissembling, but there was no straightforward admission. A long tape-recorded interview with Ian Greer the following day produced a harvest of telling quotes – 'The whole area of election expense is pretty grey'; 'I have never paid any election expenses for MPs' – but there was still nothing to the story that would get it on to the front page. An article was planned to coincide with Greer's regular, and lavish, reception at the autumn Conservative conference in Blackpool.

But as soon as the two reporters had visited him, Hamilton rushed back to his ministry and ordered officials to prepare him a list of what evidence the Department had on file about his links with Fayed. However, it was only during the party conference season – at which reporter David Hencke carried on questioning other lobbyists about Ian Greer Associates – that the minister's nerve appeared to crack. He sent Peter Preston a letter on 1 October. It was a good example of Hamilton's public style: self-confident to the point of bravado, blustering – and untruthful.

NEIL HAMILTON MP
House of Commons
London SW1 0AA

1 October 1993

The Editor
The *Guardian*
119 Farringdon Rd
London EC1R 3DA

Dear Sir,
I know from an interview with David Hencke in July and from reports of several people interviewed more recently he is preparing an article on Ian Greer Associates and the firm's alleged improper influence on ministers and MPs.

I have been told Mr Hencke intends to feature me prominently and has been boasting that I will 'get into a lot of trouble' as a result ... Almost all my time as a backbencher I was a trade and industry committee officer. Sir Peter Hordern MP was consultant to House of Fraser and in 1984 invited the officers to lunch at Harrods to meet Professor Roland Smith [then chairman] and fellow directors. The main issue was the continuing Lonrho offensive in the wake of the prohibition of the Lonrho takeover by the Government.

My view was that there was no public interest or consideration for the purposes of competition policy in the ownership of Harrods/House of Fraser. I supported the 1985 Tebbit doctrine (I still do as Competition Minister) that competition is the main test of public interest.

Peter Hordern asked me and fellow committee officers to accompany him two or three times over the next few years to see Trade and Industry ministers to discuss the public policy implications of the issue. This I was happy to do as I knew a lot about competition policy both as an economist and a lawyer. From what I knew about the Lonrho/Fayed feud, I sympathised with the Fayeds whom I felt were being unfairly treated.

At some time during these three years, Ian Greer Associates were engaged by House of Fraser to promote their case to parliament. My interest in this dispute predates such involvement.

Mohammed al-Fayed was refurbishing the Duke of Windsor's villa in Paris and invited me as part of a group of MPs, to go and see it, but to the best of my knowledge no such trip took place and if it did I did not go on it.

In 1987, my wife and I planned a motoring holiday in Alsace. I had come to know Mohammed al-Fayed reasonably well and, as a convivial person, I liked him. Talking about holiday plans, I told him what we intended, and he pressed us to drive via Paris, see the villa and stay in his private rooms at the Ritz. I accepted and we stayed several days.

Under the circumstances therefore, it is surprising that Mr Hencke claims to have a copy of a bill – which he declines to show me – if there is such a document, it can only be a notional transaction for internal accounting purposes as Fayed owns the hotel.

Clearly, Mr Hencke intends to criticise me also for not registering the Fayed hospitality in the Register of Members' Interests. There is more attention to the subject about registration of interests today than there was six years ago. The visit was, in effect, to his private residence in Paris, and therefore the question of registering the interest did not, I believe, arise.

He also intends, I gather, to make something out of the fact that subsequent to my stay at the Ritz I put down two PQs for written answer relating to the House of Fraser – copies enclosed. These are the only references to House of Fraser/Lonrho under my name in the *Hansard* index since 1987. It would seem rather difficult to justify any implication of impropriety on my part arising out of material so anodyne. The costs of investigation are always matters of public record.

It seems pretty clear that Mr Hencke is trying to weave a conspiracy along the lines of 'Greer lobbies for Fayed and persuades Hamilton to put down PQs etc. as a backbencher. Hamilton then goes into government as competition/company investigations minister and uses influence to promote interest of Greer client, Fayed.'

This falls down as I met Fayed through Peter Hordern before Greer was taken on. My interest in House of Fraser dispute predates Greer's involvement. I have taken no part of any kind in House of Fraser/Fayed matters since I joined the Government in July 1990 – in fact not since the summer of 1988.

In particular, almost as soon as I arrived at the DTI and discovered there were currently issues involving the Fayeds which fell within my responsibilities, I instructed officials not to send me any papers relevant to such matters; not to involve me in any way in meetings and if ministerial decisions were necessary another DTI minister should take them – which is what has happened.

This was on my own initiative. I felt it was wrong that I should have any part to play in a dispute where I had supported one of the parties in respect of some questions albeit those questions were now disposed of and the period concerned was several years prior to my assumption of office. In law I would be entitled to perform ministerial functions in this matter, but I have bent over backwards to avoid putting myself in a position where I could be criticised (however erroneously) for acting unfairly.

... You will note that I refer this matter to my solicitor and no doubt, you receive many such statements. I would only add that although litigation is both time-consuming and expensive for all parties, I fought a successful libel action against BBC Panorama some years ago – costing the BBC a total of £500,000. You may wish to check your cuttings. I will have no hesitation in pursuing the legal route again, which might be more necessary now because of my present ministerial position, if your newspaper prints any of the untrue facts and insinuations that Mr Hencke appears to be planning.

c.c. Messrs Peter Carter-Ruck and Partners

This long and considered letter avoided all mention of Hamilton's own connections with Ian Greer. It gave a wholly misleading impression of what had gone on. The letter also contained five direct lies. There were no 'private rooms' at the Ritz. There was indeed an itemised hotel bill, and Hamilton had signed for it. And – a blatant lie – it was untrue that Hamilton and Fayed were acquainted before Greer came on the scene. The whole relationship had been generated by the lobbyist. Hamilton had met Fayed at a lunch Greer himself organised. The fourth lie was that Hamilton had done nothing for Fayed after mid-1988. He had lobbied and pressured ministers on Fayed's behalf for a much longer period after the DTI report had been published, until December 1989. And the fifth lie was that Hamilton the minister had excused himself from Fayed-related matters 'on my own initiative'. He had done so only after an unwise letter to the Department from Fayed, and a considerable delay.

The two *Guardian* reporters, Hencke and Mullin, nervously put their heads round the door of the hall at the Pembroke Hotel in Blackpool on 5 October 1993. The hubbub of the annual Ian Greer Associates reception at the Conservative party conference was at its height. They need not have been fearful. As Hencke ruefully recalls: 'Ian Greer greeted us with open arms.' The lobbyist had decided, shrewdly, to treat the massive article that had appeared in that morning's *Guardian* as valuable publicity for the firm. 'THE POWER AND PRESTIGE OF IAN GREER' was the headline. Greer was probably right to take it calmly. It would do him nothing but good to have a major story in a liberal left newspaper, unenthusiastically pointing out his friendly relationship both with the Prime Minister and with his 1990 leadership campaign manager, Norman Lamont. The impressive list the journalists published of Greer's blue-chip clients and contacts – British Airways, British Gas, ASDA supermarkets, Kingfisher (who owned Woolworths) and Cadbury Schweppes, was, from one view, as good as free advertising. No-one was accused of cash for questions. The references to Greer's homosexuality were muted: 'Greer, who is unmarried, started a political consultancy business with his close friend John Russell ... Then came a bitter split ... Some say their personal relationship had disintegrated.'

Neil Hamilton himself, although he flung over his shoulder at the party the threat that he had already been on the phone to his libel lawyer, could not be pinned down. A passing paragraph mentioned he had stayed 'at a European hotel' at the expense of 'a leading British company' without declaring it. An elaborate verbal confection contrasted this behaviour with Smith and his attempts to declare a teddy bear. But there could be no wounding thrust. The *Guardian* was hog-tied by its inability to quote its source.

The original cause of that first encounter – Saudi funding for the Tories – faded away. Preston had become convinced that the story could not be made to stand up in essential detail. The *Guardian* eventually settled, and apologised.

Fayed and his advisers were reassured by the Ian Greer background article. The paper had not played fast and loose with a source. But essentially the *Guardian* was still on its own. Fayed was repeatedly told how much grief going public – with, say, Hamilton's Ritz bill – could cause to his business and especially to the French hotel he loved.

A couple of weeks later a very different stay at the Ritz – by Jonathan Aitken MP, then the minister in charge of arms sales – came to Fayed's attention, and he helped open a second line of inquiry with another pair of reporters from the paper. The question of who paid Aitken's Ritz Hotel bill – himself, his wife, or his Saudi associates – began to occupy the *Guardian*. Again, though, it was a question of trying to tease facts into the open independently of a 'deep background' source.

Mohammed al-Fayed was a problem and a puzzle. Why, the editor repeatedly asked himself, was he getting involved? Was there a motive beyond the wrath of an investor who had paid kilos of cash to MPs and lobbyists – and £250,000 to the Conservative party 1987 election effort after the wooings of its treasurer, Alistair McAlpine? (He had even, he said, interceded with the Sultan of Brunei to make sure that the McAlpine construction company landed the lush contract to refurbish the Dorchester Hotel.) Was the DTI report, with its catalogue of condemnations, a just reward for all this expense and friendship? Where were the promises now? 'They have taken away my family honour.' To be sure, Fayed was bitter. The Cabinet minister Michael Howard, in particular, lay at the heart of his resentment. That did not, however, seem the whole of it.

Public perceptions of Fayed – drawn from the pages of the DTI report – did not always sit neatly with the private man, especially with the protective shield of his aides around him. Then he was more the naughty schoolboy sent out to fetch a teddy bear while the hard men got weaving. Among many other things, Mohammed al-Fayed was still an Egyptian inno-cent abroad. He reminded one observer of a lad up from the country in a Ben Jonson comedy, immediately surrounded by the smart operators of Bartholomew Fair seeking to empty his purse.

Fayed, the hero of the Ritz rescue and restorer of the Duke of Windsor's Paris home, could have been a French citizen for the asking. Jacques Chirac was a personal friend. Fayed and his brother Ali, however, only wanted to be British. It seemed to Preston to be an emotional thing. 'The English ships passing, with the officers on the deck in their white uniforms ... men of efficiency and men of honour ... I dreamed of being like them.'

There was no more rational explanation. Fayed seemed to have set his heart on Britain. He spoke endlessly about the strengths of the ordinary British people – then contrasted those with his firsthand experiences of the political classes. Scorn and expletives mingled again. Were the disgust and disillusion genuine? There seemed no reason to doubt it. No conversation – even with his aides – passed without it. The rulers of Britain he had encountered wore soiled and grubby suits.

Nothing of substance that Fayed told the *Guardian* in the summer of 1993 changed over the next 14 months. But he was still constrained by those around him. He could prompt, but he would not finish. One day, perhaps in the future, the *Guardian* hoped, he would put on a white suit himself and walk the open deck.

It was late afternoon one day in January 1994, when Maurice Chittenden received the call that gave every *Sunday Times* executive that sinking feeling in the pit of the stomach: 'Andrew would like to see you now. Can you step in?' Crossing the open-plan newsroom, Chittenden wondered if he had done something to displease his notoriously ill-tempered editor, Andrew Neil. Six weeks previously, Neil had given Chittenden a plum job as head of the paper's investigative Insight team, with instructions that he and his colleagues should 'be like Rangers and Celtic and play four times a year'. One story every three months was a rare luxury in modern journalism.

Neil would probably soon become impatient. On the editor's wish-list for the new Insight team had been a quite unrealistic target: the 'head of a Government minister'. So far it was only the tabloids who had brought down ministers with revelations about sex scandals. Serious financial improprieties were rarely ever proved. But Neil was adamant. And now he was calling Chittenden into his office.

Fortunately, Neil was in good spirits. He had lunched with a 'prominent businessman' that day. The man was Fayed, who insisted that his name should not be disclosed (the *Sunday Times* never disclosed his identity then or later). He claimed that he had paid Members of Parliament to table written questions. Furthermore, he said he had been advised by his lobbyist that this was common practice. The going rate for a question was apparently £1,000. Neil may not have realised it, but at the time of their lunch, Fayed's brother's citizenship application was being blocked at the Home Office. That January, Fayed's *bête noire*, Michael Howard, now Home Secretary, and junior minister Charles Wardle, had been personally discussing the Fayed application. It may have impelled the Harrods proprietor to stir things up.

The Insight office sits in the converted Docklands warehouse at Wapping which houses Rupert Murdoch's *Sunday Times*. It was there that investigator Jonathan Calvert began the job of verifying Fayed's allegations. During subsequent conversations with 'the source', it appeared that the businessman had personally been involved with four MPs. But they could not be approached. This was an onerous condition and there were several attempts to persuade Fayed to drop it. But he was adamant. He wanted no publicity. Calvert was not completely disheartened. There were confirmatory Westminster rumours that MPs were secretly taking cash to ask questions. Indeed, there had been an academic work suggesting such a practice as long ago as 1985. The going rate was then £150 according to Professor Philip Norton in the book *Parliamentary Questions*. He wrote: 'Allegations have been flying about . . . It is not a criminal offence, but an MP would be an idiot to do it.' Six box files were amassed with computer print-outs of parliamentary questions dating back to 1983. Patterns emerged, with MPs showing an unusual interest in the most curious commercial causes. But none was conclusive.

Meanwhile, a second strand to the investigation was developing. The rumours said that Ian Greer Associates were paying MPs. Calvert rang the firm and said he was looking for someone to act as a lobbyist. Clive Ferreira, 'barrister at law' and director, was quickly summoned to the phone. Calvert explained his cover story. He was the owner of a Welsh haulage company called Red Dragon Transport which had suffered greatly because of the cost of tolls on the Severn Bridge. He wanted to create a parliamentary campaign to abolish them. Oily smooth and keen to impress, Ferreira said Calvert could not have come to a better place. 'If you look at the Early Day Motions and adjournment debates that we have introduced, I think you will find that it is a pretty impressive record.'

A few days later, inside the smart town house where Greer had his headquarters, Calvert was understandably nervous. Around the boardroom table Greer had assembled their six leading executives including Ferreira, Andrew Smith, Angela Bray and Jeremy Sweeney. They had clearly done their homework. Dressed in tweed suit, Bray, ex-Conservative Central Office, introduced the executives one by one and then reeled off a detailed history of the Severn Bridge. Andrew Smith, the neat, quietly-spoken young man at the end of the table, said that IGA's lobbying would begin by enlisting the support of local MPs.

Bray suggested that they would also approach MPs with a known interest in free trade. 'Perhaps we could arrange for you to meet Sir Michael Grylls. He is the chairman of the back-bench trade and industry committee and is keen to help business flourish,' she said. No mention was made, of course, that Grylls was on the firm's payroll. Indeed, all the talk was of persuading MPs by simply arguing a just cause. Sensing that little would be revealed in the initial meeting, Calvert decided to go for broke. He enquired whether they would able to arrange for questions to be asked in the House by MPs? The answer was yes. Calvert continued: 'I am very new to this. Would you have to pay the MP?' Sometimes a naive question elicits the most surprising of replies. But it can also fall flat.

Embarrassed laughter rippled around the table and quizzical looks were exchanged. Their suspicions had been raised. It was left to Bray to explain: 'We would never pay MPs.' The sting stalled. It was abandoned when the *Sunday Times* journalists learned that they were not the only ones trying to trap Greer. The tabloid TV investigators of 'The Cook Report' were also mounting a sophisticated sting operation against the lobbyist at the same time.

Squashed together on a sofa in March 1994, Ian Greer and his two colleagues appeared to have few qualms as they made their pitch to the openly gay president of the 'Ecocon' company and his young and handsome black assistant, 'Ben'. The antique-style tables and plush carpets made the £2,000-a-week No 43, Hyde Park Residence at 55 Park Lane, a plausible address for a wealthy international company looking for new business in Britain. Indeed Greer had instructed his colleagues Jeremy Sweeney and Richard Green to 'camp it up' in order to get this lucrative contract.

What they were not to know, as they glanced past the television screen opposite the sofa, was that inside the video recorder underneath was a tiny camera recording their every gesture. Another camera was in an ice dispenser on the window ledge, trained on them in case they moved. And the heavy curtains were wired for sound. The second journalistic sting to try to expose Greer was under way: once again, however, it failed.

At a lunch at the Tate Gallery, Sylvia Jones, former *Daily Mirror* crime reporter, had first recruited David Hencke of the *Guardian* for the 'Cook Report' sting, suggesting his original piece on Greer had told only half the story. 'If you read between the lines, it suggests the lawyers have had a good go at it,' she said. A tough blonde pro, she and ex-*Sunday People* reporter, Clive Entwhistle, had hatched a clever scam to hook Greer. They recruited Richard Roberts, a television agent who had worked in Los Angeles and Moscow, and interviewed various young black actors to play the part of Ben. The aim was to set up a company run by former Russian KGB men who had made $40 million from the sale of icons.

Jones wrote a scenario:

> Gay businessman and black 'personal assistant' front a new US company (probably registered in Delaware where regulations are lax), backed by black-market money from Russia ... He telephones the House of Commons, asks for the chairman of the trade and industry committee and will be put through to Sir Michael Grylls' office to seek advice about investing/buying one of the many Government agencies up for grabs under the Deregulation Bill ... Grylls, if he is true to form, will introduce our man to Greer ... Greer is homosexual with a special weakness for dark-skinned young men ... So our team should fit in well with the general Greer scene ... The gay network operates brilliantly throughout Whitehall and a phone introduction from another known gay is usually enough to elicit detailed confidential information from most government departments.

The memo went on to describe potential 'investments':

> The National Insolvency Agency would be particularly good because it is ... the direct responsibility of junior DTI Minister Neil Hamilton, who is also in charge of the Deregulation Bill ... Greer often asks for donations to the Tory party to oil the wheels for business deals ... once Greer is hooked, he apparently has fairly indiscreet conversations, so it should be possible to get him to explain where our 'fee' is going.

The scam was launched. A fake Los Angeles address, 15400 Chaplin (after Charlie) Way was created with a genuine telephone number placed inside a cupboard in a television station. An answering machine would handle all calls. On 2 March, Sir Michael Grylls MP agreed to meet 'Richard' and 'Ben' in the Commons. After listening to their plans, he suddenly remembered there was a company, within walking distance from parliament and, apparently trying to recall the name – finally said: 'At St Catherine's Place called Greer' – spelling it G-R-E-E-R. He then had to find his notebook before giving them the full address and telephone number. 'They know everybody. They are public affairs consultants. They have their finger on the pulse,' he said.

Events moved almost too fast, and exactly to script. Ian Greer took a personal interest, never seemed to suspect, and started boasting of his contacts with Lord Moore, John Major ('He's a good friend'), Michael Portillo and Neil Hamilton. He started admitting that he could table parliamentary questions: 'We would never go out and say we can arrange to have a question tabled, but actually we can.' Greer suggested they should meet Neil Hamilton. The Cook team made plans to hire a Spanish castle for such a meeting, to tempt the man who enjoyed freebies in Paris.

All went swimmingly until panic struck the team the following month. 'There's been a leak in the TV world,' Sylvia was warned. Rushed meetings led the team to decide it was too dangerous to continue for now. They beat an orderly retreat, paid Greer a £10,000 first instalment in cash, and pretended they were temporarily going back to Russia.

Worse was to come. *Guardian* editor Peter Preston had a Carlton Television encounter where it became clear to him that the 'Cook Report' sting had not just been delayed but abandoned. It later transpired that Carlton Television themselves had been clients of Ian Greer. Their PR man, Peter Ibbotson, had been close to him. A reluctant David Hencke was pressed by Peter Preston to write up the available transcripts of 'The Cook Report' tale without informing the television team. The tale of the aborted sting was a good story, but far from fatal to the sleazers. Following publication, Greer called in a team of high-priced security experts, Ian Johnson Associates, to sweep his premises for bugs. The sleaze machine had once again had a mysterious escape.

Stimulated – or perhaps stung – by 'The Cook Report' affair, the *Sunday Times* returned in June to their frustrating tip from the 'prominent source' about cash for questions. Mark Skipworth, the deputy Insight editor, spent a Saturday afternoon reviewing the earlier work and was struck by a thought. Why not approach some MPs directly? After consulting the Press Complaints Commission Code of Practice, it was decided that the exercise could be defended in the public interest. Ten Tory MPs and ten Labour were chosen. All had previous records of outside interests but they were, otherwise, selected at random. They were to be offered £1,000 to table a written question, which would be of benefit to no-one other than the person who was paying the money.

Calvert handled the Conservative MPs. Graham Riddick, the member for Colne Valley, was at his home in West Yorkshire when he received the call from a mysterious businessman called Jonathan Calvert. The undercover reporter explained that he was looking for somebody to do public affairs consultancy work and that Riddick had been suggested by a neighbour. 'It might require, say, a parliamentary written question,' Calvert added. Rather than sending this suspicious character away with a flea in his ear, Riddick arranged to meet him at the House of Commons at 10 am the following Tuesday. He said: 'Look forward to seeing you then. Bye bye.'

In London, 5 July 1994 was a sunny day. Riddick met Calvert at the St Stephen's entrance in the Commons and led him through to the terrace overlooking the Thames. While Riddick sipped his cup of tea, Calvert outlined his proposal. He said he was about to buy a company called Githins Business Resources and wanted Riddick to table a question asking the value of contracts the company had with the DSS. Calvert said he was willing to pay for it and Riddick enquired what it was worth. Calvert replied £1,000 and Riddick said, 'That's fine.'

Sitting on the District Line tube afterwards, Calvert's heart sank. A pause button of his tape recorder had clicked on by mistake as he concealed it in his pocket before the meeting with Riddick. None of the meeting had been recorded. So after returning to the Insight office, he immediately phoned Riddick under the pretext of discussing a CV the MP had requested. This time the tape recorder was running.

On the tape, Calvert asks: 'What do you want me to do about paying you the £1,000? Would you like me to put the cheque in with the résumé or would you rather do it after the question has been raised?' Riddick replies: 'I don't really mind. I mean, why don't you just send that – why don't you just send it to me? Do you want my home address?' Later Riddick was to post back the cheque, saying on reflection it was inappropriate. By then he had been told that the Department of Social Security had no knowledge of the company.

On Thursday, Calvert was back on the Commons terrace, this time to meet David Tredinnick, Tory MP for Bosworth. Tredinnick was handed a question about how many times a drug called Sigthin (another anagram of Insight) had been prescribed on the National Health Service. Calvert said he wanted to invest in the company making the drug.

Tredinnick asked: 'I thought this was going to be consultancy?'

Calvert: 'I don't know if this is the sort of work you do.'

MP: 'It's hardly work.'

Calvert: 'But I mean I will pay for it.'

MP: 'I'm not sure whether I . . .'

Calvert: 'It's worth about £1,000 to me, partly because I can negotiate with them and, really, I don't want to put in a lot of money and find at the end of the day that I have wasted my money.'

MP: 'Okay. Well, I'm just going to check on the upstairs office to see what they think of it. I don't see any reason why I shouldn't proceed with it.'

Later that day, Calvert's handwritten question was tabled. It said: 'To ask the Secretary of State for Health, how many times the drug Sigthin has been prescribed on the National Health Service over the past three years.'

The splash headline in the *Sunday Times* that weekend read – 'REVEALED: MPS WHO ACCEPT £1,000 TO ASK A PARLIAMENTARY QUESTION'. It went on:

Senior MPs are abusing parliamentary privilege . . . An investigation by the *Sunday Times* Insight team found two leading Tories willing to table official questions in the House of Commons in return for £1,000 . . . Sir John

Gorst, MP for Hendon North, a director of his own consultancy business, offered to do it for free, but said he was happy to discuss a future 'arrangement'. He said: 'It's legal but it doesn't look very nice if you simply ask questions because you have been paid to do so.' None of the Labour MPs would take part in arrangements to 'buy' a written question. 'Members of parliament do not deal with it in that way. I would see your local MP,' said Gordon Oakes, MP for Halton.

John Major was in Naples for the G7 summit of leading industrial states when he heard from the Chief Whip, Richard Ryder. Before the day was out, both Riddick and Tredinnick were suspended as Parliamentary Private Secretaries to ministers. Fayed was quite impressed with Andrew Neil's newspaper coup. 'He's got balls,' the Harrods boss said. In parliament, the Speaker referred complaints against the MPs to the Privileges Committee. But the conduct of the *Sunday Times* was also to be investigated.

The Privileges Committee had its usual in-built Conservative majority. Tony Newton, the Leader of the House, had the chairman's casting vote. Considerable pressure was put on the Tory members to exonerate the MPs who had tabled questions for cash. But this was not so easy. A radio telephone poll taken in the immediate aftermath of the cash-for-questions story showed that 79 per cent of callers supported the paper and did not regard what had happened as entrapment. But if the MPs were to be punished, the trade-off for the Tories was to be strong disapproval of the actions of the *Sunday Times*. The mood was hostile when John Witherow – now the editor – and his team appeared before the assembled MPs on 25 January. The desks formed a U-shape with the Tories on the left and Labour on the right. David Alton, the lone Liberal Democrat, sat among the Tories, who also dominated the top of the table where Newton was flanked by Attorney General Sir Nicholas Lyell and Dame Jill Knight.

Tory Sir Marcus Fox – arms folded and body swivelled with his back to the witnesses – tutted as each member of Insight spoke. In an earlier session dealing with Graham Riddick, his only contribution had been to plant a favourable question about the failed tape-recording. He asked Riddick: 'To put it mildly, I think there is something fishy about these missing tapes . . . how helpful would these missing tapes have been for you?'

Ironically, one of the senior members of the Privileges Committee was the Labour MP for Warrington, Doug Hoyle, who had taken elections funds from Greer. Hoyle's most striking contribution was an ill-tempered attack on the Insight editor for refusing to disclose his own salary at the *Sunday Times*. Hoyle did also mount a robust assault on the MP Riddick for his 'consultancy' with the Brewers' Society. And he might have considered that the hearings had nothing directly to do with Greer or lobbyists. Nonetheless, it seems wrong that Hoyle should not have disclosed his links to Greer. The journalists concerned would certainly have had very different emotions had they known about his connections.

After private deliberation, the conclusions of the committee were perhaps predictable. Riddick and Tredinnick were both briefly suspended from the House, but the final attack was reserved for the journalists. 'We conclude that, taken as a whole, the *Sunday Times*' conduct fell substantially below the standard to be expected of legitimate investigative journalism.' The same might have been said about the standard of conduct of parliament's self-regulating committees.

By September 1994, nothing was moving. The *Guardian* effort to expose the sleaze machine seemed becalmed. There had been no contact with Harrods for months. Then Mohammed al-Fayed's office called Peter Preston. Could he fix a time to pop round on the evening of the 19th? The fifth floor was not quite as the editor remembered it. There were fewer people around; it was somehow darker and chillier. Fayed himself was alone. Michael Cole and Mark Griffiths were away somewhere or other, unspecified. Mohammed looked a little dishevelled, shirt undone, jacket discarded, grim and upset. They drank whisky. Only a young Spanish girl seemed to be on the scene: she was sent down to the food hall to see what canapés were left.

For years, Fayed had put faith in his case to the European Court of Human Rights to demolish the Department of Trade investigation. A formal verdict was expected within 48 hours. It did not look as though it would be good news. Suddenly the constraints of what could or couldn't be said publicly began to burst apart. 'Now we show the bastards, now I right behind you,' he said. Preston did not doubt that. One interesting conclusion from over a year of Fayed experiences was that Mohammed did what he said he would do and delivered on promises – in this affair, he was a man of his word.

The reason why Ian Greer had first caught Preston's attention was that the testimony about him was firsthand. Fayed himself had engaged Greer and the associates. Fayed himself had met Smith and Hamilton one by one and, in his own words, passed over the cash envelopes. He was not a second-hand source.

The crux was whether, at last, Fayed would be prepared to step into the light and put the undoubted documentary proof he possessed – that Ritz bill signed by Neil Hamilton, and probably much more – on the record. Fayed said, unhesitatingly, that he would. It was not where he had started: but he took the prompt. At last, perhaps, the *Guardian* was about to grasp the thread that would unravel everything. Yet Preston was more thoughtful than celebratory in the taxi back to the office. He thought: 'We have all been here before.' There had been moments in 1993 when Fayed had appeared ready to take a chance and open the can of worms himself. But always his protectors had pulled him back. Once his fury about the Europe case faded, would that all happen again? Nothing could prudently be done until Cole (Fayed's PR man), Griffiths (his aide), and Webb (his lawyer), were back in town and back on the case.

Over a week passed. The *Guardian*, once slightly bitten (or at least over-enthusiastic) was feeling twice shy. Fayed, it subsequently emerged, was ploughing on elsewhere regardless. He called in the lobbyist on 22 September and gave him a tongue-lashing for all the money which Greer had separated him from over the years. Fayed was also calling in opposition politicians and giving them the full treatment on Michael Howard, his Cabinet 'Public Enemy Number One'.

Fayed summoned Brian Hitchen, the editor of the *Sunday Express*, too. Hitchen was on friendly terms with Preston.

They were both members of the Press Complaints Commission, and the *Guardian* editor rather admired the way the short, stocky, bald tabloid survivor waved a big cigar and encouraged lay members of the Commission to confront a world he helped to make real for them. Fayed was another admirer. Hitchen was highly spoken of as a bulldog, and had supported a charity for which Fayed – characteristically – had opened his cheque book wide.

There is a tape transcript of the Hitchen-Fayed meeting on Tuesday 27 September, which might form the basis of a textbook on mutual misunderstanding. Fayed delivered, for the umpteenth time, his standard British corruption lecture, including his complaint about Hamilton's snubs. 'And still there's lot of things I'm researching and a lot of shit's going to come out, especially Margaret Thatcher, right?' Hitchen took it as something else, as an ultimatum to Major that Fayed would blow the gaff unless the Prime Minister found a way of scrapping the hated DTI report. It was a ludicrous misreading. Fayed had already offered the Hamilton story to Preston to print on the record eight days before. The gaff had long since been blown. A queue of politicians were, in any case, also getting the tale from Fayed day by day.

The tabloid editor went to Major in Downing Street on Thursday the 29th. He said he wanted to tip him off about Fayed's plans, behind the Egyptian's back, and named Michael Howard, Jonathan Aitken, Neil Hamilton and Tim Smith as ministers who were the targets of Fayed's ire. Hitchen's version, both of the allegations and of cause and effect, was full of error. And after his 'tip-off', what followed was a saga of confusion, dilatoriness and ineffectiveness at No 10.

The Prime Minister, in a lather of propriety, summoned his Cabinet Secretary, Sir Robin Butler, and told him to investigate. Later, Major was to go to the House of Commons and denounce Fayed as having made a crude attempt at blackmail, which he asked the Director of Public Prosecutions to examine. In any event, the Cabinet Secretary was hardly Sherlock Holmes: more Inspector Clouseau with a public school accent. He had earlier in the year already exonerated Jonathan Aitken. The *Guardian* editor, Peter Preston, had actively sought and secured a Butler inquiry, while trying to clear up the baffling minutiae of payment for Aitken's own stay at the Ritz (not paid for by Fayed). Butler's investigation turned out to consist largely of the mandarin calling in the minister in question and receiving a personal assurance. Sir Robin began his new 'work' on Friday 30 September. He dismissed the names of Howard and Aitken at once, saying that any abuse coming from Fayed about them was well known and incorrect: there was nothing to investigate. In any case, as he correctly established, no question arose of either of them taking money for asking parliamentary questions.

Both Hamilton and Smith, the records showed, had indeed lobbied and asked PQs on Fayed's behalf as backbenchers. Major and Butler had to deal personally with these potential scandals, and also devise a strategy for Hitchen – the tabloid editor would have been acting out of professional character if he did not try to milk the PM for information in return for his hot tip. The politician's nightmare would be for a story to break during the pending party conferences.

The obvious minimum step was for Butler to seek out the two junior ministers. The pair would have been down at the party conference in Bournemouth, not far away. But in a display of apparent dithering, more than a fortnight went by while Sir Robin 'investigated'. Eventually, he discovered that the allegations against Tim Smith were true, and against Hamilton at least partly true.

Smith, the obscure little accountant, whom no-one had ever found interesting before, confessed and shocked his colleagues. Knowing he had declared fees from Fayed on his tax returns, he was unprepared to bluff it out a second time – his encounter with the *Guardian* must have been traumatic. Hamilton was far more truculent. Sir Robin, following his usual laid-back routine, gave him ample advance notice to prepare his account. When Hamilton eventually arrived at the Cabinet Office, he repeated to Sir Robin the 'cover-story', as told in his original lying letter to the *Guardian* – that he had met first Fayed through Sir Peter Hordern, the House of Fraser backbench consultant, and not through Greer. He tried once more to give the impression that he had asked only a handful of PQs on Fayed's behalf, and that he had merely stayed in Fayed's 'private accommodation' at the Ritz. But, however much Hamilton denied taking cash, there was no doubt he had enjoyed an undeclared hotel visit.

The stocky figure of editor Brian Hitchen could have been seen making his way towards Downing Street, on the evening of Tuesday 18 October, hoping for an up-date from Major's office. Alex Allan, Major's civil service Chief of Staff, stalled him until the weekend. This suggests that no-one at 10 Downing Street really knew what to do. There were repeated further meetings with the Chief Whip, Richard Ryder, who ordered Hamilton to write out and sign a personal statement that he had done nothing discreditable. However, what none of the politicians realised was that they had already run out of time.

The *Guardian* had not been idle since Fayed had offered to blow the whistle. Peter Preston had seen the Harrods proprietor – and his returned team of advisers – twice during the first three weeks of October. It was clear that the Harrods watchdogs had been called off – indeed, better than that. As Michael Cole put it: 'Mohammed is just very clear that this is what he wants and what he believes in. He's prepared to put himself on the line, and we accept that.'

Accordingly, a search through the Harrods files began and, almost daily, letters and questions put by Neil Hamilton and Tim Smith were starting to arrive at the *Guardian* – often by fax. There was no single file. There were constant new finds. But Preston's earlier anxiety about lack of documentation was soon blowing away. He called David Hencke at the Labour party conference to tell him to stand by for more action. A week later, both he and Hencke were at the Conservative conference in Bournemouth when a call from the editor's secretary told them of another bumper bundle of letters pouring through the fax.

On 18 October, as parliament resumed and Hitchen returned to Downing Street vainly asking for an up-date, Peter Preston had one last meeting with Fayed. 'Do you absolutely realise,' he asked him, 'how much shit is about to hit the fan?' On the morning of the 19th, Hencke went to Harrods and conducted a formal interview with Fayed for the story he would write that afternoon. He came away with the key quote in his book: 'Greer told me "you need to rent an MP just like you rent a London taxi".' At last, virtually 15 months from the beginning, the *Guardian* would be printing the story it had been looking for.

Preston himself went through Hencke's first draft and took over the newsroom terminal for a few minutes to fiddle with the intro. Then came the long wait until 8.30 pm, when the first edition of the paper was flashed to the printers. At 8.40, the die was cast.

'TORY MPs WERE PAID TO PLANT QUESTIONS SAYS HARRODS CHIEF'

In newspapers, you can tell when you have got a sensation on your hands. The other papers and television stations start to call up with questions as soon as the first edition hits the street. By midnight at the *Guardian* that night, all the phones were ringing.

Next morning, a fax from Greer Associates denied the report in every particular and called down a plague of writs from the feared legal firm of Carter-Ruck. This was not unexpected, but not heartening either. The *Guardian* had, of course, no idea that Downing Street had been in a fever for weeks, and was already rapidly despatching the wretched Tim Smith to the crocodiles. The dam of anxiety only broke at the newspaper when the official announcement came that Smith was resigning as Northern Ireland Minister. He had indeed taken fees from Fayed.

If the story was 'entirely without foundation' according to Greer in the morning, it was looking pretty well founded by early afternoon. John Major was under fire in the House. Smith was allowed to pass into backbench obscurity rather gently as a stalwart chap whose offer to resign had already been made and accepted. The Prime Minister did not say why at least four days of silence had then supervened.

But in an ante-room in the Cabinet Office, Neil Hamilton, by perhaps predictable contrast, was hanging tough, denying everything, and ringing up Carter-Ruck on his own behalf to issue writs against the *Guardian*. The Chief Whip suggested he resign too, but Hamilton insisted he could stay and fight the libel case. Out in the Commons corridors and bars that afternoon, the Whips reported that feelings were distinctly mixed. Quite a number of Hamilton's colleagues were unhappy about his stay at the Ritz: many wanted him to step down 'to clear his name'. More ominously, whispers began on the day of the article that Hamilton had also been mixed up with a collapsed company. The rumour-mill was undermining him.

What saved Hamilton from the sack on Day One was a crucial lie he told to Michael Heseltine. The President of the Board of Trade was a veteran political operator, with an impressive history for smelling possible cover-ups and distancing himself from them. While at the Ministry of Defence a decade before, he had arranged a departmental search to unearth the facts about Mrs Thatcher's controversial sinking of the Argentine cruiser *Belgrano* during the 1982 Falklands War. When the scandal of that decision was investigated, Heseltine looked clean. Also, during the infamous Matrix Churchill case over exports to Iraq, ministers were told by Government lawyers to sign highly questionable Public Interest Immunity certificates to conceal the way British intelligence had been using businessmen. When the Scott Inquiry about arms to Iraq investigated, there on the records was the fact that Heseltine alone had refused to sign. He was clean again.

And during the BMARC affair, when there were allegations that a company linked to his Cabinet colleague Jonathan Aitken had been selling arms to Iran, it was Heseltine who stood up in the Commons and announced he had personally discovered intelligence reports about the destination of the arms, which it was his duty to disclose. He took very good care to maintain a reputation as Mr Clean.

On the day of the *Guardian* article, Heseltine, who was Hamilton's boss at the DTI, rang him and asked the one question Butler and Ryder had not previously had the wit to raise. Hamilton denied taking cash directly from Fayed. But had he had any financial relationship with Ian Greer, his lobbyist? Heseltine's question was spot on. Hamilton had taken thousands from Greer, not to say several expensive items of garden furniture. Hamilton responded with a direct lie to the question. He said 'No'. (Later he said the call was 'fraught' and he had misunderstood.) Heseltine withdrew his objections to Hamilton staying on. It was in the end to prove a lie too far. But for now, it worked. John Major, however reluctantly, fell in on grounds of 'natural justice' with Hamilton's stubborn refusal to quit.

For the rest of that week the minister, and his omnipresent, strong-willed wife Christine, lay low. But by the weekend, they were out in his Tatton constituency for a fête, with Hamilton bizarrely waving a ginger biscuit he had been given for a mêlée of photographers and offering 'to declare it'. Such jokes are dangerous. The charges were grave but he seemed merely frivolous. He gave an interview to his local paper and compared his decision not to resign and to fight a libel case, with John Major's own pursuit – in office – of *Scallywag* magazine about allegations of an affair with a catering lady which never happened. That was no joke at all. Conservative MPs winced in private at the way Hamilton had seemed to yoke himself and the Prime Minister together. This man had been stood by at the outset; he had been given the benefit of the doubt. But was he seriously worth defending if he behaved like this?

Only five days after the original story, Hamilton was summoned back – over lunchtime – to London. Butler and Heseltine and Richard Ryder, the Chief Whip, faced him at the Chief Whip's office in No 12 Downing Street. They said that three more disclosures gave them concern and Hamilton would simply have to go. Since he had refused to quit, newspapers had revealed that Hamilton had joined the South-African-backed lobbying firm, Strategy Network International (SNI) without declaring it. The Whip planted on the Members' Interests Committee, Andrew Mitchell, had discreetly reported back the committee's possible reaction. He had spoken to the registrar who managed the committee: 'He does not think they would like it.'

Secondly, one of the backbenchers had reported an allegation to the Whips: a friendly tax accountant had tipped him off that Hamilton had also taken money from Mobil Oil to ask PQs.

Neil Hamilton's £10,000-a-year non-executive directorship of the shady Plateau Mining Company (whose shares dropped from 90p to 13p), taken up in 1990, had not been an illustrious qualification for the top Government job in corporate affairs. Especially when Hamilton's own department were now investigating Plateau and a number of its directors. Plateau – part-owned by the Welsh blue-chip mining consultancy Robertson Research – had raised £16 million with Hamilton on the board before its collapse.

And although Hamilton had resigned his post when he joined the Government as a Whip in July 1990 (he appeared to draw his pay from Plateau until September), the mining company came back to haunt the minister.

Before the DTI's investigations team reported on the company, word came in that Harlech Television in Wales was about to blow the lid on the whole scam. As a result, the Conservative Whips made their own inquiries, only to find that the minister's directorship had linked him to a potentially murky operation, and a criminal investigation against directors of the parent company, Robertson.

The Whips learned to their gloom that Hamilton had attended a Plateau annual general meeting while a minister ('for a good lunch', he explained). Moreover, he had also given a reference to John Bird, the former managing director of Plateau who was applying for the job of chairman of the Coal Authority – a DTI appointment. Unsurprisingly, Bird failed to clinch the post.

But the real concern was an investigation by the Serious Fraud Office into another company which had Robertson as its parent – a sort of commercial 'cousin' to Plateau: Butte Mining, which had wanted to go into the gold mining business in Montana. There were irregularities in this company's flotation, and charges ensued against the former head of Robertson's minerals consultancy, Malcolm Clewes, and Clive Smith, an entrepreneur connected to Robertson. More damaging to the Government was another charge against Roy Bichan, a former non-executive chairman of Robertson, whom the Conservatives had appointed in 1993 as deputy chairman of the Welsh Development Agency. Bichan had resigned his post, the day before the charges were made.

Hamilton had explanations. He had registered as a consultant to Mobil Oil, at least in 1990. He had not registered SNI because the job stopped when he went into Government. He had declared Plateau Mining, and knew nothing of any irregularities. But he could not continue as minister in charge of corporate probity with so many allegations swirling around.

Hamilton fought back as he always fought back. But the Government had decided to dump him, and that was that. By teatime on 25 October, Neil Hamilton had ceased to be a minister.

John Major announced grimly that he was forming a new Committee on Standards in Public Life to clean up Westminster, and that Lord Nolan – a quietly rigorous High Court judge – would head it. Yet the full corruption of Westminster was still concealed. And as far as Hamilton the embittered ex-minister was concerned, 'down' was not necessarily going to mean 'out'. As he later said in an unusual moment of insight: 'Few accept their fate gracefully. I know I didn't.'

With the vengeful ranks of the Tory right cheering him on, he pushed off on a roller-coaster ride to dish the *Guardian*, circumvent parliament, change the Constitution itself, and prevail over the courts. It was a performance entirely worthy of Alan B'stard MP. Grandiose as ever in his predictions, Hamilton quoted to journalists what Randolph Churchill said of Disraeli's career as a Victorian Prime Minister: 'Failure; failure; failure; partial success; renewed failure; ultimate and complete triumph.'

Geraldine Proudler, the *Guardian*'s solicitor,
who second-guessed the Hamilton–Greer hand

11

The Weed Through the Tarmac

'Like the toughest weeds which will burst through the tarmac to reach the light, I can't suppress the instinct to fight my way back.'

Neil Hamilton, 16 May 1995

Geraldine Proudler is a person you would want to take to Las Vegas to play poker. It is a place where there is no day or night, only winning and losing for high stakes – and in that unforgiving world, Proudler could probably second-guess the opponent's hand. That is what makes her one of the most head-hunted of libel lawyers. Most British libel cases are games of bluff-poker which only the rich can play. But Neil Hamilton's intended comeback was to test the guile and intellectual resources Proudler had at her command to the absolute limit.

Born near the little Yorkshire port of Whitby, Proudler has one of those ageless, vivacious faces – could be 20, could be 40 – which are almost as attractive to women as they are to men. She dresses in a way that looks smart even when casual, uses her hands while talking and wears spectacles, but prefers contact lenses when having her photograph taken. She displays a combination of mischief and authority when talking about the mountains of legal documents piled up on the floor of her smart, airy office on the third floor of the First Chicago building in Covent Garden. The *Guardian* likes to blend mischief and authority, and so it makes sense that Geraldine Proudler should be the paper's solicitor.

One of a headmistress's six children, who went to Nottingham University, she has become among the most accomplished libel specialists of her generation ('although it's only my mother who accepts such a description'). Her handsome town house, off the King's Road in Chelsea, is in London's most fashionable quarter, and if there is one shop with which she is intimately familiar, it is that West End store over which rich men had already spent a decade quarrelling – 'Harrods is down the road from where I live. I spend quite a lot of time in there.'

Her most recent trip to Harrods in October 1994 had not been with a shopping bag, however, but with a legal briefcase. As the *Guardian* prepared to publish its cash-for-questions story, she had convened a surreal meeting on the fifth floor there, with Peter Preston and Mohammed al-Fayed. In the middle of these earnest proceedings, Fayed rose to his feet and left the room; Proudler presumed 'he'd gone to the loo'. To her dismay, he re-appeared bearing an outsize Harrods teddy bear, which he duly presented to the only lady in the room.

'It was utterly bizarre. Of course, this was a present, so I couldn't put it on the floor. That would look as though I didn't appreciate the gift. So I sat there talking about the case with this giant teddy bear on my knee. The teddy and I, with all those suits around me.'

Proudler knew this would be one of the *Guardian*'s most exceptional stories. There was always drama when Peter Preston phoned her in person as he had on 19 October 1994: 'He'd say, "Hello, how are you? . . . Good, excellent . . . Er, I wonder if you could just pop up the road." That meant something serious was going on. I knew when the article went into the paper (a) that we could expect to get sued, and (b) that we would have to justify and prove that what we had said was true.'

As the writs from Hamilton and Greer descended on the *Guardian,* the paper found itself embroiled in two other conflicts with prominent Conservative figures.

One was with Cabinet minister Jonathan Aitken, who re-appeared on the paper's front page as Fayed went public about *his* hotel bill at the Paris Ritz. The bill confirmed that Aitken, although he had never taken hospitality from Fayed himself, had stayed at the hotel with an Arab friend, in circumstances where it was unclear which of them had paid for what. In order to obtain a copy of the room bill without implicating the reluctant Fayed as the source, the *Guardian* had originally sent a fax to the Ritz on Aitken's Commons notepaper. That document now became described as the 'cod fax' as Aitken and the Cabinet Secretary Sir Robin Butler – who had known about it six months before – saw it fall into the *Sunday Telegraph*'s hands. Peter Preston was violently attacked for 'forgery' and made the subject of another Privileges Committee inquiry.

Meanwhile, the Conservative party's former Central Office director, multimillionaire Paul Judge, pressed ahead with a separate libel action against the *Guardian*, for reporting his unhelpfulness to accountants seeking to recover donations made to the party by the fugitive Polly Peck businessman, Asil Nadir.

Was the empire striking back? Maybe it was only paranoia that told Peter Preston so; but it seemed to be shouting at the top of its voice. For the embattled editor, 1994 slumped to a weary end. Preston and Hugo Young had had lunch in the summer of 1994 and the editor – appointed in 1975 and by this time the longest server on Fleet Street – had said that 20 years in the chair would be enough. He didn't want to keep the obvious successor waiting around for ever. In January 1995, therefore, Preston became editor-in-chief of the *Guardian* and the *Observer*, and Alan Rusbridger took over editorship of the *Guardian*.

By a strange twist, the day that Rusbridger was named as the new editor was also the longest day of Preston's long tenure. It was 24 January 1995. He waited, through that day, for the High Court jury to come back with a verdict at the end of the potentially catastrophic Paul Judge libel case. It was not until late in the afternoon that they returned. The paper had won. The millionaire had been sent packing. Newspapers rarely win in the British libel courts – right or wrong – and there was huge relief and celebration in the first-floor newsroom at Farringdon Road.

But minutes later, Preston had to leave the party. The car was waiting to take him to Westminster, where he was due for a grilling by MPs. Preston was to face a private hearing of the Select Committee on Members' Interests (chairman: Sir Geoffrey Johnson-Smith), who had been asked to investigate the Hamilton allegations. Preston had already supplied a copy of Hamilton's Ritz bill and a thick file of the parliamentary questions and letters Hamilton had fronted on behalf of Fayed. Now he was there, alone, to give evidence.

Unnervingly, Hamilton himself was also there, slipping into the ornate, portrait-hung room off the Commons committee corridor, and standing silently simmering at the back. When Preston began to give evidence, Hamilton moved to a chair two feet from the editor's back, glaring fixedly so that his eyes seemed to drill a hole. Throughout his 90 minutes of testimony, Preston could feel a cloud of loathing seeping over him.

The *Guardian* editor could see that this small 'jury' of MPs, with a majority from the ruling party, did not look remotely like the genuine High Court version he had experienced earlier in the day; and that its chairman, Johnson-Smith, a waxen political grandee whose golden hair seemed neither to have thinned nor faded since Preston had first met him 30 years earlier in the East Grinstead by-election, was a curious judge. He knew, too, that the previous June a Conservative Whip, Andrew Mitchell, had been slipped into the committee's ranks as the Government's eyes and ears. What Preston did not know – and did not find out until much later – was the way the committee had already been nobbled.

The very day the *Guardian*'s exposé broke, with the Commons in a ferment as one minister resigned and another battled for his skin, Geoffrey Johnson-Smith talked in the corridors to one of the Government Whips, the Prime Minister's confidant, David Willetts. In a piece of skulduggery which was to cause a huge parliamentary row when it surfaced, the Whip was reassured, according to Willetts' scrawled entry in the notorious Whips' 'black book', that a Hamilton inquiry could be either blocked by saying it was *sub judice*, or hurried through to an acceptable conclusion 'exploiting good Tory majority at present'. Of the alternatives, wrote Willetts unwisely: 'We were inclined to go for (1), but he wants our advice.'

The committee, with its Tory majority and its talkative chairman, did indeed refuse to investigate the main Hamilton allegation – that he had taken cash – claiming, as suggested, it was *sub judice*. So much for self-regulation by Honourable Members, which was plainly not something likely to stand in the way of Hamilton's comeback. But the second part of the story – Hamilton's admission that he had stayed at the Ritz for free – was not so easy to kick into touch. Instead, the committee were going through the motions of investigating it, with that exploitable 'good Tory majority'.

In the hot seat at the hearings, Preston watched the Whip Andrew Mitchell's eyes darting around the room as the editor's evidence continued. Mitchell asked no questions. Instead, Tories like Peter Griffiths and James Clappison went off on what was to become a familiar tack, painting him as a Fayed stooge. Why, Clappison asked, had the *Guardian* believed someone it had joined in dubbing a liar after the DTI report? Preston explained that he had not written everything ever published in the *Guardian*; he had come to this fresh. Why anyway, he asked back, had Tim Smith come calling on Fayed for more campaign money two years after the publication of that DTI report? If the Tories weren't put off when it came to cash, weren't they overdoing the moral outrage? The questioning grew a little more careful. Hamilton glared on.

'Not quite the new spirit of Nolan,' Preston said when he got back to his office. He saw nothing more of Hamilton until, in mid-summer, the Privileges Committee summoned him on the separate Aitken case, and there, pacing outside the committee room, was the MP for Tatton, still glaring. When the committee began, it went into closed session almost immediately. Could Hamilton be allowed in to watch? By the time they had decided he could not, the corridor was bare. The glare had gone elsewhere.

It took five more months and eleven meetings for Sir Geoffrey's inquirers after truth to decide, on rigidly party lines, that Neil Hamilton had been 'imprudent' not to declare his Paris holiday, but was perhaps understandably confused by the rules of the interests register at the time. No further action. Parliament may have been a soft touch, but for his comeback to succeed, Hamilton needed to crush the *Guardian* legally, and force it to retract. He may have thought the oppressive vagaries of British libel law were on his side. But to his initial dismay, he found that for once they were not.

Hamilton had raised the legal stakes about as high as he could. Quite apart from denying the payments, he had pleaded that he had been sacked as a minister purely because of the *Guardian* article (choosing to ignore the accusations about Mobil Oil and Plateau Mining). Proudler's legal response denied this claim and pointed the case firmly in one direction if it ever came to court: the Prime Minister, his departmental chief Michael Heseltine and the Chief Whip would all have to appear and be asked: 'Well, why did you ask for Hamilton's resignation?' The subpoenas were historic documents. They gave notice that the defendants 'intend to adduce' from John Major 'an account of all discussions the Prime Minister had with government members, the Cabinet Secretary and other government staff, including Neil Hamilton MP, of and concerning Neil Hamilton MP in the period 19–25 October 1994'. Heseltine was to be asked for particulars of 'the meeting held on the afternoon of 25 October 1994', with Sir Robin Butler, the Cabinet Secretary. The case might turn into a political striptease act.

Could there actually be a case at all, however? Both Hamilton and the paper naturally assumed so: Preston had always imagined that Neil Hamilton would want to see him in the witness box. However, when Proudler hired libel specialist James Price QC, an expert in constitutional law, he pronounced at once: 'This case can never come to court.' Price saw that the arcane rules of parliamentary privilege, recently freshly interpreted, and designed to give MPs immunity from the courts, made the case un-tryable. Under them, the paper, it seemed, could show that Hamilton took money, but it could not mention that he had done anything parliamentary for it, let alone asked questions at Westminster. Would any judge think that either fair or possible? Everyone wanted the situation clarified; Hamilton because he wanted to go to court, and the *Guardian* because Proudler dreaded a situation in which:

> . . .everyone turned up in court all ready for a trial and the judge said 'hang on a minute, what about parliamentary

privilege?' It clearly hadn't been sorted out, and we didn't want some half-baked order as a result of which the *Guardian* wouldn't have been able to call its evidence because so much of the evidence we wanted to call was of Hamilton asking questions in the House of Commons around the time he was getting money from Fayed. That was absolutely crucial. We would have been fighting with one hand tied behind our back.

At the High Court on 25 July 1995, Mr Justice May sensationally confirmed that the case could not be heard without infringing parliamentary privilege. Hamilton's motives for asking questions could not be admitted as evidence. The defence could turn to an edition of *Hansard* and show that the questions had been asked, but it could not ask why. Any evidence on that would have been an inquiry into the affairs of the House of Commons, he said, which was prevented by privilege. The paper could present evidence that Hamilton had received money, but the link between the money and the questions would have been a breach of that privilege. These restrictions made a fair trial impossible, and he therefore 'stayed' the case. The libel suit was frozen, and Geraldine Proudler, with some relief, oversaw the packing-up of the Hamilton case papers into cardboard boxes – she hoped for ever.

But Hamilton, the self-styled 'weed through the tarmac', did not give up the struggle. Instead, he went on to demonstrate a persistence which certainly would have taken a large dose of weedkiller to stop. Some fellow politicians backed him, for the halting of Hamilton's case came only a week after a judge had used similar arguments to halt a libel action by Rupert Allason, Conservative MP for Torbay. Almost as soon as the news broke, his heroine Lady Thatcher was on the phone to Hamilton, declaring herself 'horrified and outraged' that he had been 'denied access to justice'. Other MPs were quick to note that the judge's ruling could have implications for their precious selves. 'This leaves every MP open to the most enormous accusations levelled against them without any possible legal recourse,' clamoured Sir Marcus Fox, the megaphone chairman of the Tory 1922 committee, who had tutted and pursed his lips so ostentatiously while the *Sunday Times* cash-for-questions investigators were put on the parliamentary rack the previous year. Allason, who rarely resorted to understatement if exaggeration would suffice, predicted that: 'Newspapers will just say that their defence relies on a piece of paper which can only be found in parliament, or they will write stories in such a way as to link any misdemeanour about an MP with his parliamentary activity.' Even David Alton, the sometimes-liberal Liberal Democrat MP, described the ruling as 'a licence to print anything about an MP'. He said: 'It was surely never the intention that the rights of an MP should be less than those of an ordinary citizen.'

It is true that MPs' libel winnings over the years have provided a welcome supplement to many a parliamentary salary. However, as the long history of the cover-ups in the Hamilton affair showed, many instances of wrongdoing by MPs and other public servants which ought, in the public interest, to be made known, never see the light of day. The huge cost of defending a libel action, let alone the prospect of phenomenal damages, means that newspapers generally err on the side of caution. The European Court of Human Rights recognises this, and has repeatedly ruled that politicians in a democracy must be broad-shouldered and readier to take criticism than private individuals. In the United States, the Supreme Court has adopted a similar view, arguing that in a democracy the need for vigorous debate takes precedence over the hurt feelings of public servants. In American courts, the onus is on plaintiffs such as Hamilton to show that a newspaper which exposed them had known the story to be false or had published it with reckless disregard for the truth.

From time to time, the British media have tried to persuade judges to move in the American direction, as has Australia, though with little success. Only in a 1993 ruling that a local authority could not sue for libel did the House of Lords partially apply the ideas behind the American Supreme Court to justify its decision. The great difficulty in bringing about reform is that the people in a position to change the law are those who stand to gain personally from the status quo: the politicians. In any event, the Bill of Rights had rarely prevented Members of Parliament from defending their reputations; during the 300 years since it was passed, an estimated 2,000 MPs have succeeded in bringing libel actions against publishers. The idea that Mr Justice May's ruling amounted to a licence to defame MPs with impunity was ludicrous. The problem occurred only where allegations concerned an MP's parliamentary activity – and Mr Justice May's ruling made clear that the parliamentary connections would have to be so central to the case that their exclusion would make a fair trial impossible.

But encouraged by the baying of his colleagues, Hamilton began to look for alternative ways to force the *Guardian* to retract, while making a sizeable tax-free sum for himself. The Privileges Committee of the House of Commons had the power, if necessary, to subpoena all relevant documents and witnesses. But although the committee, if it found in Hamilton's favour, could impose an unlimited fine on the *Guardian* and conceivably imprison its editor, it had no power to award compensation to Hamilton or Greer.

Andrew Smith, managing director of Ian Greer Associates, began to organise another lobbying operation: this time for his own boss and Hamilton. His first PR project was to seek support to stage a full-scale libel trial under the auspices of parliament in the Palace of Westminster. Although such a procedure was unheard of in modern times, Smith argued, eccentrically, that there were ancient precedents. 'The same rules and regulations would apply as in a normal libel case,' he said. Response was sceptical: David Alton, a member of the Privileges Committee, warned: 'A procedure that is dragged up under some medieval piece of statute unused for centuries is always going to be open to subsequent challenge. For parliament to start taking literal judicial powers to ourselves would be an error of judgement.'

Geraldine Proudler, trying to unpack and set up the new office in Covent Garden to which she had recently moved, was startled to receive a pompously elegant piece of calligraphy from Hamilton's and Greer's solicitors, Carter-Ruck, on a huge sheet of paper – a hand-scripted 'humble petition' addressed 'to the Honorable the Commons [sic] of the United Kingdom of Britain and Northern Ireland, in Parliament assembled ...' At first she was baffled: 'It was going to be a parliamentary court, which is a novelty anyway. He was basically suggesting that parliament was going to sit and hear evidence on oath. Completely unheard of, we were on new territory now. Then I began to think – this is ridiculous, they're taking the bluff too far, suspiciously far.'

Hamilton wrote to Peter Preston himself, on 24 July 1995.

> My proposal is this ... The appropriate parliamentary procedures be set in train as soon as possible, with the parties agreeing to legal representation, and for evidence to be given upon oath in the same way as in a court of law. Were I to be vindicated, you would undertake to publish a full apology, to pay me damages to be assessed by an independent arbitrator if not agreed, and legal costs.

Preston replied dryly:

> Thank you for your letter which, by coincidence, I read in conjunction with your press release of the same date. In that release you variously state that the *Guardian* 'has perverted the purpose of the Bill of Rights and turned it into a Charter for Wrongs'; that we have 'relied on a technicality' to deny you access to justice; and that we are clearly 'scared stiff of exposing our case to the rigours of a High Court judge and a British jury'. Such claims, as their rhetoric makes clear, seem to me more rooted in politics than legal reality, which inevitably somewhat contaminates the substance of your letter.

Preston repeated the paper's charges against Hamilton and, on the question of trial by parliament, continued:

> I have recently, in a separate matter, had the experience of appearing before the House of Commons Privileges Committee and have great difficulty in visualising how and whether that committee could change its procedures to parallel 'the rigours of a High Court judge and a British

jury'. Could it sit continuously in public over a period of several weeks? Could it provide the right to subpoena documentation and witnesses to the list we have already provided? Could it enforce rules of evidence as to cross-examination of witnesses so as to ensure both sides are bound by the same procedures? How could we address the fundamental tenet of British justice that plaintiffs or defendants in a case should not be known to the judge or jury when, in this matter, all the MPs on the committee would know you, many would know Mr Greer personally from his lobbyings, and a majority would, like yourself, be Members of Parliament belonging to the Conservative party?

Hamilton's eventual reply was an unfocused rant:

In spite of your attempts to provoke me there is clearly no point in debating with you in correspondence the issues of fact ... The points you make about House of Commons committees apply equally to the Press Complaints Commission [of which Preston had been a member]. I do not recall your saying that it is wrong for representatives of the press to hear and deal with complaints against the press. You advocate principles of self-regulation for the press but are not prepared to accept it for MPs. I am not surprised by this, as your concern for fair play and natural justice does not extend to your own victims. ... Clearly, you regard the *Guardian* as exempt from the rules that govern ordinary mortals.

Preston showed this to Proudler. 'Great letter,' she said. 'Completely mad.'

The project for the 'trial by parliament' found insufficient takers. An even more remarkable scheme was now cooked up by Hamilton, about which the *Guardian* side first heard from a short article planted in *The Times* on 15 September, entitled: 'MP ASKS COMMONS TO BACK LIBEL FIGHT'. Hamilton had thought of a simpler – if far more drastic – plan: he would change the British Constitution so that he could have his day in court after all. In this, Lord Hoffmann, a distinguished judge and cross-bench member of the upper house, was to be unwitting stooge.

By coincidence, the Lord Chancellor's department had recently published a draft of a new Defamation Bill. Although the Bill proposed a number of minor changes to the libel law, the main impetus behind it had come from the sprawling growth of the Internet. Companies which provide Internet services, along with universities, hospitals and Government departments, were worried that they might be classed as 'publishers' under existing law and unfairly held responsible for defamatory messages transmitted by users of their facilities. The Bill aimed to exclude them from responsibility.

Hamilton and Greer set themselves the task of inserting a new clause into this Bill, amending the seventeenth-century Bill of Rights which governed the relations between parliament and courts, and allowing individual MPs such as Hamilton the right to waive their parliamentary privilege. Then he could re-start his libel case.

Their success was an astonishing lesson in lobbying – and in the event became a clear demonstration of the evils which result from allowing lobbyists to pervert parliament on behalf of private interests. One imagines that, in this make-or-break situation, Greer called in every one of his outstanding political favours, every large lunch at Wiltons, every contribution to campaign funds, every commission cheque. The amendment to the Defamation Bill was presented as non-party political and would be decided on a free vote. In the Lords, where it began, Lord Finsberg, a former Tory minister, rose on 8 March 1996 to support: 'an issue which concerns two friends of mine, Mr Neil Hamilton, Member of Parliament, and Mr Ian Greer, the lobbyist – from whom I had better say straightaway I have never received or sought any financial reward. Both have a case against the *Guardian* newspaper for defamation. I have known them as friends for well over 20 years.'

By the time the Bill reached the committee stage in the Lords on 2 April, Lord Hoffmann had been enlisted to propose the necessary amendment. This helped to maintain the illusion that the 'Hamilton clause' was a non-party issue. After an illustrious legal career, Hoffmann had become a Law Lord the previous year at the (relatively) youthful age of 61. The Hamilton clause was not his own initiative. 'It was as a result of a conversation with the Lord Chancellor. The Lord Chancellor felt he wanted the matter debated,' he said later. He was provided with parliamentary counsel to assist in the drafting.

Hoffmann emphasised that the new clause was 'an attempt at a constructive solution' which was not necessarily the last word on the matter: he was proposing it in order to initiate debate. Under pressure from peers who were sceptical about the amendment, the Lord Chancellor suggested that it was of such fundamental importance that it should be considered by the whole house after the committee stage and that in the meantime Lord Hoffmann should withdraw it – which he did.

The next attempt to insert the Hamilton clause into the Bill, at the report stage a fortnight later, descended into farce. Lord Hoffmann was no longer in the chamber when his time came to propose it – he was in the lavatory. So Lord Finsberg – Hamilton's and Greer's friend of more than 20 years – proposed it instead, saying that he did so 'in the momentary absence' of his Lordship, ad libbing until Hoffmann returned. The top of column 648 of the *Hansard* records an apology from Lord Hoffmann for 'choosing to leave at precisely the wrong moment'.

As before, the amendment had to be withdrawn, against Finsberg's protests. A number of peers were still unhappy about it, arguing that since it affected both houses of parliament, but mainly the Commons, it should not – as the Law Lord, Lord Simon put it – be 'just passed by one house and laid on the plate of the other ... It is hardly possible to exaggerate the constitutional importance of this matter,' he said, and it would be 'highly inappropriate' to attempt to pass it at such short notice and in an empty chamber. The only remaining opportunity in the Lords was during the Third Reading of the Bill. This was normally forbidden by the procedural rules of the House, but in order to indulge Hamilton's wishes, they were temporarily set aside.

After two sparsely attended debates on the Hamilton clause, this third and final attempt to insert it into the Defamation Bill, on 7 May, played before a remarkably packed house – at least on the Government side. This was such brazen party political business that Tory peers, including Lady Thatcher herself, outnumbered those on the opposition benches by roughly three to one. Watching over the scene from the public gallery, his grey hair neatly combed over his receding hairline, was the man for whom all this was being done: Neil Hamilton. The stooge, Lord Hoffmann, glanced around with consternation. 'The very large number of people who turned up made it look as if some sort of Whip-like activity had gone on. It looked like it was becoming politicised,' said this Merlin of the law, with new insight. 'Because I saw all these people, including Mrs Thatcher, I thought: "this is now becoming a political issue".' Party Whips were not supposed to drum up support for a free vote. To preserve the fiction, Conservative peers had instead been phoned directly from Downing Street. One said: 'It was made absolutely clear to me that ... the Prime Minister was relying on my support.' The Conservative party continued to deny any intervention: 'Neither the Prime Minister nor his office has ever been involved.' Only much later was Major himself to admit he had indeed 'steered through' the Bill, believing in Hamilton's innocence.

At the sight of the massed ranks of Tory peers, the now-enlightened Lord Hoffmann recoiled: 'I do not see myself in the role of a partisan advocate for this amendment,' he insisted. Lord Simon, a former Appeal Judge, objected: 'What will the public say if the Lords were to approve of a measure which allows a member to pick and choose to stand on his privilege when it suits him but to waive it when that suits him?' But Lord Aldington, a former Tory minister who fought and won a marathon libel case against Count Nicolai Tolstoy in 1989, spoke up for the Hamiltonites' private interest: 'Having decided to subject himself to the ordeal of libel proceedings, Mr Hamilton now finds he has come to a dead stop ... These proceedings have been stayed. For as long as they have been stayed, Mr Hamilton's character is stained.' Another Hamiltonite was the Labour Baroness Turner of Camden. 'I believe the allegations to be totally without foundation,' she said, to the surprise of none. She was herself on the board of Ian Greer Associates. Turning a blind eye to the packed Tory benches, the Lord Chancellor asserted that the Government was neutral but urged the peers to support the amendment. Lord Hoffmann absented himself again and ended up not voting for his own amendment. It was carried without him by 157 votes to 57.

In the Commons on 24 June, Labour spokesman Paul Boateng's prescient warnings of conflict between the MPs Neil Hamilton and Tim Smith were ignored: 'If another member who is involved in the proceedings is not prepared to waive his privilege, what will happen?' MPs glossed over the existence of their own immunities, under which they can recklessly defame other people, fully protected from lawsuits. It was a privilege Neil Hamilton himself had often exploited. Instead, the Tory Peter Tapsell painted a fantastical picture of the need to amend the Bill of Rights to protect cowering MPs against journalists. 'Individual members can be subjected to persecution, not from the executive or from the sovereign, but from what many people regard as an over-mighty press.' A secret whipping operation left Tory backbenchers in no doubt of the Government's view.

One unimpressed Tory informed the *Guardian* he had been accosted by an excited Hamilton and urged to vote for the amendment because 'The *Guardian* will never fight it. They'll back off – end of case.' The Commons divided almost entirely along party lines, voting 264 to 201 for Hamilton. Neil Hamilton voted in his own cause, along with the Prime Minister and a large part of the Cabinet. It was a masterly – if indefensible – piece of lobbying.

Hamilton was so excited and confident of victory that in July, after the amendment to the Bill of Rights had been approved by parliament, he held a very special dinner party at his London flat. Oddly, Ian Greer, his lobbyist friend, was not invited. The other illustrious guests at the mansion block included his comrade-in-arms against the BBC – Gerald Howarth and his wife, Julie. But Hamilton's coup was his guest of honour: Margaret Thatcher, accompanied by Denis. Waiters served at table and a special menu was printed which so impressed some of the guests that they later framed it. After numerous toasts, the celebrations were slightly marred when Lady Thatcher fell asleep, waking up to warm to her favourite subject, Germany's domination of Europe.

The vast Gothic entrance hall of the law courts in the Strand was almost deserted and echoed more than usual when the plaintiffs, defendants and their lawyers trooped in and headed up the stone staircase to Court 12, where Mr Justice May had been summoned back from holiday. Officially, by the middle of August, the legal world was in recess but, with the Defamation Bill due to become law in September, Hamilton and Greer assured the judge that they wanted to get their case back on the road as soon as possible.

Lord Williams of Mostyn spoke for Hamilton and Greer; James Price QC for the *Guardian*. Behind them, on the public benches, sat Neil Hamilton and his wife Christine, and Ian Greer with his partner, former airline steward Clive Ferreira. Hamilton, who found himself sharing a bench with the *Guardian*'s managing editor, Brian Whitaker, kept his distance by placing on the seat between them a case prominently displaying a British Airways Executive Club membership tag which, on closer examination, had passed its expiry date. After an hour and a half of legal argument, the Hamilton case was suddenly back on the jury list with the stay lifted – and scheduled for trial on 1 October.

Whether with forethought or not, Hamilton's and Greer's insistence on a trial at the earliest possible date placed it in the midst of the party conference season. The first week of the case was likely to be taken up with preliminary arguments – not the sort of stuff that would deprive Labour of its conference headlines. The interesting part – and potentially the most embarrassing for the Government – would begin in the second week, the week of the Tory conference.

In the meantime, both sides had little more than six weeks to prepare their cases. The *Guardian* also faced a further problem: allowing Hamilton to waive his privilege had not created a level playing field. Hamilton had waived his parliamentary privilege, but Tim Smith, the other MP in the original cash-for-questions story, still refused to do so. There were other MPs, too, whose evidence might help the *Guardian* to prove its case, all of whom were entitled to refuse to co-operate on the grounds of privilege.

'It was crucial,' Geraldine Proudler argued, 'to be able to say to the jury that Fayed was making payments to two MPs, and that one of them had resigned the day the article came out.' The *Guardian* could present Fayed saying that he paid Smith. And it could present Smith's letter of resignation, and John Major's reply. But after that, Proudler was back at the stage of a year earlier when Mr Justice May had stayed the case: the *Guardian* could not enter into the motive for Smith's parliamentary behaviour. If asked in the witness box (were it possible to get him there), Smith could simply refuse to answer, and be perfectly within the law. It was a nightmare of unfairness.

Besides that, none of the QCs who had worked on the case to date, on either side, was available for a trial on 1 October. The Hamilton side were apparently untroubled at having to find a new QC for the trial: they were presumably banking on a *Guardian* collapse. The *Guardian* had originally booked the acclaimed cross-examiner George Carman but he was embroiled in a three-month trial and unavailable. Whoever was going to take this brief would have to be ready to examine the Prime Minister, Heseltine and the Conservative Chief Whip.

Geraldine Proudler drew up 'a very short shortlist' of the few silks she thought might be available and up to the task, and sent it to the *Guardian*. On it was Charles Gray, as his name suggests the *éminence grise* of libel law. He too was unavailable. 'We were scrambling around in August with every barrister worth their salt in Chianti,' she said, '– and we needed a real gladiator.'

It was a fair summer in London. England performed estimably in the soccer championships, accompanied by some oafish xenophobia in the press. A heatwave bared and reddened the shoulders and legs of the capital, whose citizens were drinking coffee and beer along on the pavements of the city centre. The Conservative papers were talking about the 'feel-good' factor – a sort of counterfeit version of the swinging sixties, with Oasis, the poor man's Beatles, all the rage. But no-one was feeling very good in Farringdon Road at the offices of the *Guardian*.

Geoffrey Robertson QC, counsel to the *Guardian*,
dressed for a trial that never happened

12

A Liar and a Cheat

'God does not pay debts in money.'

Mohammed al-Fayed

The sweet evening light of the Tuscan sun was still stroking the valleys and cypress trees of Chianti-shire when the phone rang. The venerable stone of John Mortimer's villa, in the hills between Siena and Florence, was a fitting place for Geoffrey Robertson QC to be summering with the novelist Kathy Lette, his wife and Australian compatriot. This was the building Mortimer had rented in order to write *Summer Lease*, his infamously funny and self-deprecating portrait of the English colonisation of Chianti. And Mortimer's legendary character in his 'Rumpole of the Bailey' series had served as something of a role model for the young Robertson as he made his way to prominence at the Bar to become one of Britain's leading civil rights lawyers; indeed the omnibus edition of Rumpole yarns was dedicated to him.

When the phone call came in, Robertson and Lette were sharing a delightful moment on the terrace, the sun still up, the valley sweeping below them, pouring out the Chianti, ruby-red as it caught the hue of oncoming dusk. But they were not alone: they were in the company of some prominent Britons, in an ambience far removed from the Monday Clubbery of the Hamiltons and their friends. Chianti – as renowned for wine as for its Elysian scenery – was the favourite colony for the Red Raj of Britain's new Labour intelligentsia and its allied oper-atives in the liberal arts. By day in Tuscany, one could savour the musky scent of the frescoed churches, picnicking on olives in the cradle of Renaissance humanism, with the Penguin edition of *Vasari's Lives of the Artists* to hand. And in the balmy evenings – to complete the satisfaction of Labour's aristocracy

– one could relax in the knowledge that this blessed corner of the planet had been governed for half a century by the civic wisdom of Italy's Gucci-clad Communist party, which had recently, to the great convenience of all, changed its symbol from the now awkward hammer and sickle to an oak tree.

Neil Kinnock, former Labour leader and target of so many of Hamilton's parliamentary jibes, was there with his wife Glenys. The Robertsons had also teamed up for their summer break with two prominent luvvies-for-Labour: Jeremy Irons of *Brideshead* and Sinead Cusack, his actress wife. This was to be an especially agreeable evening, since the Blairs had popped over for drinks and a spot of dinner – Cherie and Tony taking what might be a last summer holiday before his intended step over the threshold of Downing Street. When the phone rang on 7 August, it was a call from London, from the clerks at Robertson's chambers off Theobalds Road. In the kitchen, the cook picked up the receiver and passed it to Kinnock. The former Labour leader took the news with the next bottle of Chianti out to Robertson on the terrace. The *Guardian* newspaper, where Geoffrey had many friends, was in a panic. Its solicitors had a date for a libel hearing in the horribly near future and needed a good barrister instantly. Would Robertson take it on? The offer was £30,000 for the brief plus £2,000 a day: the kind of money Italian footballers earn.

Geoffrey Robertson QC, born in Sydney, Australia, has a shock of greying hair and wears designer shirts. A degree of detachment from the pompous assumptions and claustrophobia of the British legal system had helped him to shine at the London Bar, both as a master craftsman and radical theoretician of the law. Few would accuse Robertson of bashfulness. Recently, he had been the media star of the Matrix Churchill trial, securing the dramatic acquittal of his client, Paul Henderson, whom the Government had tried to make a scapegoat for the undercover export of arms to Saddam Hussein's Iraq. In the process, the acquittal brought about the traumatic judicial inquiry by Lord Scott which was to reveal how Major's ministers had lied. Robertson achieved this stunning result by doing something very unlikely: he got one of the ministers in Her Majesty's Government to tell the truth. In a cross-examination of the then Minister for Trade, maverick millionaire Alan Clark – recent publisher of his own sex-preoccupied diaries – Robertson revealed the Government's hand in the whole smutty business.

But in Chianti, Robertson was mellowing out. There was his holiday, a book in prospect and his upcoming 50th birthday. He was currently reading about the death of Shelley, and Kinnock had produced a CD of Phil Ochs, a lachrymose folk singer they had both once liked as students. Now the *Guardian* was butting in with some flap over corrupt politicians. If he took the case, Robertson realised he would have to postpone his birthday celebrations. 'It'll make me feel younger anyway,' he said to his wife. He accepted at once on the phone, with little idea what lay ahead. The party only vaguely remembered the Hamilton affair.

'I've just been hired to defend the *Guardian*,' Robertson told Tony Blair, the Downing Street dauphin. 'Oh you poor chap,' Blair replied, 'I only hope they've been more accurate about Neil Hamilton than they are about me.' Kinnock, now pouring champagne, offered a Welsh warning: 'Hamilton's a tough nut and a smart nut. He's clever, don't underestimate him; he was parliamentary wit of the year in 1989.'

'Well,' said Robertson, 'let's make him parliamentary shit of the year in 1996.'

Back in England nine days later, Robertson had a prior engagement – Sunday luncheon at Saltwood Castle, Kent, the stately home inherited from his father by Alan Clark. What a curious creature the establishment is: Clark was, of course, the man Robertson had hung out to dry in the witness box during the Matrix Churchill trial: and now it was time for lunch at the castle. Clark's cultivated view of his interlocutor was 'a frightfully intelligent chap, and excellent company'. At table, Robertson was sandwiched between two Conservative politicians, former Chancellor Norman Lamont and Home Secretary Michael Howard.

The next day, when he opened his brief, Robertson discovered that both men would be dragged into the *Guardian* case: Lamont's election expenses had been subsidised by Greer and Howard was the target of allegations by Fayed. Ironically, the only Tory at the lunch and in the clear would be

Alan Clark, who as Defence Minister had answered Hamilton's queries without realising that the MP had been bribed to ask them.

Family time in Sussex was the first casualty. 'The children's holiday is a washout,' Robertson told Kathy Lette as he buried himself in Geraldine Proudler's 24 lever-arch 'Hamilton' files fetched up from her storage vaults and hastily dusted down.

The picture of Hamilton and Greer emerged gradually from the pages. At his first meeting with Brian Whitaker, the *Guardian*'s managing editor, the QC had found his clients anxious about the sudden setting of an immediate trial date. The fact that Carter-Ruck had chosen the time, date and place of battle gave them 'a terrific advantage', Robertson agreed. But he advised that the *Guardian* had a reasonable case because of what he called Hamilton's astonishing 'greed gene' – a £200-plus Ritz dinner every night without once going out to the bistro. The Hamiltons were not a couple a juror would want to invite to his or her own house, he said. The QC was, however, worried by the 'beautiful craftsmanship' of Hamilton's statement describing how he had suffered from the *Guardian*'s 'campaign of lies'. 'It reads like a dream, and is almost plausible. It is only when you begin to unpick it that you realise every line is a half-truth.' He described Christine's accompanying statement as a real tearjerker. 'This will be the fragrant witness.' Every libel case worth its salt had one, named after politician Jeffrey Archer's wife, Mary. After she had once testified in her husband's support, a besotted libel judge told the jury: 'Is she not fragrant?'

Robertson by then had read every speech Hamilton had made in parliament, and even his 'dull little volume' on double taxation. A whole page of one Commons speech on privacy was lifted from a book Robertson himself had written – *The People Against The Press*. Robertson said wrily: 'He can't be wholly bad. He was just what my grandmother would have called a smart-aleck.'

The QC read on, through the interminable 750-page DTI report on Fayed and his credibility. He was a man who had been branded a liar by the Government and who, Robertson felt, 'talks in broad brushes', apparently saying sweepingly that he had paid bribes at all the 12 meetings with the MP. All it took was an alibi to start to shoot through the armour – and the plaintiffs had duly produced a journalist called O'Sullivan who had been present at one of the meetings. The original details from Fayed in the article – how much money, when, to whom, exactly what for – seemed vague. The *Guardian*'s perceived closeness to Fayed, internal *Guardian* memoranda which contained 'some pretty brutal assumptions' and 'a lot of cynical humour' – there was much that the other side could make a meal of in court.

Guardian solicitor Geraldine Proudler was less gloomy, and sought to reassure the QC on the merits of the case. Her view was that the paper had been presented with an unfair problem because all the material about Tim Smith, which had been before them when they took the decision to publish, might now be withheld from the jury. When the *Guardian* ran the original story they had been right in all the major respects – Tim Smith had taken money to plead for Fayed in parliament, and the paperwork in the *Guardian*'s hands bore that out. He admitted it and resigned as a minister the day the *Guardian* published. Neil Hamilton had, as a mass of documentary evidence showed before publication, lied extensively about the amount of work he had done for Fayed.

And Fayed had been proved completely accurate in one of his central charges – that Hamilton had taken a free holiday at the Ritz. Proudler was also conscious that a crucial element in her full case strategy was to demolish the plaintiffs' lies by cross-examination. This was the burden she was laying on a QC who was new to the case.

Proudler asked Robertson – as a 'hand-holding exercise' – to talk to the clients. With only a month to go before the trial, he came to Farringdon Road with a bleak assessment. The editor Alan Rusbridger was flanked by Caroline Marland, the paper's managing director and a group of anxious executives facing a major crisis at their newpapers. Rusbridger had taken over the *Guardian*'s helm only a year back. He was 41 and looked even younger, but he had a reputation for keeping his cool. True, it was not he who had dealt with Fayed in the first instance, but Preston, his predecessor. But it would, ultimately, be his decisions – and his alone – that would dictate the course of the coming weeks. Rusbridger knew the barrister from the days when he had been a newspaper diarist facing the threat of writs from the politician Cecil Parkinson. He greeted him characteristically: 'I hope you're enjoying yourself.'

'It's not quite the words I'd choose,' Robertson replied.

The QC gave the meeting a worst-case analysis which he knew was over-gloomy. Part of his aim was to ensure that the *Guardian* put massive effort into what he felt would be a battle against time. If he was to have a fighting chance, the QC demanded that he be allowed to commandeer the *Observer* journalist, David Leigh – with whom he had worked on Matrix Churchill and on arms-smuggling in Antigua – as an aide. It was agreed. The *Guardian*'s main investigative reporter David Pallister was drafted, as were David Hencke, two researchers – Jamie Wilson and Jane Mulholland – and managing editor Brian Whitaker. The platoon marshalled, the main meeting broke up and Rusbridger saw Robertson out, saying: 'Good. Good to see you again. Keep in touch.' As soon as he had left, Proudler said: 'He wasn't that pessimistic yesterday.' Brian Whitaker reminded them that Hamilton did not actually deny attending any of the dozen private meetings that Fayed had described. This showed that Fayed was credible on the bigger picture. Rusbridger decided that he would provide all the resources the QC needed: whatever it took. He would commit the *Guardian* to battle. There would be no cave-in.

'Catch the next plane back to London.' The phone rang in the Canadian Rockies with Robertson's brisk orders to Heather Rogers to abandon her family holiday. As a trainee barrister, she had been Robertson's first pupil long before; now a leading light herself at the libel bar, she was to be junior counsel in the case. They took over the spacious first floor conference room in Robertson's Doughty Street chambers (from which the Matrix Churchill case had been won), and turned it into a warehouse of paper. Robertson installed a sofa bed, a carousel containing what had grown by now to 40 lever-arch files, and his desk belonging to Clifford Mortimer – John's father – the blind barrister from his book *A Voyage Round My Father*. For everyone, the 18-hour working days began. Geraldine Proudler would only make it back to her big Chelsea town house long after midnight – 'just in time to open the Scotch, sleep and then get up after a few hours to begin again'.

An early climbdown by Hamilton and Greer looked impossible to the QC. They had invested everything in their case, and persuaded a lot of weighty people of their innocence. 'The oldest trick in the book of the guilty,' he told Rusbridger. 'You impress everyone by the lengths to which you will go.' It did not seem they would behave like Princess Diana, who had cried off five days before the start of her action against a New Zealand gym owner who had filmed her working out, and whom Robertson had also represented.

The QC went to Harrods, and its maddeningly 'broadbrush' proprietor who was so vague with dates, to seek help with evidence. The Knightsbridge experience immediately strengthened his belief in Hamilton's guilt. As he and Proudler went up the escalator, they tried to visualise Hamilton floating through this Aladdin's cave of temptation. Robertson said: 'I just can't imagine him resisting it.' In Fayed's office, a tidal wave of gift silk ties began to make their way across the table in Robertson's direction. The QC told Fayed that the gift envoked an image of the courtroom collapsing with laughter at an opponent's last question to him: 'And what did you give my learned friend?' The silken tide ebbed back along the table. Robertson's pitch was clear. He knew that there were smoking guns somewhere at Harrods – on bits of paper, letters, notes scrawled by secretaries, on the message pads. He wanted Fayed to make a systematic search and help convict Hamilton.

British libel law forces defendants to do the proving: in effect, it puts them on the defensive from the start. But Robertson – who had always had a hankering to be a prosecutor – decided to take the offensive. In any case, it could be argued that Hamilton was being accused of a criminal offence, which meant the judge could demand proof to a high standard – not just guilty 'on the balance of probabilities', but guilty 'beyond reasonable doubt', as in a criminal court.

Robertson's move, now working more like a continental examining magistrate than a libel lawyer, was to create a detailed chronology of all that had happened over the years – dates, letters, speeches, question, trips, payments. He also – in the style of Inspector Maigret – began to build psychological profiles of his quarry.

Proudler's strategy, meanwhile, was to define and find the documents. It was in the papers that the key to this case could – and would – be unearthed. She had the right to claim 'discovery' of papers from the other side's files, if they were relevant, if they existed, and if she could work out what they might contain. In this game of poker, Proudler would have to guess the cards in the other players' hands. Each time a new crop of papers arrived, Proudler would have to look, in her mind's eye, at what was *not* included even more closely than what was, second-guessing every particle ever committed to paper. Proudler's blindfold journey was to begin with the microns of accountancy and end up with the headed note-paper of 10 Downing Street. She was cautiously confident: the higher the other side raised the stakes, the more she was convinced that they were protecting a weak and defeatable hand.

For this expedition, Proudler assembled the team at her new law firm, Olswang, to which she had moved that summer. They included Marcus Barclay, a partner with a hawk's eye for figures, who would concentrate on Greer's £10 million special damages claim, and Fergus Falk, from accountants Deloitte Touche. Nicki Schroeder, a solicitor, would work as an assistant on the main case and Tom Beezer, who was just about to qualify, would act as link man, ferrying the documents over to Robertson and the *Guardian*. Proudler told her team: 'You dig for it. Stand back and say: "What documents are there likely to be?" '

They already had a taste of the likely obstacles to be placed in their path. On demanding Hamilton's diaries between 1987 and 1990, the defence team had been chagrined to get a letter from Carter-Ruck saying their client had only been able to locate diaries from 1984 to 1986. He had lost the rest. 'If you have a suspicious mind,' thought Proudler, 'that's just up until he starts receiving the money.'

The first bundles of Hamilton's bank statements were uni-lluminating. It was Greer's greed that opened a chink in the armour – by filing his claim that the business had lost £10 million, compared to its previous level of activity. Number-cruncher Marcus Barclay saw his opportunity: 'The special damages claim was tactically a mistake by them. It enabled us to legitimately insist on having discovery of all the financial records of all Greer companies ... We agreed with Carter-Ruck to look at all the accounts from 1990 onwards. What we wanted to see was the auditors' working files. These gave a summary of the company's internal documents and a schedule of the invoices. The files were kept at the Greer accountants, Stoy Hayward, who were preparing the expert report alleging the loss of £10 million. The reason I went was to see if there was anything in the special damages claim that would be of use in the main action. I had a list of names to look out for'. Marcus Barclay, as events would show, had been handed the key to, and invited to rummage around in, a treasure chest. Proudler says:

> We were wading through paper, huge amounts of documents which were boring and irrelevant, to work out if any had any relevance at all. You're drowning in documents, endlessly boring stuff, whittling it down, sending it to the accountants for analysis. We were extracting anything that seemed relevant to Greer's way of operating ... The tempting thing is to send down a junior trainee to go and organise the documents, but if we had done that, we would never have got to the truth. Marcus went there himself, every time. Just to look.

And Marcus Barclay started to get results.

> The first file I looked at was Schedule 28, the 'fees payable'. That looked interesting. Lots of money was changing hands. The left-hand margin of the schedules showed the fees paid the previous year. I had spent about three afternoons, ten hours, going through reams of stuff. The accounts for 1990, the earliest we had, showed in the left-hand margin there had been a fee paid to Neil Hamilton the previous year – in 1989. When I found this first payment to Neil Hamilton, it felt great. I immediately went and copied it to put straight in front of Geraldine.

These were the first figures the team saw revealing the details of Hamilton's cash.

At Doughty Street, Robertson's chambers, the new haul of names and payments was being entered into his vast chronology. Fayed's office message pads and diaries were emerging from Knightsbridge. The chronology showed the ebb and flow of the conspiracy: the gentlemanly MP Michael Grylls at the hub of the wheel, linking up with what Robertson described as 'Greer at the centre of a spider's web of corrupting influence'.

The QC was already preparing a 50-page draft of his opening speech, which had been circulated to Rusbridger and Preston for their comments:

> These MPs latched on to the wealthy Egyptian, they stroked and rubbed and polished the Harrods lamp so that its genial and generous genie would make their day – and their weekends at the Ritz. They prostituted their parliamentary privileges to serve in his private war against Tiny Rowland . . . Hamilton is a politician, libelling others is his stock-in-trade. His wife shares his politics as she shared his bedroom at the Ritz, and his gluttony at the Espadon restaurant: they shared the fun with Greer and now must face up to the reckoning. A wise American president once said of politics: 'If you can't stand the heat, get out of the kitchen.' These plaintiffs now stand in the kitchen with peeled onions held to their face. They got everything they deserved from the *Guardian* article. They got what they had so cunningly hidden from ministers, from parliament, from the Register of Members' Interests and from the public: the truth.

Proudler, meanwhile, was cutting to the heart of the Conservative party. She served a subpoena on the Party Chairman, Brian Mawhinney, for documents he possessed on payments made to Tories by Greer. Central Office resisted. They said Greer had made payments to individuals, but none at the relevant time to central party funds, so Mawhinney had no evidence to supply. Proudler countered immediately: how did Central Office know these facts? Mawhinney had not been Chairman at the time, so he could only have known about it through reading an internal file. Hand over that file, she said, and the embarrassing demand for Mawhinney to go in the witness box would be dropped. It was sheer poker. And back across the table came a glorious pile of winning chips.

A one-page memo was delivered to Proudler via Central Office solicitors. Written in 1995, it was from the former director general of Central Office, millionaire Paul Judge, the same man who had unsuccessfully taken the *Guardian* to court for libel on behalf of the party. It informed the Party Chairman of the embarrassing fact that Greer had forwarded £18,000 of Fayed's money and another £11,000 from the DHL courier company to 21 MPs, for their 1987 election expenses. Greer had shown Paul Judge a list naming the MPs. The politicians, he warned, in writing, included prominent figures like Michael Portillo, Michael Hirst and Gerry Malone. Judge even added icing to the devastating cake: 'This issue clearly does have the potential to embarrass the party ... It is clear that the *Guardian* could generate considerable "sleaze" by portraying these payments ... as being designed to buy influence.'

'This,' thought Proudler, 'is a breakthrough. If he admits payments to MPs, why is it so incredible that he should have a financial relationship with Hamilton? And so we followed the trail. Back to Carter-Ruck and say: "Where's the list of 21 MPs? You haven't disclosed it." '

The faxed bombardment of requests for documents was followed up by telephone calls to Carter-Ruck each afternoon to say 'Where are they, then?' The correspondence itself fills several thick files. There are requests, request lists, replies, reply lists, counter lists. A letter of 9 September lists eight outstanding points to be dealt with. 'Confirmation of document inspection taking place tomorrow,' reads Proudler. She recalls: 'They refused to give us what we wanted, so we write back ... The letters were criss-crossing at a rate of five a day.'

On 13 September, the list of Greer's election payments to the 21 politicians arrived. 'Why was all this money being paid out to so many MPs?' Proudler wondered. 'Now, we've got a system. A parliamentary lobbyist running what appeared to be a very scientific operation, making donations to MPs. Not just a question of one particular friend who says, "Can you chip in, on my election expenses?" It's a great list of names, and all the names were players on key committees, or significant in some way.'

Proudler was worried that the focus would start to dissipate as disclosure of Greer's accounts brought more and more politicians into the frame, to general excitement at the *Guardian*: 'It would turn the jury against the *Guardian* if this began to look like some kind of general attack against Conservative MPs,' she warned. 'Part of my job was to rein-in journalistic enthusiasm, channel it into the case ... and to make sure that everything relevant that was coming back was being fed out again to get maximum benefit from all the brains that were being applied to it.'

The team review meetings would begin at 10 pm, and sometimes last until shortly before dawn. Two working weeks left. '17 September, pretty close to trial,' Proudler thought, 'so we can't afford to assume anything about what we're going to get.' The memoranda and counter-memoranda in search of documents were becoming a flood tide.

Typically, a five-page letter in from Carter-Ruck began 'Thank you for your five faxes of 17 September ...' Meanwhile, Robertson was faxing lists of 'random queries', 40 or 50 at a time, which included such questions as 'What was the name of Ian Greer's poodle?' The barristers had also applied for a court order that Greer and Hamilton comply with their discovery obligations. They asked for 'all documentation evidencing all payments, including commission payments, made by Ian Greer to Members of Parliament'. This would cover any payments made to Hamilton while he was a minister and any payments made while he was active in the service of Fayed. They also demanded Hamilton's tax returns. On the evening before the hearing, due for 19 September, their opposing counsel, Victoria Sharpe, called to offer a deal: her clients were prepared to hand the material over – a binding undertaking to obtain the crucial evidence. This seemed to be a significant break, for previously documents had only arrived at a snail's pace, with occasional gems buried in a welter of irrelevant paper.

It was the response to these discovery applications which produced, on 20 September, records of the payments to Hamilton: the 'commissions' for his work on behalf of US Tobacco and the National Nuclear Corporation. A letter of the same day promised to deliver Hamilton's tax returns (they never came). But here was a copy of the bill Greer settled for the watercolours bought by the Hamiltons from Tony Sanders Antiques of Penzance, and the series of invoices from the Peter Jones department store in Sloane Square, for the wrought-iron garden furniture, costing more than £950. Some of the chairs had been collected and signed for by Christine Hamilton herself. 'The fragrant witness!' Robertson snorted delightedly when he heard about the discovery: 'More like the flagrant witness!'

The journalist David Leigh, wading through the stack of red files in the *Guardian* 'bunker' – a squashed cluster of executive cubby-holes – was trying to piece together Hamilton's psychology. Peter Jones? What kind of shopping-spree was this? A reasonably-priced store which will refund the difference if anything they sell is found cheaper elsewhere is hardly in the go-for-broke spirit of the Hamilton pig-out at the Paris Ritz. The answer, he reasoned, must have been this: when there is a blank cheque, Hamilton reaches for the champagne breakfast, the full works, no matter how over-priced. But a sudden attack of thrift tells him to head for the spot where he gets the best value for money if he has a ceiling. Ergo, Greer had probably named a figure, told him he could spend up to £1,000. The mosaic was filling in.

The more documents that arrived at the Long Acre offices of Olswang, the more incomprehensible it seemed that Hamilton and Greer could carry on with the case. But, far from hauling up the white flag, Greer went for what seemed to be a dazzling act of chutzpah. On Monday 23 September came proposals for a settlement. Greer would refer the £10 million special damages claim to arbitration if the *Guardian* would admit their mistake and agree to pay up to £2.5 million. 'What!' said Proudler. 'This is Alice in Wonderland. This is not in touch with reality.' She picked up the phone, dialled and found it hard to keep a straight face as she conveyed the proposal to Rusbridger. 'What do they think we're working all day and all night for, if they think we're going to concede liability?' Since no appropriate response suggested itself, no response was sent. Robertson's intelligence about the other side was that Hamilton and Greer were running out of money. Carter-Ruck were charging them large sums, taking £250,000 from Greer (£100,000 for the special damages claim) and £150,000 from Hamilton. And this time, Sir James Goldsmith was *not* paying.

In the High Court itself, on 26 September, with the trial due the following week, all eyes focused on a formal hearing about the subpoenas sent to the Government. Although the *Guardian* did not realise it, and nor, certainly, did the Prime Minister's office themselves, 10 Downing Street were holding in their possession perhaps the most devastating document of all.

Charles Gray QC, representing a crowd of clients – Major, Heseltine, Robin Butler, Richard Ryder, the Home Office, the DTI, and the Defence Ministry – produced some large red files and sat them on the bench. These were the Government documents that had been collected together. The Government had agreed to release those papers it considered directly relevant, but everything on the papers that was not directly pertinent to the case would be blacked out, including material about other MPs. As yet, though, officials had not taken their felt-tip pens to the documents in question. Robertson demanded that delivery take place before the day was out, and the judge agreed.

Returning from the Law Courts in the Strand that afternoon, David Leigh encountered the originator of the exposures – Peter Preston – coming out of his office on the top floor at Farringdon Road. Leigh said to him: 'I had a funny feeling, watching the body language in that courtroom. I don't think this trial will ever happen.' Brian Whitaker, managing editor of the *Guardian*, had also become puzzled. While the *Guardian*'s lawyers had been busy with subpoenas for thousands of documents, the opposing side had demanded almost nothing.

Mounting the escalators at Harrods again, Proudler and Robertson were increasingly pleased with the way the case was going, but they still hoped for a 'smoking gun' from Harrods. Once in the boardroom, they were inspecting some statements that had been requested by Robertson – requests that had fallen on deaf ears until, a week earlier, the QC had met Fayed's Washington lawyer, Doug Marvin. Both Marvin and Robertson had acted for the *Washington Post*. Robertson beseeched him to overcome Fayed's reluctance to involve his former staff and to obtain statements from them. 'Whether they are helpful to the *Guardian* or not, we must have written and signed accounts by these people of their dealings with Hamilton and Greer. What did they understand Hamilton to mean when they took down his messages to Fayed about wanting his "envelope"?'

'The secretaries,' said Robertson, 'the secretaries must have known. When we cracked government corruption in Antigua, it was because the secretaries must have known what was going on.'

Marvin speaks with a slow, exact and meticulous drawl. A partner with the illustrious Washington firm of Williams and Connolly, he had dealt with Fayed for some 18 years, and acted for him in the US and the Middle East. Now, as he said, he was being 'brought into the case at the last minute'. It was, he thought, 'a credibility contest'.

He had sought out Fayed's secretary first, on 23 September. 'I didn't get more than 30 seconds into my explanation,' he recalled, 'when she said, "Neil Hamilton's a liar." She made it clear that she had read the *Guardian* article and she knew the facts to be as stated in that article. And when Neil Hamilton said he did not receive any payments he was lying. She was very clear and very strong.'

Fayed's secretary had made the note of a message from Greer in the telephone book for Fayed's attention, which had already been discovered: 'You owe July, August, September.' She now testified that the note 'confirms my recollection that quarterly payments of £5,000 in cash were made to Ian Greer'. In addition, she said: 'Mr Neil Hamilton was a frequent visitor ... at one time as frequent as three times a month ... I remember on several occasions that prior to a meeting with Mr Hamilton, Mr Fayed would make a remark to the effect that he was coming to collect his money, and would prepare an envelope for him with a bundle of £2,500 in notes in my presence.'

After speaking to her, Marvin asked her who else might be aware, and she mentioned Fayed's former PA. This woman was no longer employed by Fayed and had since become a trainee solicitor at a prominent City firm. She had been on holiday in France, and Marvin had met her on the evening of her return, Wednesday 25 September. 'She was just as clear in her recollection,' Marvin said. Fayed's former PA testified:

> In addition to payments made to Mr Greer following receipt of invoices from his office, Mr Greer would also receive cash. Sums of £5,000 in cash were paid to Mr Greer on a quarterly basis. Both my colleague and I were responsible for making for arranging these cash payments at various times. Mr Greer would often phone and ask whether Mr Fayed had left an envelope for him. Sometimes he would ask bluntly whether Mr Fayed had his money ready ... Mr Greer was very persistent and would sometimes phone four or five times asking for the envelope. Mr Fayed would occasionally ask me to remind him to get an envelope for Mr Greer in preparation for meeting him. On occasions, Mr Fayed would ask me to place amounts of cash in an envelope for Mr Greer, and I recall putting amounts of between £2,000 and £5,000 in envelopes at various times. On several occasions I delivered an envelope containing cash at the reception desk at 60 Park Lane to await collection by Mr Greer.

As far as Hamilton was concerned:

> Mr Hamilton came to Park Lane quite often to see Mr Fayed, usually about once every four to six weeks, although there were times when the visits may have been as frequent as once a week. Mr Hamilton phoned the office on numerous occasions enquiring whether Mr Fayed had an envelope ready for him. If an envelope was prepared by either Mr Fayed or me, I would tell Mr Hamilton and he would come over to 60 Park Lane and

pick it up ... This happened on several occasions ... Mr Hamilton was as persistent as Mr Greer, if not more so, in asking for his envelope. He would sometimes phone saying he was stopping by at very short notice to pick up his envelope.

There was one nugget which made Geoffrey Robertson chuckle out loud when he reached it:

> Mr Hamilton telephoned me and said that he would visit the Ritz Hotel in Paris and that his wife Christine would be in touch to make the necessary arrangements ... Mrs Christine Hamilton telephoned me and told me the dates that they intended to travel to Paris. I then booked a room at the hotel for the Hamiltons through the hotel manager. Prior to Mr Hamilton's departure for Paris, Mr Fayed asked me to leave an envelope containing between £2,000 and £3,000 at the reception desk for his trip.

Marvin had completed the hat trick, he said, by questioning Fayed's doorman at Park Lane. He well remembered Hamilton and his 'envelopes'. The security man gave a statement that at least twice, 'when I was sitting at the front desk, an envelope was brought down to me from Mr Fayed's office'. He continued: 'I was informed that Mr Hamilton would be stopping by to collect the envelope. On each of these occasions, Mr Hamilton personally came to the front desk ... Because I recognised Mr Hamilton, I would hand the envelope over to him.'

Robertson told Marvin: 'I asked for a smoking gun and you've given me a Kalashnikov.'

The lawyers left Harrods. Proudler returned to Olswang, Robertson to his chambers, at 8.30 pm – to wait for the Government bundle. Back at Covent Garden, still nothing. Proudler's assistant, Nicki Schroeder, had been calling the Treasury Solicitor's office. They said they were having trouble with their black-out pen. The confidential passages were still legible. So they were having to black them out all over again. 'This is supposed to be a Government department, for God's sake,' said Proudler. By 9.30, still nothing. Schroeder found herself speaking on the phone to a doorman, who said everyone had left the building apart from someone in the immigration office. Through to the immigration official, then, who said the Treasury Solicitors were actually at the photocopying machine. Geoffrey Robertson and Heather Rogers were drumming their fingers on the conference table at Doughty Street. Leigh sat by the phone at the *Guardian*. Shortly after 10 pm, the Government courier arrived at Proudler's office. The first task was to get the documents copied – 'Literally whole pages of blacked-out lines,' recalls Proudler. 'I assumed there was going to be nothing in them. But there was.'

Neither at Olswang, nor at Doughty Street, did anyone get much sleep that Thursday night. And by the time dawn broke over central London, the contents of the Government bundle had finished off Neil Hamilton. It turned out that, on the very day that the *Guardian*'s article of 20 October 1994 was published, Hamilton had solemnly promised Trade Secretary Michael Heseltine that he had had no financial relationship with the lobbyist Ian Greer. And this promise had been recorded within the Cabinet Office, in one of those Whitehall memoranda designed not so much to inform the reader as to protect the back of the writer.

Early on Friday morning, Robertson called Proudler. He was in an upbeat mood. 'We are now as certain as we can be of victory. We can prove Hamilton lied to the Deputy Prime Minister, and that will help to persuade the jury that he is lying to the court.'

The lawyers agreed an urgent timetable for the day. Robertson and his junior, Heather Rogers, would prepare amendments to the defence pleadings to incorporate the most important revelations from the Government documents (these included further details of his shady associations which had contributed to his being sacked as a minister). Proudler would concentrate on getting the witness statements signed and sent to Carter-Ruck, while Rogers would spend the afternoon with her opposite number, Victoria Sharpe, agreeing a bundle of documents to be placed before the jury. But Friday did not happen as planned. The first sign that something was wrong in the enemy camp was that Victoria Sharpe was suddenly 'not available' to sort out the jury bundle. What could this mean?

Meanwhile, on Friday afternoon, a man appeared in the marbled lobby of the First Chicago building, where Olswang is based, wearing green regalia, braid and buttons. This was Rodney, aged 82, the longest-serving employee of Harrods store. When he was not holding open the Harrods door for Princess Diana (who knew him quite well), Rodney was Fayed's personal messenger. And on Friday 27 September, he had a package, which he insisted on delivering personally to Miss Geraldine Proudler, on the chairman's authority. The parcel did not contain a giant teddy bear this time. It contained the three signed witness statements taken by the lawyer Marvin, corroborating the cash payments to Hamilton. 'Euphoria,' said Proudler, 'was starting to set in.'

As Friday afternoon ran on, it became clear that not only had Victoria Sharpe become 'unavailable', but that the solicitors working on the case at Carter-Ruck were not taking any calls either. Proudler was unable to communicate with her opposing solicitor; this was incredible. On the Friday before a mammoth libel trial, there is always a flurry of last-minute preparation and consultation between opposing teams of solicitors. Robertson said he was duty bound to get the new witness statements somehow to his opposite number, Richard Ferguson QC, 'to spoil his weekend'.

On touch-down at the City Airport in Docklands from an appointment in Brussels, Alan Rusbridger found an urgent message telling him to go straight to Olswang. An hour later he was sitting across a table with Proudler and the paper's managing editor, Brian Whitaker, reading the devastating batches of paper from the Treasury Solicitor and from Fayed. Suddenly there was not one smoking gun, but four. Robertson was due to phone at any minute to provide an assessment of the new evidence. Outside, the light was fading and offices were shutting up for the weekend. Proudler uncorked a bottle of Chablis and the three of them sat back and wondered. Never mind the envelope-stuffers for the moment. Could Hamilton contemplate letting the Deputy Prime Minister and the Prime

Minister be examined on oath when he knew that they would be confronted with evidence that Hamilton had lied to them? There could be nothing more ruinous to Hamilton's political career than to bring about the public humiliation of John Major in a court of law.

When Robertson eventually rang in – at 5.55 pm on Friday 27 September – it was with momentous news; Proudler put him on the speakerphone for the *Guardian* editors to hear. He said he had just had the most extraordinary phone conversation with Richard Ferguson, the tough Ulster-born QC for Hamilton and Greer whose most recent client had been Rosemary West, the serial killer of Cromwell Street, Gloucester. 'I was just ringing him to warn him of the new evidence coming his way,' said Robertson. Suddenly the QC reported Ferguson had interrupted to ask whether there was any chance of both parties 'walking away' from the trial, each party paying their own costs. He had revealed that a conflict of interests had arisen, which had required him to consult the Bar Council. It was a startling development.

And this had happened *before* they had seen the new witness statements from Harrods. 'Ferguson,' said Robertson, 'doesn't even want to read them.' Robertson explained that Ferguson's phrase 'consulting the Bar Council' was code for an irreconcilable conflict of interest between his two clients, Greer and Hamilton.

More Chablis appeared in the solicitor's office where the *Guardian* team were clustered round the speakerphone. This was bewildering stuff. In days, Hamilton and Greer had moved from demanding £10 million to £2.5 million to nothing. They had gone from artillery barrage to white flag in ten minutes flat. What was Ferguson talking about? Why was he offering to surrender? And still there was no-one at Carter-Ruck. The place was deserted; the Friday before the trial, *and no one was there.* (It was 7.30 pm by the time Proudler managed to contact Carter-Ruck solicitor Andrew Stephenson at home, and told him there was new material to deliver. 'No-one would read it,' he replied.

'This is getting bizarre,' said Proudler.

Hamilton's dull book on taxation had opened with the famous quotation from Benjamin Franklin: 'In this life, nothing can be said to be certain except death and taxes'; the lawyers were still waiting eagerly to see Hamilton's own tax returns. Perhaps the plaintiffs had fallen out over that. The *Guardian* still had outstanding applications for further discovery, which were due to be heard on Tuesday morning by way of an overture to the trial. Greer himself apparently had no reason to offer surrender terms. But his lawyers had certainly told him he had yet to hand over more evidence showing all payments to Hamilton, up to October 1994, including the period when Hamilton was a minister.

The party had to decide what response Robertson was to convey to Ferguson next day. The QC and solicitor advised them that, barring a perverse jury, they would almost certainly win the trial. But it could not go ahead the following week. The conflict of interests meant that new lawyers would have to be instructed by both Hamilton and Greer. It would take them three months to prepare and there were no court dates for a six-week trial until mid-1997 – after the general election. The voters at that election would never know about the sleaze if the case were adjourned. 'That,' said Rusbridger, 'would be the worst result possible.' In order to get the story out, the *Guardian* would have to give some inducement to settle now.

Plaintiffs who withdraw from a libel action have to pay most of the costs of the other side. These costs are 'taxed' so that the proportion ordered to be paid is usually 65 per cent. When the case had collapsed first time round, because of the Bill of Rights, each side had agreed to pay its own costs up to that point. So if Hamilton and Greer withdrew on Monday, they would be ordered to pay 65 per cent of the costs the *Guardian* had run up since August, which the lawyers calculated at about £60,000. To encourage them to withdraw now, rather than after the election next year, they would have to be relieved of some of that costs burden.

But the lawyers and the editor agreed nothing else would or could be offered. They would not countenance any fig-leaf for Hamilton or Greer, such as a statement in open court or an agreement to mute publicity. The *Guardian* would reserve the right to tell the full truth that it had so recently uncovered as brutally as it chose. There was another reason to offer some inducement. Robertson warned that from the evidence they had now discovered Hamilton and Greer would appear such sleazy figures that the jury might well add to their humiliation by awarding them the famous libel raspberry – one penny, 'the lowest coin in the realm', as the value put on their reputation. Since the *Guardian* had refused even to pay one penny into court, this would ironically have the effect of preventing the *Guardian* recovering any costs at all. Robertson's advice was to insist on a 'significant' contribution to costs to emphasise the fact that it had won. 'What would be significant?' asked Rusbridger. Robertson replied: 'Why not make them pay my brief fee – £30,000?'

'Done,' said Rusbridger.

The *Guardian* team reassembled at Olswang on Saturday lunchtime, *en masse*. They were waiting for a call from Robertson with news about the response to their ultimatum. He was due to talk to Ferguson at a barristers' conference where both were giving papers. Dusk began to fall; still no Robertson. By now, the *Guardian* team had been shooed out while the solicitors got on with their work; they were strolling aimlessly around the streets of Covent Garden buying kettle chips and bottles of wine, and clutching their mobile phones. Finally, at 6 pm, Robertson rang in. He had seen Ferguson and was coming over in a cab. Proudler gathered the *Guardian* team. Between mouthfuls of kettle chips, Robertson reported to his audience.

'Not a very generous offer,' Ferguson had said of the £30,000. 'More than they deserve,' grumbled Robertson, who was reluctantly settling what the press had billed as 'the libel trial of the century'. Ferguson had impressed upon him that the 'conflict of interest' which had arisen between his clients was genuine, and he could do no more than convey the *Guardian*'s response to them.

By now it was no longer clear who was acting for whom among their opponents. Hamilton and Greer appeared to have briefed different solicitors. Christine Hamilton had been frantically telephoning around solicitors' offices, trying to find new representation for her husband, reported to be 'going to pieces'. She had found Rupert Grey at Crockers, a flamboyant libel lawyer with a taste in exotic bow ties. Grey had already come on the telephone to Proudler the night before, saying, 'I must be able to contact you over the weekend in relation to the *Guardian*.'

'What for?' had asked Proudler.

'I can't tell you,' came the reply.

'This is ridiculous,' said Proudler.

Greer, meanwhile, who was understood to be in a fury on the Friday and in floods of tears on the Saturday, had made off in the direction of Mark Stephens, an astute defamation specialist whom Robertson knew well.

Sunday had barely begun when a voice asserted itself on to Geraldine Proudler's answering machine. He would like a word, he said, 'entirely without prejudice'. It was the unlikely tone of 82-year-old Peter Carter-Ruck himself. The eponymous head of the most famous libel firm in London, in his time, had been one of the most feared lawyers in Britain, consulted by any member of the establishment who felt threatened by unwelcome publicity. In 55 years in practice, he had acted on behalf of a glittering array of the great and the good and the not-so-good. His Conservative party credentials stretched from service on behalf of Randolph Churchill and Lord Beaverbrook to Norman Lamont, Michael Heseltine, Norman Tebbit, Cecil Parkinson and Edwina Currie. He had also acted for Neil Hamilton (with financial guarantees from Sir James Goldsmith) in his successful action against the BBC. His services did not come at all cheap: he billed clients at £260 an hour. The fruits of a half century of libel had been well spent: a seventeenth-century house in Essex, a croft in Argyll, a London flat, a Rolls-Royce; and a life of first-class travel, gambling, ocean racing, exotic holidays and opera.

Carter-Ruck, it became clear, had not followed this case in detail. What was not immediately clear was what attributes it was felt his personal involvement could bring to the situation. It was certainly extraordinary for a conflict of interest to become apparent at the 59th minute of the 11th hour and for a new partner to be brought in while other solicitors were briefed.

'You will be aware,' Carter-Ruck said, 'that a conflict of interests has arisen.' He would have to apply for an adjournment. (This would be no doubt be after a general election, the

Guardian's worst fear.) Or perhaps the *Guardian* would prefer to settle? Whatever the reason for Carter-Ruck's personal intervention, he was trying to negotiate a painless escape for his clients. His opening proposition was a classic piece of Carter-Ruck poker-playing: the *Guardian* would make a statement in open court in which it would (1) withdraw the allegation that there had been any cash payment to Hamilton from Fayed, and (2) withdraw the allegation that Greer had ever paid anyone for parliamentary activities. If, additionally, the *Guardian* was prepared to pay Hamilton's and Greer's costs they were prepared to waive their right to punitive damages. As a final condition, Carter-Ruck announced that Hamilton wanted to place his case before parliament's new Committee on Standards and Privileges and the *Guardian* would have to agree to hand back all copies of documents it had in its possession.

Proudler listened in bewildered silence. Did Carter-Ruck know anything about the case at all? Did he know that Richard Ferguson had already offered a walk-away on Friday, with each side paying their own costs, and with no conditions? Had he seen any of the documentation which had been compiled within the past 24 hours? She gently began to acquaint Carter-Ruck with some of the weaknesses of his clients' position. He listened and then dramatically switched tack. Perhaps a walk-away. But both sides would agree to say nothing about anything to do with the case. 'Absolutely no deal,' said Proudler, the *Guardian* had to be free to say what it wanted. And the paper not only stood by its story, it wanted a contribution to its costs. Carter-Ruck said he didn't think his clients were in much of a position to offer the *Guardian* money, but he would come back.

Rusbridger and his team were at a critical point in these discussions. It was plain by now that Hamilton, Greer and all their lawyers were in disarray. But they still had some cards left. What the *Guardian* continued to fear was that if there was no settlement by the following Monday night, delaying tactics were certain: with an adjournment, since it would take at least two months for new counsel to prepare the case, it would be nearly Christmas before they would be ready, and the state of the court lists meant that no-one could predict how long after that the case would be heard.

The other, even thornier legal issue could arise. Neil Hamilton had successfully persuaded parliament to amend the law to enable MPs to waive their privilege under the 1688 Bill of Rights in order to fight a libel case in the ordinary courts. Tim Smith, the other MP in the original case, had been lying rather low since taking the 'Good Chap' route and resigning as a minister. His reward for this had not been long coming – quietly placing him back on another select committee, the Public Accounts Committee, responsible for probity in public spending. The last thing Smith wanted now was for all the facts in his case to be dragged out in a court of law. He duly briefed counsel to tell the court that he did not waive his parliamentary privilege and that his name should be kept out of all proceedings. It was the sort of legal point which could occupy barristers for months as it meandered from High Court to Court of Appeal to House of Lords – and even to Europe.

These were the reasons for the paper to accept a settlement, but they could only hope for a fraction of their costs to be paid; they would also be left with a stack of material which they might not be able fully to publish due the technical rules covering documents obtained on discovery.

Neither outcome remained attractive. But it seemed to the *Guardian* team that there would be a better chance of getting the issues out into the open when they settled the case. They continued to be sure about one thing: any settlement had to involve a contribution, however token, by Greer and Hamilton towards the paper's costs. Anything else would be presented by the pair of plaintiffs as some kind of moral victory. They were, after all, lobbyists. They were masters of the black arts of spin. Rusbridger was already planning how to deal with that. He would produce a front page for the morning after the settlement that would be a front page to remember.

It was six hours before Carter-Ruck came back to Proudler, launching a round of attempted negotiation on Sunday. Hamilton, said the solicitor, was going to ask the newly-formed Standards and Privileges Committee to examine his case. Back to parliament. How about an agreement whereby the *Guardian* would say nothing more about the matter until after the committee reported? Proudler rejected this: Hamilton had managed to get parliament to shut up about his case while it went to court.

Now he was trying to get everyone to shut up while he went back to parliament. At one point during the discussion that followed Carter-Ruck made a telling slip when he said: 'That's a matter for Mr Greer . . . it doesn't affect my client.' He was supposedly negotiating on behalf of both men – each of whom had another solicitor – but clearly believed himself to be mainly acting for Hamilton. Proudler repeated the *Guardian*'s position: £30,000 towards the paper's costs, and no gag on the front page that Rusbridger was already designing in his mind.

Mark Stephens, meanwhile, was officially acting for Greer. Stephens said he was not expecting any money because Greer had not got any; he had spent it all at Carter-Ruck. The impression given was that Greer thought he had acted honourably as regards preparations for the trial. The Greer camp seemed hostile to Hamilton. Robertson even wondered if Greer's side might fish for a deal by offering to deliver Hamilton's head. If they were thinking of doing so, it was too late.

Carter-Ruck himself was still busy in his curious role as mediator. He came on the phone again at 8.10 pm, to say that Hamilton was ready to settle if each side covered its own costs. Proudler repeated the *Guardian* offer: £30,000 towards the paper's costs and no deal on publicity. He had until 11 o'clock next morning to accept, she said, or the trial would go ahead. Extraordinarily, Carter-Ruck was back on the line ten minutes later, at 8.20, saying he presumed the *Guardian* had accepted Hamilton's offer; 'I nearly swallowed the phone,' recalls Proudler. She told Rusbridger: 'He's not making sense.'

Rusbridger asked about the advisability of letting their opponents walk away.

Proudler said: 'Not yet. Push them really hard and get a contribution towards costs. It's a point of presentation.' At 8.40, Mark Stephens now said he wanted to look at the Harrods secretaries' witness statements urgently. He had not yet seen their contents. At 9.05, he was back on again, trying for a statement in open court by the *Guardian* that let Greer off more lightly than Hamilton. Robertson and Proudler insisted: no deal.

In the end, it went to the wire. All Monday the ball was kicked around between Carter-Ruck and Proudler, between Proudler and Grey, between Grey and Stephens. Hamilton and Greer were desperate not to pay the *Guardian* anything, because they knew that any payment would be interpreted by the outside world as crucial evidence that they had thrown in the towel. The *Guardian* held firm. The sum didn't matter. The principle did. No money, no deal.

By then, those at the paper knew that they would lose a fair amount of cash on the case. It had begun with a simple and modest desire to tell the truth about a corrupt pair of MPs. It had turned into a huge saga involving dozens of lawyers, the Prime Minister, the Lord Chancellor, the Whips' office, the Bill of Rights – and a legal bill of unmentionable proportions still growing by the minute. Having got this far, the only thought in the minds of Rusbridger and Preston was that the story must come out. Whether it emerged through parliament, the press or the courts (or a mixture of all three) no longer mattered very much.

At 3.15 pm, 75 minutes before the court closed, Carter-Ruck called Proudler to offer £15,000 towards costs. The *Guardian* had already agreed they would accept this lesser sum, if pressed. One minute later, the phone rang again: it was Rupert Grey, also representing Hamilton, to confirm that the *Guardian* knew about the new offer from his side. Yes, said Proudler, £15,000 towards costs. And the deal over statements? 'What deal?' said Proudler, aghast. 'That there should be no statements from either side,' said Grey – this had been plucked from mid air. 'Completely unacceptable,' said Proudler. 'This is a deal-breaker.' By now the whole *Guardian* was working on the next day's front page. At 3.50 pm., Proudler's record shows Grey back again to try the middle ground, that both sides could make a press statement. 'He obviously thinks the *Guardian* is just going to put out a press release – little did he know!'

If the case were to be settled that day, the papers had to be lodged with the judge, His Honour Michael Morland, by 4.30 pm. At 4.10 pm, Rusbridger was still waiting in his office for the phone call that said Hamilton and Greer had finally caved in. The shape of that night's paper – and much else – hung on that phone call. Teams of editors and sub-editors needed to know whether the first three pages were going to be devoted to the Hamilton saga, or whether they would have to find another lead to the paper – a new announcement on tax by Gordon Brown, perhaps, or another White House summit on the Middle East.

At the back of Rusbridger's mind was the suspicion that Hamilton and Greer had already prepared press releases and were ready, the moment a deal was done, to rush out whatever spin they could put on the cave-in. He drafted the *Guardian*'s press release, to be sent to the Press Association within minutes of an announcement. He also laid in some champagne. As *The Times* was to point out two days later, the week had begun with a libel suit which could, at a single stroke, have cost the *Guardian* £10 million. Now the journalists appeared to be minutes away from a complete victory. The case of Neil Hamilton and Ian Greer v. *Guardian* Newspapers Limited finally collapsed with precisely nine minutes to spare. A minute later and the waiting clerks would not have had time to rush round to the High Court to lodge the necessary papers to halt the action. They had taken it right to the precipice before blinking – but in the end they blinked. Robertson called the trial judge to tell him not to spend the evening reading the evidence against Greer and Hamilton: they had hauled up the white flag. As the splash sub-editor, Brian McDermott, started laying out the pages, the first takes of the Press Association story started running.

The *Guardian*'s version was first on the wires but Hamilton and Greer weren't far behind. Both men tugged on the heart strings. They were just little guys up against a powerful newspaper. A legal technicality meant that they simply could not afford to clear their names when confronted with a multi-million-pound media group. The fact that they were paying the *Guardian* a derisory £15,000 showed that neither side had really won. Greer went further. With a breathtaking audacity he stated baldly: 'The *Guardian* blinked first.' A last-gasp fax arrived from Rupert Grey, saying: 'We trust you won't be running the story in your newspaper.' He also rang up Rusbridger and said with an air of menace: 'You'll have to be careful.' 'It's okay,' replied the editor, 'I've got Geraldine here at my elbow.' Television crews started swarming round the *Guardian*'s newsroom as first edition time approached. The paper's deputy editors, Georgina Henry and Paul Johnson, concentrated on the story while Rusbridger gave interviews and – with the aid one or two robust legal flourishes from Geoff Robertson – wrote a 1,500-word editorial for the front page.

Shortly after 9 pm, they stood in the newsroom around the first proof of a page which the following day's *Times* predicted would become 'a classic of British journalism'. The page was dominated by a four-column picture of Neil Hamilton and an eight-column, massively large headline which in five words summarised what dozens of lawyers had been arguing about for 23 months and 18 days. It said simply: 'A LIAR AND A CHEAT'.

Exclusive extract from the revealing new biography

Pinter
His life and work
G2 with today's television

Should DB be allowed her dead husband's baby?

Whose sperm is it anyway?
G2 pages 6/7

With 22 pages of jobs

Education
Universities: one cash crisis too many

45p
Tuesday
October 1
1996
Published in London
and Manchester

The Guardian

Disgraced former minister and lobbyist abandon £10m case at last minute

A liar and a cheat

New evidence halts MP's libel suit

David Hencke, David Leigh and David Pallister

Neil Hamilton last night after he ended his libel action by paying towards the Guardian's costs

Questions for cash. . .

'Sometimes he [Mr Greer] would ask me bluntly whether Mr Al Fayed had his money ready.'

'Mr Hamilton was as persistent as Mr Greer, if not more so, in asking for his envelope.'

— Mohamed Al Fayed's ex-personal assistant

'I remember on several occasions that prior to a meeting with Mr Hamilton, Mr Al Fayed would make a remark

...that he was coming to collect his money and would prepare an envelope for him with a bundle of £2,000 (in) notes in my presence.'

— Mr Al Fayed's secretary

'On at least two occasions when I was sitting at the front desk, an envelope was brought down to me from Mr Al Fayed's office and I was informed that Mr Hamilton would be stopping by to collect the envelope.'

— Mr Al Fayed's security man

Comment

A pattern of corruption and deceit

SELDOM in the long and chequered history of the libel laws can there have been a more humiliating case in, for two years now Neil Hamilton and Ian Greer have blustered vigorously and volubly about their utter innocence and this paper's utter guilt...

The front page, Tuesday 1 October 1996

13

Postscript

'That I was conned by the wretched Hamilton fills me with shame and horror.'
Woodrow Wyatt, News of the World, *regretting his part in changing the Bill of Rights, 6 October 1996*

'It was nearly one of the greatest weeks in the *Guardian*'s history.'
Daily Telegraph *editorial, 5 October 1996*

So much for the legal battle. The struggle to establish the truth subsequently moved into two new arenas – the media and parliament. Hamilton and Greer had overnight changed the rules of engagement – and in both new forums they started with a clear advantage. Both were fluent media performers and lobbyists. Both men knew the way to play television studios and to stroke influential journalists and editors. They knew better than anyone how to co-ordinate a campaign and how to lobby. They ran this like any other campaign.

Hamilton at first played the wronged little man. He had been beaten by the big boys with the big money. Never mind that he was a barrister himself and that he had fought a massive libel action before, he pleaded that he simply could not afford to fight the case that would have cleared his name. His wife Christine ever doggedly by his side, he now repeated this sorrowful mantra to all and sundry.

Both he and Greer knew they had one massive trump card remaining. Documents 'discovered' by lawyers during the course of an action have to be returned once a case collapses and must never be published or disclosed to third parties. By pulling out of the case at the eleventh hour Hamilton and Greer had made sure that a cloud of secrecy would once more descend over the areas of their life which were just about to be exposed to glaring searchlights. The proof of their lies and their fiddles lay in the documents which were once more secret. The *Guardian* could safely call them liars – but the paper could produce little of the evidence which the journalists knew lay in the 45 bright red ring files that were even now being packed up to send back to Greer, Hamilton and to the Government.

Hamilton and Greer both exploited this legal block to the full. All stories the *Guardian* published over the next few days were denounced as 'lies' in the happy knowledge that little evidence could be publicly produced to prove them. Hamilton, in particular, attacked the *Guardian* repeatedly on every possible occasion. It was underhand and subversive, a purveyor of lies, mendacious and scurrilous, evil and wicked . . . as the days wore on he ran out of adjectives damning enough to describe the paper.

Television is a particularly effective medium for an accomplished liar when the story is complex and partly hidden. The constraints of production mean that it is often not the reporter, but a young producer or researcher who pitches up to garner the soundbites. They frequently arrive for an interview anxiously demanding into a mobile phone back to their office what questions they should ask. Hamilton found it easy to denounce all allegations as lies since he was never confronted by anyone who knew what the follow-up question was. Both he and Greer spent the first two days after the collapse of the case looking straight into lenses and declaring that black was white, hot was cold and a humiliating legal cave-in was actually a 'sound commercial decision'. Watching them, you realised they were good at what they did. You suddenly understood why businessmen in trouble flocked to them and paid them well. These boys were smooth.

But it was not all plain sailing. One of the things Hamilton knew would emerge sooner or later was that Ian Greer had paid him quite large sums of undeclared money in the late 1980s – which directly contradicted Hamilton's assurance to Michael Heseltine that he had not had a financial relationship with Greer. Greer and Hamilton tackled this by making two separate admissions to television companies late on 1 October. Greer admitted paying Hamilton on two separate occasions.

Hamilton admitted taking the money but argued, breath-takingly, that taking £10,000 from someone did not amount to a financial relationship.

As the new revelations trickled out, the complete absence of Tory MPs in the television studios became extremely notice-able. Four hundred and twenty-one peers and MPs had rallied behind him just three months earlier to help him change a 300-year-old law in order to fight the case. Others had helped out financially. The sense of bewilderment now that he had thrown in the towel and confessed to taking money was palpable. The lone supporter was Roger Gale, a former Blue Peter presenter with an obsession about media ethics, who made an eccentric rallying call on Radio Wales's 'Meet for Lunch' programme. The Conservative MP for Thanet North predicted that the *Guardian* would rue its 'Liar and Cheat' headline and appealed to the lunchtime listeners in the Princi-pality to contribute to Neil Hamilton's fighting fund so that he could re-start the case.

Hamilton was also losing the argument in even the tradi-tionally conservative newspapers. Most papers carried sympathetic interviews with Christine Hamilton, but the leader columns were universally hostile to her husband. The *Express* said the Government only had itself to blame if it were tarred by association with Hamilton and the question of sleaze. The *Daily Mail* said it was a shocking and disturbing story. Stephen Glover in the *Spectator* said the *Guardian* had not put a foot wrong. The *Standard* said it was difficult to see how Hamilton could remain an MP. *The Times* published two coruscating leaders. Even the *Sun*, not normally a great friend of the *Guardian*, gave the paper a pat on the back for its thoroughness. Only the *Daily Telegraph* affected a superior disdain for the whole business, suggesting that British corrup-tion was in the tea-cup-and-molehill class compared with Johnny Foreigner.

The climax of the first 48 hours was a confrontation between Hamilton and Rusbridger on 'Newsnight', described by the *Evening Standard* Londoner's Diary as 'the most com-pelling on-screen tussle since Alan Bates and Oliver Reed locked arms for *Women in Love*.' Bates and Reed would have been poor casting for the pair who found themselves sitting across an uncomfortably small table, as presenter Jeremy Paxman rehearsed his lines minutes before the programme went out live. Hamilton was as smoothly and expensively turned out as ever, more Alan Rickman than Oliver Reed. Rusbridger never succeeded in looking wholly groomed: he was half Angus Deayton, half Just William. Both men had minders lurking behind the scenes. Rusbridger had press officer Camilla Nicholls and his deputy, Georgina Henry, at the back of the studio. Hamilton had his wife and other supporters in the hospitality suite.

The only rules of engagement were that the two protagonists would be interviewed separately by Paxman. It was the first time Rusbridger and Hamilton had ever set eyes on each other. Hamilton looked hollow-eyed and nervous as he started protesting at Paxman's rehearsed introduction, threatening to walk out with seconds to go. Rusbridger looked a touch ropey as well: he had a gastric bug, a pounding headache and was running a temperature. He would much rather have been tucked up in bed than making a live appearance on 'Newsnight' with the man who loathed him most in the world. Paxman first accused the *Guardian* of using its riches to run a vendetta against a small individual. Then he turned his attention to Hamilton, who launched into his – by now well-practised – routine about his lack of money. The preparation for his trial had been thorough, and he had a rehearsed explanation for most of the things that Paxman threw at him. But he struggled to explain away his assurance to Michael Heseltine that he had never had a financial relationship with Greer.

'So if I buy two copies of the *Guardian*, does that mean I have a financial relationship with him?' he asked at one stage, prodding his finger at Rusbridger.

Paxman: 'Well, it depends how much money was involved, I suppose.'

Hamilton: 'Does it?'

It took another six questions from Paxman before Hamilton confessed to having accepted £10,000 ... as against 90p for two copies of the *Guardian*.

Paxman then asked if Hamilton had ever had payments in kind from Greer. The former minister slipped into the well-practised political gambit of changing the question: 'Look, I'm not getting into this kind of discussion on this programme this evening. What I want to concentrate on here . . .' The tactic worked. He changed the agenda back to the *Guardian* and the fact that the paper had denounced Fayed after the DTI report had pronounced him a liar. This was parried by Rusbridger who wanted to know why, if Hamilton was so worried by the DTI's verdict on Fayed, he had carried on acting on his behalf in parliament? 'I did not *act* for Mr Fayed,' Hamilton snapped back. 'I had a sympathy with his cause.'

Paxman switched the subject to Hamilton's stay at the Ritz. Hamilton flipped the question back to a night Peter Preston had spent in Paris (along with Charles Moore and several other editors – though not, as Hamilton claimed, at the Georges V). Pressed about the lavishness of the hospitality he and his wife had indulged in, Hamilton again turned the question – this time on Paxman himself: 'Well, I've seen *you* in restaurants eating similar dinners.' He launched into a tirade against 'smart journalists on freeloading expense accounts who like to take a high moral tone . . . I think the general public ought to be told that this is hypocrisy.'

The interview did not get much further. Asked about 21 Tory MPs taking election expenses from Greer, Hamilton hit back with claims about two Labour MPs who had done likewise. Asked if he would resign if parliament found against him, he said it would depend. Asked if he would be happy to waive his privilege and appear at the Old Bailey, he once more demanded to know why the *Guardian* was not exposing Fayed. Rusbridger was allowed one final response at the end which he used to dismiss Hamilton's claims as 'absolute tosh'.

As the programme moved on to another topic, Hamilton snapped at Paxman: 'That was disgraceful . . . an absolute disgrace.' Rusbridger detached his microphone and walked off, muttering: 'Bad loser.' An assistant producer grabbed Rusbridger as he headed for the studio door and warned him not to go down to the hospitality suite. 'There's an ugly group down there and they've been tucking into the booze. Christine Hamilton's offering to plant one on your nose. We suggest you leave by another exit.'

Neutral observers said Hamilton had come across as fluent, if blustering and evasive. But the programme had been an object lesson in how ineffective television can be in such circumstances – even with a top-class interviewer who had done a certain amount of homework and with ten minutes or so to play with. Hamilton was a practised interviewee and it was plain that his story could be dented only by someone who had spent hours, if not days, reading the thousands of papers in the case and could confront him with the evidence buried therein. As Robert Maxwell showed, an accomplished and litigious liar can go far in British public life.

The difficult job of uncovering the truth about the Hamilton and Greer affair now fell back to parliament. No-one at the *Guardian* felt terribly enthusiastic about the prospect. The cosy 'private club' described by Lord Blake did not operate by the rules which governed other institutions in public life. The more world-weary commentators shrugged off any surprise at the unwillingness of MPs to break the cosy circle. These were politicians, and they played everything by political rules. What else could you expect? John Major and Michael Heseltine knew by now that they had been lied to, but they refused to suspend Hamilton pending a full investigation, as would have happened in any school, hospital or business. Why not? Because the Government had an effective majority of one – and, as John Prescott told the Labour party conference that year, Neil Hamilton *was* that majority.

The more important reservation in the *Guardian*'s mind about the new process was the memory of parliament's last attempts to get at the truth of the various scandals involving MPs, money and lobbying, which had verged on farce. They had certainly been partisan, as even Tom King, a Conservative MP and member of the Nolan committee, later admitted. Labour MPs remained convinced that there had been a concerted effort at the highest levels to suppress diligent inquiries into Fayed's claims. In April 1995 – in the middle of the first inquiry into Hamilton – there had been an unprecedented debate in the Commons, during which several Labour MPs on the old Members' Interests Committee had expressed serious doubts about the proceedings of their own committee. One MP had publicly complained at the time: 'The whole tenor of the committee changed as soon as the Whip was appointed to the committee.'

There was yet another factor which made the *Guardian* doubly anxious about Hamilton's eagerness to place his case before his fellow MPs rather than a judge and jury. Buried among the hundreds of pages supplied on discovery by the Treasury Solicitor was that memo from Government Whip David Willetts, written after a conversation with the chairman of the Members' Interests Committee on the very day the *Guardian*'s original allegations against Hamilton had appeared. The crucial part's exact wording was: '[Sir Geoffrey Johnson-Smith] is now expecting to receive a formal complaint about Hamilton receiving money etc. He could (i) argue now sub-judice and get committee to set it aside or (ii) investigate it as quickly as possible, exploiting good Tory majority at present We were inclined to go for (i) but he wants our advice.'

The document – due to be returned to the Government – clearly suggested that the Government Whips' office had been involved in an attempt to smother the first investigation into the Hamilton/Fayed affair, just as Labour MPs suspected at the time. What made it all the more remarkable was that the two courses suggested in this conversation were precisely the two courses which the committee eventually took. The main charges against Hamilton were declared *sub judice* (even though they weren't), while Hamilton's stay at the Ritz was merely declared 'imprudent' on the casting vote of the (Conservative) chairman. It looked, on the face of it, as though the committee might well have been nobbled.

The more esoteric laws and regulations of the House of Commons are understood by few. But some of the most fundamental ones concern the privileges of parliament. One of the most important privileges involves the effective immunity from prosecution in criminal courts for MPs in relation to anything that occurs in parliament. A variety of authorities hold that MPs simply cannot be prosecuted for bribery or corruption. In return for this immunity, the High Court of Parliament convenes a quasi-judicial select committee to hear any charges against MPs. Before the Nolan reforms this function was carried out by the Privileges Committee and by the Members' Interests Committee. The function is now carried out by the joint Standards and Privileges Committee, which in October 1996 counted Sir Geoffrey Johnson-Smith among its members. In no other court in the land would a judge or jury hold a conversation with anyone outside the court, let alone the Government, about the most suitable outcome for a case. Yet that – on a straightforward reading of this document – appeared to be precisely what had happened here.

This document presented the *Guardian* with a problem. It was 'discovered', and therefore could not be published. On the other hand, it clearly suggested that the very process which Hamilton chose over the courts had itself been polluted. Sir Gordon Downey, the new Commissioner on Standards, was clearly a man of integrity. But his powers to call for witnesses and evidence were subject to the decisions of the Select Committee, with its own 'good Tory majority', in the form of the casting vote.

Rusbridger took advice from no fewer than four lawyers. One suggested an ingenious solution. The *Guardian* could never get away with publishing the document, he said. But it could do what any citizen might reasonably do in the circumstances: send it to the four most senior privy councillors in the land, pointing out the apparent abuse of parliament.

Rusbridger duly sent the memo to the Prime Minister, the Speaker and the leaders of the two main opposition parties and announced the fact on the front page of the paper the next day, with an editorial explaining to readers why it was that the paper could not publish the contents of the document. Paddy Ashdown of the Liberal Democrats immediately saw its importance and wrote to Major saying that it 'appears to show that the Government sought to pervert, and may in fact have perverted, procedures of the House of Commons'. But, without the memorandum itself, most of the television and radio organisations were puzzled by the story and left it alone for 24 hours. It was yet another instance of how – with one or two honourable exceptions – television found it hard to report 'difficult' subjects. But the silence was resoundingly broken the following morning by all four broadsheet Sunday papers, which by then had managed to get hold of the text of the memo and all of whom featured the story.

The timing could not have been worse for John Major, who was due on David Frost's television programme that morning as a curtain raiser for the imminent Tory party conference. He doubtless had thoughts of an undemanding half hour talking about Britain's economic miracle, by way of a morale-booster to the troops. The last thing he wanted that Sunday morning was to be grilled about sleaze. He was fortunate in meeting Frost at his most docile, but his displeasure showed as he launched into a long table-thumping harangue attacking those who were 'slanting' stories against his Government. Apart from his display of ill-temper, his reply was notable for two things. Firstly, he let slip that he had helped to 'steer' the Hamilton-inspired amendment to the Bill of Rights – a direct contradiction of the Lord Chancellor's claims at the time that the Government was 'neutral' in the matter. Secondly, he announced that he wanted Sir Gordon Downey to finish his inquiry in two to three weeks – a timescale that indicated that he had absolutely no idea of the complexity and scale of the case against five or six of his own MPs.

Major was fortunate that the Labour party had so far matched Sir David Frost in its docility. The prospect of putting half a dozen Tory MPs in the dock for sleaze six months before a general election – and with a roomful of documents to plunder – might have been thought a prospect which would have had them licking their lips. Instead, they seemed strangely reluctant to exploit the story at all. Indeed, when the libel case collapsed, they found themselves on the back foot for three days running defending minor sideshows relating to their own party. Twenty or more Tories had had contributions to their election expenses paid by Greer – but the Conservative spin doctors managed to focus most press attention on Doug Hoyle and Chris Smith, two Labour MPs who had also received some money, and on a trip Blair had taken to America, paid for by some companies who retained Greer. A minor Labour peeress who was removed from frontbench duties after refusing to resign from Ian Greer's board also dominated the news at a time when it should have been the Conservatives running for cover.

A variety of Labour spin doctors and MPs tried their best to explain to the *Guardian* why they were keeping a low profile. The excuses ranged from: 'Some of our chaps may have been up to the same', and 'Look, all Whips get up to this sort of thing', to 'Well, the truth is MPs just don't have much appetite for investigating each other.' Robin Cook, who had done such a brilliant forensic job on the Scott Report, was not allowed near this one by party managers. Tony Blair's closest aides, Alastair Campbell and Peter Mandelson, blew hot and cold. The cautious Labour Chief Whip, Donald Dewar, was put in charge of co-ordinating the party's response. At first this consisted of Blair and Ashdown writing to Major demanding a judicial inquiry into the Willetts memorandum. When this was contemptuously dismissed by Major, both parties rather lamely dropped the suggestion – though by now a variety of voices, including *The Times*, Andrew Neil and Professor Vernon Bogdanor, Professor of Government at Oxford, had joined the clamour for an inquiry under the 1921 Tribunals of Inquiry Act (something also proposed to the Nolan committee by the leading constitutional lawyer, Professor Sir William Wade). MPs may not have had much appetite for investigating each other – but they had even less appetite for creating a modern precedent for judges to do the job for them.

The spotlight thus fell on the quiet figure of Sir Gordon Downey, a *sotto voce* 67-year-old former civil servant who, in the wake of the Nolan Report, had been appointed the first Parliamentary Commissioner for Standards on a salary of £72,000 a year. The Nolan Report was John Major's attempt to reassure the public that he was getting a grip on sleaze. But its reforms had not yet been tested. Published in May 1995, it said: 'The House of Commons is at the heart of our democracy. The standards of conduct observed by its members are crucially important to the political well-being of the nation. Those standards have always been self-imposed and self-regulated because parliament is our supreme institution.' It then described how inadequate the measures designed to uphold those standards had been. Nonetheless, the Nolan committee maintained that self-regulation was still the answer. 'We concluded,' they said, 'that it was appropriate to United

Kingdom circumstances to tailor our recommendations closely to our largely non-statutory mechanisms,' subject only to new procedures of 'independent scrutiny and monitoring'.

It was Downey who was to embody the new notion of 'independent scrutiny', as the Commissioner for Standards. He had had a distinguished Whitehall career, rising to deputy secretary at the Treasury before moving, in 1981, into a second career as a public watchdog. He had enjoyed spells as Comptroller and Auditor General, as Chairman of Fimbra (Financial Intermediaries, Managers and Brokers Regulatory Association) and as the ombudsman of the *Independent* newspapers. People who knew of him spoke of a man of quiet determination, of humour and of integrity. It was the *Independent* which asked the crucial question: 'Does he have the wily political skills that would, for example, keep him out of the various traps set for Sir Richard Scott in his arms-to-Iraq inquiry?' But no-one doubted that he knew his way around parliament and Whitehall. He was the consummate insider's outsider.

Downey worked part-time with a staff which consisted of a couple of secretaries. It was not immediately apparent that he, any more than the Prime Minister, knew the extent of the documentation which was about to land on his desk. He was at least relieved of the necessity of looking into the Willetts affair: the Speaker referred that to the new Committee on Standards and Privileges. There were immediate problems in finding a suitable membership for the committee. Doug Hoyle, the recipient of election funds from Ian Greer, stepped down. So did Sir Geoffrey Johnson-Smith. Some eyebrows were raised at Sir David Mitchell, for whom Hamilton had been a PPS, but who showed no inclination to quit – even when, later in the proceedings, the role of his son, Andrew, on the committee became the source of heated controversy.

Even more eyebrows were raised when the Tories replaced Sir Geoffrey with Sir Archie Hamilton, the former Armed Services Minister, who had not only opposed the key Nolan reforms, but had also effectively cleared his namesake in a BBC radio interview he had given on the 'Today' programme in April 1995. In that interview, he had praised Hamilton's willingness to stand up and fight a newspaper which indulged in slur and innuendo. He went on to advocate 'a number of bits of legislation to restrict freedom of the press . . . it is going to be necessary because we cannot go on having politicians being picked on in this way, nor indeed our institutions undermined'. It was difficult to imagine any other public body in the land appointing someone to a jury who had already so clearly declared his views in advance. One vote against him from any MP would have been sufficient to hold up his nomination, but there was not a squeak from any member on either the Labour or the Liberal Democrat benches.

'The Whips don't really like challenging each other's choices,' a senior Labour figure mumbled apologetically to the *Guardian*. 'Sorry, it's outrageous, but we somehow missed it,' said a senior Liberal Democrat. A complaint to the committee's chairman, Sir Tony Newton, was met with the brusque response that he did not choose its members. A complaint to the Speaker met with the response that it was not up to her but the House. That left the wonderful possibility of a complaint to the Leader of the House (Tony Newton). It was a Looking Glass world which seemed perfectly normal to its inhabitants, but utterly impenetrable and strange to anyone outside. The state of affairs now reached was unimaginable in any other area of public life or business. Imagine it: a man in a responsible position is found, at the very least, to have lied to his boss. He is allowed to stay in his job on full pay while a committee is convened to look into his case. Someone is appointed to the committee who has already effectively announced the man is innocent, and the chairman of the committee shrugs and says, 'I didn't pick the committee.' And all this was *after* Lord Nolan said that parliamentary self-regulation could work only if 'the public [can] see that breaches of the rules by its elected representatives are investigated as fairly, and dealt with as firmly, by parliament . . . as would be the case through the legal process'.

Sir Gordon had meanwhile appointed a rising star of the Bar to help him in his task. Nigel Pleming was a QC in his forties who specialised in judicial review. His appointment suggested that Sir Gordon was more interested in establishing a *prima facie* case based on documents (in private) than exposing MPs to a gruelling cross-examination. But his attempts to get at the documentation in the case ran into early problems.

The simplest and quickest way of getting at the key documents would have been to call in the bundle of papers prepared for the aborted libel trial. That would have given him access to most (but not all) of the main papers – though he had yet to secure Hamilton's and Greer's agreement to hand over documents they knew would be incriminating. But Downey seemed reluctant to go for this course. He also decided that he could not allow the *Guardian*'s lawyers to talk him through the paperwork – something which would greatly have speeded up the process. Furthermore, he told witnesses that any material they presented to him would have to remain secret unless – at some future stage – the Select Committee agreed to its publication.

These conditions proved a severe stumbling block. Without an agreed and consolidated bundle of evidence, it was difficult to see how any inquiry could be completed in six months, never mind the two to three weeks the Prime Minister had demanded. Without lawyers to talk him through the case it would take still longer. But the main obstacle was the demand that the *Guardian* should abandon all its evidence to the tender mercies of a Select Committee which, all recent previous precedents suggested, was incapable of acting in other than a partisan manner. Sir Archie's appointment was hardly an additional incentive to a newspaper to sign over its right ever to report the story again. The *Guardian* refused to hand over any material on this basis.

It was not even apparent by November 1996 just how broadly either Sir Gordon or his committee wished to inquire into the state of affairs revealed by the *Guardian*. No-one at this stage knew if he would be questioning witnesses himself or making a judgement on the papers. What were the standards of proof? Would there be transcripts of any questioning of witnesses? Would those transcripts be available to anyone else so that evidence could be challenged or rebutted? No-one knew the answers to any of these questions. It was not difficult to imagine what an American congressional inquiry would have demanded in such a case. With evidence that a lobbyist had paid 'commissions' to a number of legislators, Congress would have called in all the lobbyist's accounts for the past ten or 15 years to see who else he had paid.

A Congressional committee would have demanded all Hamilton's tax returns. It would have wanted to know about the discrepancy between the Lord Chancellor and the Prime Minister over the changing of a 300-year-old law. It would have looked into Hamilton's behaviour as a minister and the Prime Minister's unexplored relationship with Greer. It would have demanded the tax returns of all other MPs known to be working with or for Greer and Fayed. It would have explored the vetting procedures for Tim Smith and Hamilton before they became ministers in sensitive areas of Government. It would have done all this in the open, with clear terms of reference settled in advance. Sir Gordon had no such broad terms of reference, and seemed to be having to make up his rules of engagement as he went along.

After much huddling with lawyers, House of Commons clerks and the Select Committee, Sir Gordon eventually relaxed his conditions on the documents, and even on his opposition to talking to lawyers. He finally got sight of the key documents in the case in the last week of November – a month after John Major's deadline for the completion of the inquiry.

The committee, meanwhile, was preparing for its first televised hearing. Though the implications for Sir Geoffrey were as severe as for Willetts – if not more so – all the pre-hearing hype centred on the man universally nicknamed 'Two Brains' on account of his formidable cerebral powers. Robert Harris's pen-portrait in the *Sunday Times* encapsulated him as well as any: 'Policy, policy, policy: that is the gospel according to Willetts.' At the age of 26 he was running the Treasury's monetary policy division. At 28 he was in the Prime Minister's policy unit, working for the king of all policy nerds, John Redwood.

Finally, at the age of 31 Mr Willetts had achieved a kind of policymaking apotheosis as Director of Studies at the Centre for Policy Studies. By the time he reached parliament in 1992, Willetts had not, as far as one can see, worked full time at any stage in his life in any part of the real world which he has always sought so earnestly to regulate. He is exactly the sort of professional busybody which old-style Tories used to complain the Labour party was full of: the man in Whitehall who thinks he knows best, the wet-behind-the-ears theoretician, the bossy intellectual, the political appointee – a classic member of what in the old Soviet Union would have been called the *nomenklatura*.

The committee hearing began with a mild interrogation of Sir Geoffrey, a suave, handsome former television sports presenter now routinely described as a 'grandee'. He answered the questions with a puzzled air of old-world charm. Yes, he'd chatted with young Willetts in a corridor; he'd chatted to lots of people that day. Looking back, he couldn't even be sure if he knew Willetts was a Whip at the time. He certainly didn't ask for his advice. Quite frankly, if he'd wanted advice (which he didn't) he'd have gone to the Chief Whip, not some junior new bug in his first week. He'd never used any phrase about 'exploiting a good Tory majority' and couldn't imagine why young Willetts had rushed off to write such a thing down. Better ask Willetts.

This they did, at some length and to no great effect. Willetts, too, thought it was all a storm in a tea cup. It had been a conversation of no great import, and if he had misrecorded it in the Whips' book it was simply that he was new to the job and still thinking like a policy nerd. Policy nerds felt obliged to 'give structure' to conversations rather than simply record what had been said. As the afternoon wore on and the sky outside darkened, an atmosphere of gentle torpor descended on the proceedings. The room, which had been packed, slowly emptied as reporters went off to file their pieces.

Then something remarkable happened. Quentin Davies, a dapper and intelligent old-school Conservative, decided to dismember Willetts limb from limb. In Robert Harris' words, it was 'one of the great acts of political assassination. Before it, Willetts was a figure to be reckoned with. After it, he was a wet patch on the ground.' Willetts' mistake was in imagining his huge brain power could be used to baffle the committee – and Davies, with a first at Cambridge and a spell at Harvard behind him, was not stupid. Instead of a frank apology,

Willetts attempted a casuistical explanation of the various meanings which the document could sustain. It was a spellbinding performance in which the worlds of spin doctor Peter Mandelson and the literary don F. R. Leavis collided. Most comically, Willetts claimed that the phrase 'He wants our advice' was intended to carry the archaic meaning: 'He is in want of/desirous of/in need of, our advice.' The Oxford English Dictionary gave Old Norse and Middle English derivations for this meaning, adding (even in the 1933 edition): 'now rare, arch'.

Line by line, Davies demolished Willetts' explanation for his memo. There could be no simpler sentence in the English language than 'He wants our advice.' Either Willetts had been lying in his original memo or he was lying to the committee now. For good measure, he dismissed Sir Geoffrey's claim that he might not have known that Willetts was a Whip as 'complete nonsense'. As Davies moved in for the kill, there was suddenly a growl of displeasure from two Conservative members of the committee – Sir Archie Hamilton and Sir David Mitchell. The chairman, Tony Newton, immediately intervened and suggested that the mood of the committee was that Davies had probably taken this line of questioning far enough.

It might be thought admirable that a Conservative MP cared enough about the integrity of parliament to throw partisanship to the winds and demonstrate that a select committee could, as intended, act in a quasi-judicial manner. It might be argued that this was evidence that parliament was up to the business of self-regulation. Instead, a poisonous whispering campaign was immediately launched against Davies by his own party's spin doctors and his own colleagues. He was a bitter man (it was suggested) who bore a grudge against Willetts because he believed that he, Davies, should be in Government as well as, if not instead of, Willetts.

After his mauling at the hands of Davies, Willetts knew that his chances of escaping from the clutches of the committee were thin. He was the subject of a number of sympathetic articles by friendly journalists. One, Matthew Parris, admitted that he could not stomach the sight of his inquisition, which was a perfect illustration of why self-regulation was a waste of time:

> Take it from an old parliamentary hand: this kind of investigation will never work. It runs right against the grain of the Commons ethos, as does the whole select committee system. The whips on both sides infiltrated select committee work from the start, and this episode throws a rare shaft of daylight on to the process. But nobody really wants to change it. Whether Labour, Liberal Democrat or Tory you simply do not attack your own colleagues in public unless you want to become a pariah. This is what Quentin Davies now risks. Each party has ways of disciplining, or even destroying, its own Members in private. But never in front of the children. To watch the proceedings of the Standards and Privileges Committee yesterday was to observe the clash of two cultures. The culture of party, ancient and integral to the place, versus the culture of neutral inquiry, an uncomfortable import. Party will prevail.

Shortly before Willetts' sentence was pronounced, two other journalists, Bruce Anderson and Alan Watkins, took the condemned man out for a final meal at the Connaught Hotel. Both men eventually recorded the food and drink for posterity in the pages of the *Spectator*: the occasion would certainly merit a mention of any future volume of Great Lunches of Our Time. The wines alone were of Hamiltonian proportions and quality. The three men started with champagne at £7.75 a glass. They moved on to a 'useful' '94 Montagny from Louis Latour before investing in two 'superb' £55 bottles of '88 Calon Segur and a Gelas VSOP at £12.90 a nip. The total bill topped £500 – around £170 a head. 'Unjustifiable, but most enjoyable,' wrote Anderson, who subsequently wrote a stout defence of his lunch date in *The Times*.

The Committee eventually sat for nearly 25 hours, spread over nearly two months, before they could reach a consensus on the 88-word Willetts memo. It was a pace of progress which did not bode well for the thousands of pages of evidence littering the path ahead. Tony Newton, knowing that this was the Commons' first real post-Nolan test of its appetite for self-regulation, was desperate that there should be a unanimous report. He somehow had to force through a form of word that was acceptable to the Tory loyalists, the Labour sceptics – and Quentin Davies.

The result was published at 3.30pm on Wednesday 11 December. Precisely five minutes later journalists' screens across Britain flashed with a one-line special alert from the Press Association: 'PA NEWSFLASH: Paymaster-General David Willetts resigns – official.'

Willetts had been given an advance copy of the report a couple of hours earlier – a scene surrealistically imagined in an Austin cartoon the next day. It depicted an empty desk bearing the nameplate 'Two Brains' on which lay two pearl-handled revolvers. Willetts had indeed done the decent, if inevitable, thing. Not since Lord Carrington's departure over the Falkland Islands in 1982 had there been such a swift political resignation. But Willetts did not go entirely uncomplainingly. His letter to the Prime Minister said he was sorry that his integrity had been called into question, and insisted that he stood by his evidence. In a notably warm reply Mr Major praised Willetts' dignity and said he 'very much regretted' the resignation.

The committee left open the question of whether there had been a conscious attempt by either Willetts or Sir Geoffrey to influence the conduct of the committee, let alone whether they had succeeded. But they were unequivocal in stating that neither Sir Geoffrey nor Willetts should have taken part in such a discussion. They considered that Willetts' original memo had been a broadly accurate account of the conversation that had taken place, and concluded that it was conversation which had gone 'beyond what should properly have taken place.'

All that was mildly damaging, if not terminally so. But what sank Willetts was the damning conclusion of the committee about his evidence to them, particularly his attempt to explain away the conversation with Sir Geoffrey. 'We cannot accept much of the memorandum submitted to the Committee by Mr Willetts, nor much of his oral evidence, as being accurate,' said the report. It added, fatally for Willetts: 'We are very concerned that any Member should dissemble in his account to the Committee and believe that this response by Mr Willetts had substantially aggravated the original offence.'

That word 'dissemble' sent reporters scurrying back to the very dictionaries they had so recently pored over in relation to 'want'. They found it defined as: 'To cloak or conceal; to alter or disguise the semblance of so as to deceive; to give a false semblance to; to play the hypocrite.' Most people concluded it was tiptoeing on the edge of lying. John Prescott, the deputy Labour leader, needed no dictionary as he lashed out on television: it *was* lying. Brian Wilson, another Labour spokesman, commented drily: 'Two brains and no common sense.'

Other MPs were more distressed by the final paragraph of the report, which stated that, in future, the Committee would normally ask witnesses to give evidence on oath. So that was what it had come to. A quasi-judicial select committee had decided that they could no longer rely on elected MPs to come along and tell the truth. One Tory grandee, Sir James Spicer, appeared mournfully on television that night to say he was glad he was leaving politics at the next election. He wouldn't want to be part of the parliament which couldn't trust its members.

And so the Hamilton Affair claimed its third ministerial victim. Some felt Willetts had been unlucky: he was a new boy, trying to play the game by the rules everyone else played by back in 1994. Others felt he deserved no sympathy. Hugo Young in the *Guardian* condemned his amateurish attempts to blind the committee with tortuous wordplay and said he would have done better to plead that he had behaved no differently from anyone else – and defied them to disagree. But that would have been to give the club game away.

Robert Harris, in the *Sunday Times*, was no less brutal in his assessment of Willetts' modest role in the whole sorry saga:

If this Government falls next spring, historians may well look back at this moment and discern in that answer ['He wants our advice'] what has gone wrong with politics over the past few years. And lexicographers may find here the origins of a new verb; 'to willett', meaning to place a ludicrous interpretation on a phrase or event, manifestly at odds with its true meaning . . . It was the moment when all those ghastly policy nerds, who have strutted around the Tory party for the past 20 years, at last got something they have been in want of (old meaning) for a very long time: a wonderful, well-aimed punch on the nose.

Appendix

Clients of Ian Greer Associates up to 1996.
Was your employer one of them?

3i Group plc
ABECEL
Acorn Computers Limited
ADT Group plc
Airship Industries
al-Fayed, Mohammed
Alfred McAlpine plc
AMCO
Amoco (UK) Exploration
    Company Limited
ANA
Aristuein
Arthur Andersen & Co
Article Number Association (UK)
    Ltd.
Asda Group plc
Associated Octel
Association of European Express
    Carriers
Association of International
    Courier and Express Services
AT/Comm
Automotive Technik Limited

Basingstoke & Dean Council
BDO Binder Hamlyn
BHP Petroleum Limited
Biro Bic Ltd
Birmingham International Airport
    Limited
Boeing Aerospace & Defence

Brazil
Britdoc
British Airways plc
British Alcan Aluminium plc
British Borneo
British Gas plc
British Steel Tinplate
British Telecom
Brophy Plc

Cadbury Schweppes plc
Calor Gas Limited
Calor Group plc
Camas Aggregates
Camas plc
Carlton Television
Carr-Gomm Housing Association
Century Oils Limited
Channel Four Television
Charles Church Developments
Clydeport plc
Coal Investments
Coca-Cola International
Computer Sciences Corporation
    Ltd
ComputerCab
Coopers & Lybrand
CrossRail
CSC

Derbyshire Dales District Council

THI Development
Thompson & Gow Associates
Touche Ross & Co.
Trafalgar House
Transax

UK Charity Lotteries
Unitary Tax Campaign Limited

United States Tobacco Company

Videotron

Water Services Association
Whitbread plc
Wright Johnson & McKenzie

Index